Originals

Originals

**HOW NON-
CONFORMISTS
CHANGE
THE WORLD**

Adam Grant

1 3 5 7 9 10 8 6 4 2

WH Allen, an imprint of Ebury Publishing,
20 Vauxhall Bridge Road,
London SW1V 2SA

WH Allen is part of the Penguin Random House group of companies whose
addresses can be found at global.penguinrandomhouse.com

Penguin
Random House
UK

First published in the United Kingdom by WH Allen in 2016
First published in the United States by Viking in 2016

www.eburypublishing.co.uk

A CIP catalogue record for this book is available from the British Library

Hardback ISBN 9780753556979
Trade Paperback ISBN 9780753556986

Printed and bound in Great Britain by Clays Ltd, St Ives PLC

Penguin Random House is committed to a sustainable future for our
business, our readers and our planet. This book is made from
Forest Stewardship Council® certified paper.

For Allison

Contents

Foreword by Sheryl Sandberg   ix

1
Creative Destruction

The Risky Business of Going Against the Grain   *1*

2
Blind Inventors and One-Eyed Investors

The Art and Science of Recognizing Original Ideas   *29*

3
Out on a Limb

Speaking Truth to Power   *62*

4
Fools Rush In

Timing, Strategic Procrastination, and the First-Mover Disadvantage   *92*

5
Goldilocks and the Trojan Horse

Creating and Maintaining Coalitions   *114*

6

Rebel with a Cause

How Siblings, Parents, and Mentors Nurture Originality   146

7

Rethinking Groupthink

The Myths of Strong Cultures, Cults, and Devil's Advocates   175

8

Rocking the Boat and Keeping It Steady

Managing Anxiety, Apathy, Ambivalence, and Anger   210

Actions for Impact   245

Acknowledgments   255

References   259

Index   309

Foreword

BY SHERYL SANDBERG

Chief operating officer of Facebook and founder of LeanIn.Org

Adam Grant is the perfect person to write *Originals* because he is one.

He is a brilliant researcher who passionately pursues the science of what motivates people, busting myths and revealing truths. He is an informed optimist who offers insights and advice about how anyone—at home, at work, in the community—can make the world a better place. He is a dedicated friend who inspires me to believe in myself and has helped me understand how I can advocate effectively for my ideas.

Adam is one of the most important influences in my life. Through the pages of this magnificent book, he will enlighten, inspire, and support you as well.

MYTH BUSTER

Conventional wisdom holds that some people are innately creative, while most have few original thoughts. Some people are born to be leaders, and the rest are followers. Some people can have real impact, but the majority can't.

In *Originals* Adam shatters all of these assumptions.

He demonstrates that any of us can enhance our creativity. He reveals how we can identify ideas that are truly original and predict which ones will work. He tells us when to trust our gut and when to rely on others. He shows how we can become better parents by nurturing originality in our children and better managers by fostering diversity of thought instead of conformity.

In these pages, I learned that great creators don't necessarily have the deepest expertise but rather seek out the broadest perspectives. I saw how success is not usually attained by being ahead of everyone else but by waiting patiently for the right time to act. And to my utter shock, I learned that procrastinating can be good. Anyone who has ever worked with me knows how much I hate leaving things to the last minute, how I always think that anything that can be done should be done right away. Mark Zuckerberg, along with many others, will be pleased if I can let go of the relentless pressure I feel to finish everything early—and, as Adam points out, it might just help me and my teams achieve better results.

INFORMED OPTIMIST

Every day, we all encounter things we love and things that need to change. The former give us joy. The latter fuel our desire to make the world different—ideally better than the way we found it. But trying to change deep-seated beliefs and behaviors is daunting. We accept the status quo because effecting real change seems impossible. Still, we dare to ask: Can one individual make a difference? And, in our bravest moments: Could that one individual be me?

Adam's answer is a resounding yes. This book proves that any one of us can champion ideas that improve the world around us.

FRIEND

I met Adam just as his first book, *Give and Take,* was generating buzz in Silicon Valley. I read it and immediately started quoting it to anyone who would listen. Adam was not only a talented researcher but also a gifted teacher and storyteller who was able to explain complicated ideas simply and clearly.

Then my husband invited Adam to speak to his team at work and brought him over for dinner. Adam was every bit as extraordinary in person as he was on paper. His knowledge was encyclopedic and his energy was contagious. He and I started talking about how his research could inform the debate on gender and began working together. We have done so ever since, conducting research and writing a series of op-eds about women and work. LeanIn.Org has benefited immensely from his rigorous analysis and commitment to equality.

Once a year, Facebook brings its global teams together, and in 2015 I invited Adam to give a keynote speech. Everyone was blown away by his wisdom and humor. Months later, the teams are still talking about his insights and putting his advice into action.

Along the way, Adam and I became friends. When tragedy hit and I lost my husband suddenly, Adam stepped up and stepped in as only a true friend would. He approached the worst time of my life as he approaches everything, combining his unique understanding of psychology with his unparalleled generosity. When I thought I would never feel better, he flew across the country to explain what I could do to build my resilience. When I could not figure out how to handle a particularly gut-wrenching situation, he helped me find answers where I thought there were none. When I needed a shoulder to cry on, his was always there.

In the deepest sense of the word, a friend is someone who sees more potential in you than you see in yourself, someone who helps you become the best version of yourself. The magic of this book is that Adam becomes that kind of friend to everyone who reads it. He offers a wealth of advice for overcoming doubt and fear, speaking up and pitching ideas, and finding allies in the least likely of places. He gives practical guidance on how to manage anxiety, channel anger, find the strength in our weaknesses, overcome obstacles, and give hope to others.

———

Originals is one of the most important and captivating books I have ever read, full of surprising and powerful ideas. It will not only change the way you see the world; it might just change the way you live your life. And it could very well inspire you to change your world.

Originals

1

Creative Destruction

The Risky Business of Going Against the Grain

"The reasonable man adapts himself to the world;
the unreasonable one persists in trying to adapt the world to
himself. Therefore all progress depends
on the unreasonable man."

George Bernard Shaw

On a cool fall evening in 2008, four students set out to revolutionize an industry. Buried in loans, they had lost and broken eyeglasses and were outraged at how much it cost to replace them. One of them had been wearing the same damaged pair for five years: He was using a paper clip to bind the frames together. Even after his prescription changed twice, he refused to pay for pricey new lenses.

Luxottica, the 800-pound gorilla of the industry, controlled more than 80 percent of the eyewear market. To make glasses more affordable, the students would need to topple a giant. Having recently watched Zappos transform footwear by selling shoes online, they wondered if they could do the same with eyewear.

When they casually mentioned their idea to friends, time and again they were blasted with scorching criticism. No one would ever buy glasses over the internet, their friends insisted. People had to try them on first. Sure, Zappos had pulled the concept off with shoes, but there was a reason it hadn't happened with eyewear. "If this were a good idea," they heard repeatedly, "someone would have done it already."

None of the students had a background in e-commerce and

technology, let alone in retail, fashion, or apparel. Despite being told their idea was crazy, they walked away from lucrative job offers to start a company. They would sell eyeglasses that normally cost $500 in a store for $95 online, donating a pair to someone in the developing world with every purchase.

The business depended on a functioning website. Without one, it would be impossible for customers to view or buy their products. After scrambling to pull a website together, they finally managed to get it online at 4 A.M. on the day before the launch in February 2010. They called the company Warby Parker, combining the names of two characters created by the novelist Jack Kerouac, who inspired them to break free from the shackles of social pressure and embark on their adventure. They admired his rebellious spirit, infusing it into their culture. And it paid off.

The students expected to sell a pair or two of glasses per day. But when *GQ* called them "the Netflix of eyewear," they hit their target for the entire first year in less than a month, selling out so fast that they had to put twenty thousand customers on a waiting list. It took them nine months to stock enough inventory to meet the demand.

Fast forward to 2015, when *Fast Company* released a list of the world's most innovative companies. Warby Parker didn't just make the list—they came in first. The three previous winners were creative giants Google, Nike, and Apple, all with over fifty thousand employees. Warby Parker's scrappy startup, a new kid on the block, had a staff of just five hundred. In the span of five years, the four friends built one of the most fashionable brands on the planet and donated over a million pairs of glasses to people in need. The company cleared $100 million in annual revenues and was valued at over $1 billion.

Back in 2009, one of the founders pitched the company to me, offering me the chance to invest in Warby Parker. I declined.

It was the worst financial decision I've ever made, and I needed to understand where I went wrong.

———

orig•i•nal, adj *The origin or source of something; from which something springs, proceeds, or is derived.*

orig•i•nal, n *A thing of singular or unique character; a person who is different from other people in an appealing or interesting way; a person of fresh initiative or inventive capacity.*

Years ago, psychologists discovered that there are two routes to achievement: conformity and originality. Conformity means following the crowd down conventional paths and maintaining the status quo. Originality is taking the road less traveled, championing a set of novel ideas that go against the grain but ultimately make things better.

Of course, nothing is completely original, in the sense that all of our ideas are influenced by what we learn from the world around us. We are constantly borrowing thoughts, whether intentionally or inadvertently. We're all vulnerable to "kleptomnesia"—accidentally remembering the ideas of others as our own. By my definition, originality involves introducing and advancing an idea that's relatively unusual within a particular domain, and that has the potential to improve it.

Originality itself starts with creativity: generating a concept that is both novel and useful. But it doesn't stop there. Originals are people who take the initiative to make their visions a reality. The Warby Parker founders had the originality to dream up an unconventional way to sell glasses online, but became originals by taking action to make them easily accessible and affordable.

This book is about how we can all become more original. There's a surprising clue in the web browser that you use to surf the internet.

Finding the Faults in Defaults

Not long ago, economist Michael Housman was leading a project to figure out why some customer service agents stayed in their jobs longer than others. Armed with data from over thirty thousand employees who handled calls for banks, airlines, and cell-phone companies, he suspected that their employment histories would contain telltale signs about their commitment. He thought that people with a history of job-hopping would quit sooner, but they didn't: Employees who had held five jobs in the past five years weren't any more likely to leave their positions than those who had stayed in the same job for five years.

Hunting for other hints, he noticed that his team had captured information about which internet browser employees had used when they logged in to apply for their jobs. On a whim, he tested whether that choice might be related to quitting. He didn't expect to find any correlation, assuming that browser preference was purely a matter of taste. But when he looked at the results, he was stunned: Employees who used Firefox or Chrome to browse the Web remained in their jobs 15 percent longer than those who used Internet Explorer or Safari.

Thinking it was a coincidence, Housman ran the same analysis for absences from work. The pattern was the same: Firefox and Chrome users were 19 percent less likely to miss work than Internet Explorer and Safari fans.

Then he looked at performance. His team had assembled nearly three million data points on sales, customer satisfaction, and average call length. The Firefox and Chrome users had significantly higher sales, and their call times were shorter. Their customers were happier, too: After 90 days on the job, the Firefox and Chrome users had customer satisfaction levels that Internet Explorer and Safari users reached only after 120 days at work.

It's not the browser itself that's causing them to stick around, show up dependably, and succeed. Rather, it's what their browser preference signals about their habits. Why are the Firefox and Chrome users more committed and better performers on every metric?

The obvious answer was that they're more tech savvy, so I asked Housman if he could explore that. The employees had all taken a computer proficiency test, which assessed their knowledge of keyboard shortcuts, software programs, and hardware, as well as a timed test of their typing speed. But the Firefox and Chrome group didn't prove to have significantly more computer expertise, and they weren't faster or more accurate typists. Even after accounting for those scores, the browser effect persisted. Technical knowledge and skill weren't the source of their advantage.

What made the difference was *how* they obtained the browser. If you own a PC, Internet Explorer is built into Windows. If you're a Mac user, your computer came preinstalled with Safari. Almost two thirds of the customer service agents used the default browser, never questioning whether a better one was available.

To get Firefox or Chrome, you have to demonstrate some resourcefulness and download a different browser. Instead of accepting the default, you take a bit of initiative to seek out an option that might be better. And that act of initiative, however tiny, is a window into what you do at work.

The customer service agents who accepted the defaults of Internet Explorer and Safari approached their job the same way. They stayed on script in sales calls and followed standard operating procedures for handling customer complaints. They saw their job descriptions as fixed, so when they were unhappy with their work, they started missing days, and eventually just quit.

The employees who took the initiative to change their browsers to Firefox or Chrome approached their jobs differently. They looked for novel ways of selling to customers and addressing their concerns. When they encountered a situation they didn't like, they fixed it. Having taken the initiative to improve their circumstances, they had little reason to leave. They created the jobs they wanted. But they were the exception, not the rule.

We live in an Internet Explorer world. Just as almost two thirds of the customer service reps used the default browser on their computers, many of us accept the defaults in our own lives. In a series of provocative studies, a team led by political psychologist John Jost explored how people responded to undesirable default conditions. Compared to European Americans, African Americans were less satisfied with their economic circumstances but perceived economic inequality as *more* legitimate and just. Compared to people in the highest income bracket, people in the lowest income bracket were 17 percent more likely to view economic inequality as necessary. And when asked whether they would support laws that limit the rights of citizens and the press to criticize the government if enacting such legislation was necessary to solve our nation's problems, twice as many people in the lowest income bracket were willing to give up the right to free speech as those in the highest income bracket. After finding that disadvantaged groups consistently support the status quo more than advantaged groups, Jost and his colleagues concluded: "People who suffer the most from a given state of affairs are paradoxically the least likely to question, challenge, reject, or change it."

To explain this peculiar phenomenon, Jost's team developed a theory of system justification. Its core idea is that people are motivated to rationalize the status quo as legitimate—even if it goes directly against their interests. In one study, they tracked Democratic and Republican voters before the 2000 U.S. presidential election. When George W. Bush gained in the polls, Republicans rated him as more desirable, but so did Democrats, who were already preparing justifications for the anticipated status quo. The same happened when Al Gore's likelihood of success increased: Both Republicans and Democrats judged him more favorably. Regardless of political ideologies, when a candidate seemed destined to win, people liked him more. When his odds dropped, they liked him less.

Justifying the default system serves a soothing function. It's an emotional painkiller: If the world is *supposed* to be this way, we don't need to be dissatisfied with it. But acquiescence also robs us of the moral outrage to stand against injustice and the creative will to consider alternative ways that the world could work.

———

The hallmark of originality is rejecting the default and exploring whether a better option exists. I've spent more than a decade studying this, and it turns out to be far less difficult than I expected.

The starting point is curiosity: pondering why the default exists in the first place. We're driven to question defaults when we experience *vuja de*, the opposite of déjà vu. Déjà vu occurs when we encounter something new, but it feels as if we've seen it before. Vuja de is the reverse—we face something familiar, but we see it with a fresh perspective that enables us to gain new insights into old problems.

Without a **vuja de** event, Warby Parker wouldn't have existed. When the founders were sitting in the computer lab on the night they conjured up the company, they had spent a combined sixty years wearing glasses. The product had always been unreasonably expensive. But until that moment, they had taken the status quo for granted, never questioning the default price. "The thought had never crossed my mind," cofounder Dave Gilboa says. "I had always considered them a medical purchase. I naturally assumed that if a doctor was selling it to me, there was some justification for the price."

Having recently waited in line at the Apple Store to buy an iPhone, he found himself comparing the two products. Glasses had been a staple of human life for nearly a thousand years, and they'd hardly changed since his grandfather wore them. For the first time, Dave wondered why glasses had such a hefty price tag. Why did such a fundamentally simple product cost more than a complex smartphone?

Anyone could have asked those questions and arrived at the same answer that the Warby Parker squad did. Once they became curious about why the price was so steep, they began doing some research on the eyewear industry. That's when they learned that it was dominated by Luxottica, a European company that had raked in over $7 billion the previous year. "Understanding that the same company owned Lens-Crafters and Pearle Vision, Ray-Ban and Oakley, and the licenses for Chanel and Prada prescription frames and sunglasses—all of a sudden, it made sense to me why glasses were so expensive," Dave says. "Nothing in the cost of goods justified the price." Taking advantage of its monopoly status, Luxottica was charging twenty times the cost. The default wasn't inherently legitimate; it was a choice made by a group of people at a given company. And this meant that another group of people could make an alternative choice. "We could do things differently," Dave suddenly understood. "It was a realization that we could control our own destiny, that we could control our own prices."

When we become curious about the dissatisfying defaults in our world, we begin to recognize that most of them have social origins: Rules and systems were created by people. And that awareness gives us the courage to contemplate how we can change them. Before women gained the right to vote in America, many "had never before considered their degraded status as anything but natural," historian Jean Baker observes. As the suffrage movement gained momentum, "a growing number of women were beginning to see that custom, religious precept, and law were in fact man-made and therefore reversible."

The Two Faces of Ambition

The pressures to accept defaults start much earlier than we realize. If you consider the individuals who will grow up and make a dent in the universe, the first group that probably comes to mind is child prodigies. These geniuses learn to read at age two, play Bach at four, breeze through calculus at six, and speak seven languages fluently by eight. Their classmates shudder with jealousy; their parents rejoice at having won the lottery. But to paraphrase T. S. Eliot, their careers tend to end not with a bang, but a whimper.

Child prodigies, it turns out, rarely go on to change the world. When psychologists study history's most eminent and influential people, they discover that many of them weren't unusually gifted as children. And if you assemble a large group of child prodigies and follow them for their entire lives, you'll find that they don't outshine their less precocious peers from families of similar means.

Intuitively, this makes sense. We assume that what gifted kids have in book smarts, they lack in street smarts. While they have the intellectual chops, they must lack the social, emotional, and practical skills to function in society. When you look at the evidence, though, this explanation falls short: Less than a quarter of gifted children suffer from social and emotional problems. The vast majority are well-adjusted— as delightful at a cocktail party as in a spelling bee.

Although child prodigies are often rich in both talent and ambition, what holds them back from moving the world forward is that they don't learn to be original. As they perform in Carnegie Hall, win the science Olympics, and become chess champions, something tragic happens: Practice makes perfect, but it doesn't make new. The gifted learn to play magnificent Mozart melodies and beautiful Beethoven symphonies, but never compose their own original scores. They focus their energy on consuming existing scientific knowledge, not producing new insights. They conform to the codified rules of established games, rather than inventing their own rules or their own games. All along the way, they strive to earn the approval of their parents and the admiration of their teachers.

Research demonstrates that it is the most creative children who are the least likely to become the teacher's pet. In one study, elementary school teachers listed their favorite and least favorite students, and then rated both groups on a list of characteristics. The least favorite students were the non-conformists who made up their own rules. Teachers tend to discriminate against highly creative students, labeling them as troublemakers. In response, many children quickly learn to get with the program, keeping their original ideas to themselves. In the language of author William Deresiewicz, they become the world's most excellent sheep.

In adulthood, many child prodigies become experts in their fields and leaders in their organizations. Yet "only a fraction of gifted children eventually become revolutionary adult creators," laments psychologist Ellen Winner. "Those who do must make a painful transition" from a child who "learns rapidly and effortlessly in an established domain" to an adult who "ultimately remakes a domain."

Most prodigies never make that leap. They apply their extraordinary abilities in ordinary ways, mastering their jobs without questioning defaults and without making waves. In every domain they enter, they play it safe by following the conventional paths to success. They become doctors who heal their patients without fighting to fix the broken systems that prevent many patients from affording health care in the first place. They become lawyers who defend clients for violating outdated laws without trying to transform the laws themselves. They become teachers who plan engaging algebra lessons without questioning whether algebra is what their students need to learn. Although we rely on them to keep the world running smoothly, they keep us running on a treadmill.

Child prodigies are hindered by achievement motivation. The drive to succeed is responsible for many of the world's greatest accomplishments. When we're determined to excel, we have the fuel to work harder, longer, and smarter. But as cultures rack up a significant number of achievements, originality is increasingly left to a specialized few.

When achievement motivation goes sky-high, it can crowd out originality: The more you value achievement, the more you come to dread failure. Instead of aiming for unique accomplishments, the intense desire to succeed leads us to strive for guaranteed success. As psychologists Todd Lubart and Robert Sternberg put it, "Once people pass an intermediate level in the need to achieve, there is evidence that they actually become less creative."

The drive to succeed and the accompanying fear of failure have held back some of the greatest creators and change agents in history. Concerned with maintaining stability and attaining conventional achievements, they have been reluctant to pursue originality. Instead of charging full steam ahead with assurance, they have been coaxed, convinced, or coerced to take a stand. While they may seem to have possessed the qualities of natural leaders, they were figuratively—and sometimes literally—lifted up by followers and peers. If a handful of people hadn't been cajoled into taking original action, America might not exist, the civil rights movement could still be a dream, the Sistine Chapel might be bare, we might still believe the sun revolves around the earth, and the personal computer might never have been popularized.

From our perspective today, the Declaration of Independence seems inevitable, but it nearly didn't happen due to the reluctance of key revolutionaries. "The men who took commanding roles in the American Revolution were as unlikely a group of revolutionaries as one can imagine," Pulitzer Prize–winning historian Jack Rakove recounts. "They became revolutionaries despite themselves." In the years leading up to the war, John Adams feared British retaliation and hesitated to give up his budding law career; he only got involved after being elected as a delegate to the First Continental Congress. George Washington had been focused on managing his wheat, flour, fishing, and horse-breeding businesses, joining the cause only after Adams nominated him as commander in chief of the army. "I have used every endeavor in my power to avoid it," Washington wrote.

Nearly two centuries later, Martin Luther King, Jr., was apprehensive about leading the civil rights movement; his dream was to be a pastor and a college president. In 1955, after Rosa Parks was tried for refusing to give up her seat at the front of a bus, a group of civil rights activists gathered to discuss their response. They agreed to form the Montgomery Improvement Association and launch a bus boycott, and one of the attendees nominated King for the presidency. "It had happened so quickly that I did not even have time to think it through. It is probable that if I had, I would have declined the nomination," King reflected. Just three weeks earlier, King and his wife had "agreed that I should not then take on any heavy community responsibilities, since I had so recently finished my thesis, and needed to give more attention to my church work." He was unanimously elected to lead the boycott. Faced with giving a speech to the community that evening, "I became possessed by fear." King would overcome that trepidation soon enough that in 1963 his thundering voice united a country around an electrifying vision of freedom. But that only happened because a colleague proposed that King should be the closing speaker at the March on Washington and gathered a coalition of leaders to advocate for him.

When the pope commissioned him to paint a fresco on the ceiling of the Sistine Chapel, Michelangelo wasn't interested. He viewed himself as a sculptor, not a painter, and found the task so overwhelming that he fled to Florence. Two years would pass before he began work on the project, at the pope's insistence. And astronomy stagnated for decades because Nicolaus Copernicus refused to publish his original discovery that the earth revolves around the sun. Fearing rejection and ridicule, he stayed silent for twenty-two years, circulating his findings only to his friends. Eventually, a major cardinal learned of his work and wrote a letter encouraging Copernicus to publish it. Even then, Copernicus stalled for four more years. His magnum opus only saw the light of day after a young mathematics professor took matters into his own hands and submitted it for publication.

Almost half a millennium later, when an angel investor offered $250,000 to Steve Jobs and Steve Wozniak to bankroll Apple in 1977, it came with an ultimatum: Wozniak would have to leave Hewlett-Packard. He refused. "I still intended to be at that company forever," Wozniak reflects. "My psychological block was really that I didn't want to start a company. Because I was just afraid," he admits. Wozniak changed his mind only after being encouraged by Jobs, multiple friends, and his own parents.

We can only imagine how many Wozniaks, Michelangelos, and Kings never pursued, publicized, or promoted their original ideas because they were not dragged or catapulted into the spotlight. Although we may not all aspire to start our own companies, create a masterpiece, transform Western thought, or lead a civil rights movement, we do have ideas for improving our workplaces, schools, and communities. Sadly, many of us hesitate to take action to promote those ideas. As economist Joseph Schumpeter famously observed, originality is an act of creative destruction. Advocating for new systems often requires demolishing the old way of doing things, and we hold back for fear of rocking the boat. Among nearly a thousand scientists at the Food and Drug Administration, more than 40 percent were afraid that they would face retaliation if they spoke up publicly about safety concerns. Of more than forty thousand employees at a technology company, half felt it was not safe to voice dissenting opinions at work. When employees in consulting, financial services, media, pharmaceuticals, and advertising companies were interviewed, 85 percent admitted to keeping quiet about an important concern rather than voicing it to their bosses.

The last time you had an original idea, what did you do with it? Although America is a land of individuality and unique self-expression, in search of excellence and in fear of failure, most of us opt to fit in rather than stand out. "On matters of style, swim with the current," Thomas Jefferson allegedly advised, but "on matters of principle, stand like a rock." The pressure to achieve leads us to do the opposite. We find surface ways of appearing original—donning a bow tie, wearing bright red shoes—without taking the risk of actually being original. When it comes to the powerful ideas in our heads and the core values in our hearts, we censor ourselves. "There are so few originals in life," says renowned executive Mellody Hobson, because people are afraid to "speak up and stand out." What are the habits of the people whose originality extends beyond appearance to effective action?

The Right Stuff

To be an original, you need to take radical risks. This belief is embedded so deeply in our cultural psyche that we rarely even stop to think about it. We admire astronauts like Neil Armstrong and Sally Ride for having "the right stuff"—the courage to leave the only planet humans have ever inhabited and venture boldly into space. We celebrate heroes like Mahatma Gandhi and Martin Luther King, Jr., who possessed enough conviction to risk their lives for the moral principles they held dear. We idolize icons like Steve Jobs and Bill Gates for having the audacity to drop out of school and go for broke, holing up in garages to will their technological visions into existence.

When we marvel at the original individuals who fuel creativity and drive change in the world, we tend to assume they're cut from a different cloth. In the same way that some lucky people are born with genetic mutations that make them resistant to diseases like cancer, obesity, and HIV, we believe that great creators are born with a biological immunity to risk. They're wired to embrace uncertainty and ignore social approval; they simply don't worry about the costs of non-conformity the way the rest of us do. They're programmed to be iconoclasts, rebels, revolutionaries, troublemakers, mavericks, and contrarians who are impervious to fear, rejection, and ridicule.

The word *entrepreneur*, as it was coined by economist Richard Cantillon, literally means "bearer of risk." When we read the story of Warby

Parker's stratospheric rise, this theme comes through loud and clear. Like all great creators, innovators, and change agents, the quartet transformed the world because they were willing to take a leap of faith. After all, if you don't swing for the fences, it's impossible to hit a home run.

Isn't it?

———

Six months before Warby Parker launched, one of the founders was sitting in my classroom at Wharton. Tall and affable, with curly black hair and a calm energy, Neil Blumenthal hailed from a nonprofit background and genuinely aspired to make the world a better place. When he pitched the company to me, like many other doubters, I told him it sounded like an interesting idea, but it was hard to imagine people ordering glasses online.

With a skeptical consumer base, I knew, it would require a herculean effort to get the company off the ground. And when I learned how Neil and his friends were spending their time preparing for the launch, I had the sinking feeling that they were doomed.

The first strike against them, I told Neil, was that they were all still in school. If they truly believed in Warby Parker, they should drop out to focus every waking hour on making it happen.

"We want to hedge our bets," he responded. "We're not sure if it's a good idea and we have no clue whether it will succeed, so we've been working on it in our spare time during the school year. We were four friends before we started, and we made a commitment that dealing with each other fairly was more important than success. But for the summer, Jeff got a grant to focus on the business full time."

What about the other three of you? "We all got internships," Neil admitted. "I was in consulting, Andy was in venture capital, and Dave was in health care."

With their time scarce and their attention divided, they still hadn't built a website, and it had taken them six months just to agree on a name for the company. Strike two.

Before I gave up on them entirely, though, I remembered that they were all graduating at the end of the year, which meant they'd finally have the time to go all in and dedicate themselves completely to the business. "Well, not necessarily," Neil backpedaled. "We've hedged our bets. Just in case things don't work out, I've accepted a full-time job for after graduation. So has Jeff. And to make sure he would have options, Dave did two different internships over the summer, and he's talking with his former employer about rejoining."

Strike three. They were out—and so was I.

I declined to invest in Warby Parker because Neil and his friends were too much like me. I became a professor because I was passionate about discovering new insights, sharing knowledge, and teaching the next generations of students. But in my most honest moments, I know that I was also drawn to the security of tenure. I would never have had the confidence to start a business in my twenties. If I had, I certainly would have stayed in school and lined up a job to cover my bases.

When I compared the choices of the Warby Parker team to my mental model of the choices of successful entrepreneurs, they didn't match. Neil and his colleagues lacked the guts to go in with their guns blazing, which led me to question their conviction and commitment. They weren't serious about becoming successful entrepreneurs: They didn't have enough skin in the game. In my mind, they were destined to fail because they played it safe instead of betting the farm. But in fact, this is exactly why they succeeded.

I want to debunk the myth that originality requires extreme risk taking and persuade you that originals are actually far more ordinary than we realize. In every domain, from business and politics to science and art, the people who move the world forward with original ideas are rarely paragons of conviction and commitment. As they question traditions and challenge the status quo, they may appear bold and self-assured on the surface. But when you peel back the layers, the truth is that they, too, grapple with fear, ambivalence, and self-doubt. We view them as self-starters, but their efforts are often fueled and some-times forced by others. And as much as they seem to crave risk, they really prefer to avoid it.

———

In a fascinating study, management researchers Joseph Raffiee and Jie Feng asked a simple question: When people start a business, are they better off keeping or quitting their day jobs? From 1994 until 2008, they tracked a nationally representative group of over five thousand Americans in their twenties, thirties, forties, and fifties who became entrepreneurs. Whether these founders kept or left their day jobs wasn't influenced by financial need; individuals with high family income or high salaries weren't any more or less likely to quit and become full-time entrepreneurs. A survey showed that the ones who took the full plunge were risk takers with spades of confidence. The entrepreneurs who hedged their bets by starting their companies while still working were far more risk averse and unsure of themselves.

If you think like most people, you'll predict a clear advantage for the risk takers. Yet the study showed the exact opposite: Entrepreneurs who kept their day jobs had 33 percent lower odds of failure than those who quit.

If you're risk averse and have some doubts about the feasibility of your ideas, it's likely that your business will be built to last. If you're a freewheeling gambler, your startup is far more fragile.

Like the Warby Parker crew, the entrepreneurs whose companies topped *Fast Company*'s recent most innovative lists typically stayed in their day jobs even after they launched. Former track star Phil Knight started selling running shoes out of the trunk of his car in 1964, yet kept working as an accountant until 1969. After inventing the original Apple I computer, Steve Wozniak started the company with Steve Jobs in 1976 but continued working full time in his engineering job at Hewlett-Packard until 1977. And although Google founders Larry Page and

Sergey Brin figured out how to dramatically improve internet searches in 1996, they didn't go on leave from their graduate studies at Stanford until 1998. "We almost didn't start Google," Page says, because we "were too worried about dropping out of our Ph.D. program." In 1997, concerned that their fledgling search engine was distracting them from their research, they tried to sell Google for less than $2 million in cash and stock. Luckily for them, the potential buyer rejected the offer.

This habit of keeping one's day job isn't limited to successful entrepreneurs. Many influential creative minds have stayed in full-time employment or education even after earning income from major projects. *Selma* director Ava DuVernay made her first three films while working in her day job as a publicist, only pursuing filmmaking full time after working at it for four years and winning multiple awards. Brian May was in the middle of doctoral studies in astrophysics when he started playing guitar in a new band, but he didn't drop out until several years later to go all in with Queen. Soon thereafter he wrote "We Will Rock You." Grammy winner John Legend released his first album in 2000 but kept working as a management consultant until 2002, preparing PowerPoint presentations by day while performing at night. Thriller master Stephen King worked as a teacher, janitor, and gas station attendant for seven years after writing his first story, only quitting a year after his first novel, *Carrie,* was published. *Dilbert* author Scott Adams worked at Pacific Bell for seven years after his first comic strip hit newspapers.

Why did all these originals play it safe instead of risking it all?

Why Risks Are Like Stock Portfolios

Half a century ago, University of Michigan psychologist Clyde Coombs developed an innovative theory of risk. In the stock market, if you're going to make a risky investment, you protect yourself by playing it safe in other investments. Coombs suggested that in their daily lives, successful people do the same thing with risks, balancing them out in a portfolio. When we embrace danger in one domain, we offset our overall level of risk by exercising caution in another domain. If you're about to bet aggressively in blackjack, you might drive below the speed limit on your way to the casino.

Risk portfolios explain why people often become original in one part of their lives while remaining quite conventional in others. Baseball owner Branch Rickey opened the door for Jackie Robinson to break the color barrier, but refused to go to the ballpark on Sundays, use profanity, or touch a drop of alcohol. T. S. Eliot's landmark work, *The Waste Land*, has been hailed as one of the twentieth century's most significant poems. But after publishing it in 1922, Eliot kept his London bank job until 1925, rejecting the idea of embracing professional risk. As the novelist Aldous Huxley noted after paying him an office visit, Eliot was "the most bank-clerky of all bank clerks." When he finally did leave the position, Eliot still didn't strike out on his own. He spent the next forty years working for a publishing house to provide stability in his life, writing poetry on the side. As Polaroid founder Edwin Land remarked, "No person could possibly be original in one area unless he were possessed of the emotional and social stability that comes from fixed attitudes in all areas other than the one in which he is being original."

But don't day jobs distract us from doing our best work? Common sense suggests that creative accomplishments can't flourish without big windows of time and energy, and companies can't thrive without intensive effort. Those assumptions overlook the central benefit of a balanced risk portfolio: Having a sense of security in one realm gives us the freedom to be original in another. By covering our bases financially, we escape the pressure to publish half-baked books, sell shoddy art, or launch untested businesses. When Pierre Omidyar built eBay, it was just a hobby; he kept working as a programmer for the next nine months, only leaving after his online marketplace was netting him more money than his job. "The best entrepreneurs are not risk maximizers," Endeavor cofounder and CEO Linda Rottenberg observes based on decades of experience training many of the world's great entrepreneurs. "They take the risk out of risk-taking."

Managing a balanced risk portfolio doesn't mean constantly hovering in the middle of the spectrum by taking moderate risks. Instead, successful originals take extreme risks in one arena and offset them with extreme caution in another. At age twenty-seven, Sara Blakely generated the novel idea of creating footless pantyhose, taking a big risk by investing her entire savings of $5,000. To balance out her risk portfolio, she stayed in her full-time position selling fax machines for two years, spending nights and weekends building the prototype—and saving money by writing her own patent application instead of hiring lawyers to do so. After she finally launched Spanx, she became the world's youngest self-made billionaire. A century earlier, Henry Ford started his automotive empire while employed as a chief engineer for Thomas Edison, which gave him the security necessary to try out his novel inventions for a car. He continued working under Edison for two years after building a carburetor and a year after earning a patent for it.

And what about Bill Gates, famous for dropping out of Harvard to start Microsoft? When Gates sold a new software program as a sophomore, he waited an entire year before leaving school. Even then he didn't drop out, but balanced his risk portfolio by applying for a leave of absence that was formally approved by the university—and by having his parents bankroll him. "Far from being one of the world's great risk takers," entrepreneur Rick Smith notes, "Bill Gates might more accurately be thought of as one of the world's great risk *mitigators*."

It was this kind of risk mitigation that was responsible for Warby Parker's breakthrough. Two of the cofounders, Neil Blumenthal and Dave Gilboa, became the company's co-CEOs. They rejected advice to conform to the norm of selecting a single leader, believing it was safer to have a pair at the helm—indeed, evidence shows that having co-CEOs elicits positive market reactions and increases firm valuation. From the start, their number-one priority was reducing risk. "Warby Parker wasn't the basket that I wanted to put all my eggs into," Dave says. After starting the company he continued exploring other business opportunities by scouting scientific discoveries on campus to see if they had any commercial potential. Having backup plans gave the founders the courage to base their business on the unproven assumption that people would be willing to buy glasses online. Instead of just acknowledging that uncertainty, they actively worked to minimize it. "We talked constantly about de-risking the business," Neil says. "The whole journey was a series of go/no-go decisions. At every step of the way, we had checks and balances."

As part of their protection against risk, the four friends took an entrepreneurship class together and spent months honing their business plan. To make customers more comfortable with the unfamiliar concept of ordering eyewear over the internet, they decided to offer free returns. But in surveys and focus groups, people were still hesitant to buy glasses online. "There were a lot of people who just wouldn't do it. That really made us question the whole premise of the business," Neil recalls. "It was a moment of severe self-doubt. That took us back to the drawing board."

After discussing the problem at length, the team came up with a solution—a free home try-on program. Customers could order the frames alone without any financial commitment, and simply send them back if they didn't like the feel or look. This would actually be less costly than free returns. If a customer bought the frames with lenses and then returned them, Warby Parker would lose a lot of money, as the lenses were unique to the customer. But if customers tried on only the frames and returned them, the company could reuse them. By now Dave was confident and committed: "By the time we were ready to launch, and I had to make the decision this was something we were ready to do full time, it didn't seem risky. It didn't feel like I was taking a big leap of faith." The free home try-on program was so popular that Warby Parker had to temporarily suspend it within forty-eight hours of launch.

A growing body of evidence suggests that entrepreneurs don't like risk any more than the rest of us—and it's the rare conclusion on which many economists, sociologists, and psychologists have actually come to agree. In one representative study of over eight hundred Americans, entrepreneurs and employed adults were asked to choose which of the following three ventures they would prefer to start:

(a) One that made $5 million in profit with a 20 percent chance of success

(b) One that made $2 million in profit with a 50 percent chance of success

(c) One that made $1.25 million in profit with an 80 percent chance of success

The entrepreneurs were significantly *more* likely to choose the last option, the safest one. This was true regardless of income, wealth, age, gender, entrepreneurial experience, marital status, education, household size, and expectations of how well other businesses would perform. "We find that entrepreneurs are significantly more risk-averse than the general population," the authors conclude.

These are just preferences on a survey, but when you track entrepreneurs' real-world behavior, it's clear that they avoid dangerous risks. Economists find that as teenagers, successful entrepreneurs were nearly three times as likely as their peers to break rules and engage in illicit activities. Yet when you take a closer look at the specific behaviors involved, the adolescents who went on to start productive companies were only taking calculated risks. When psychologists studied American twins and Swedish citizens, they found the same results.

Across all three studies, the people who become successful entrepreneurs were more likely to have teenage histories of defying their parents, staying out past their curfews, skipping school, shoplifting, gambling, drinking alcohol, and smoking marijuana. They were not, however, more likely to engage in hazardous activities like driving drunk, buying illegal drugs, or stealing valuables. And that was true regardless of their parents' socioeconomic status or family income.

Originals do vary in their attitudes toward risk. Some are skydiving gamblers; others are penny-pinching germophobes. To become original, you have to try something new, which means accepting some measure of risk. But the most successful originals are not the daredevils who leap before they look. They are the ones who reluctantly tiptoe to the edge of a cliff, calculate the rate of descent, triple-check their parachutes, and set up a safety net at the bottom just in case. As Malcolm Gladwell wrote in the *New Yorker*, "Many entrepreneurs take plenty of risks—but those are generally the failed entrepreneurs, not the success stories."

A disregard for social approval doesn't differentiate people who take original paths, either. In a comprehensive analysis of 60 studies covering more than 15,000 entrepreneurs, people who had little concern for pleasing others weren't more likely to become entrepreneurs, nor did their firms perform any better. We see the same pattern in politics: When hundreds of historians, psychologists, and political scientists evaluated America's presidents, they determined that the least effective leaders were those who followed the will of the people and the precedents set by their predecessors. The greatest presidents were those who challenged the status quo and brought about sweeping changes that improved the lot of the country. But these behaviors were completely unrelated to whether they cared deeply about public approval and social harmony.

Abraham Lincoln is usually regarded as the greatest of all American presidents. When experts rated the presidents on the desire to please others and avoid conflict, Lincoln scored the highest of them all. He devoted four hours a day to holding office hours with citizens and pardoned deserters during the Civil War. Before signing the Emancipation Proclamation, Lincoln agonized for six months over whether he should free the slaves. He questioned whether he had the constitutional authority; he worried that the decision might lose him the support of the border states, forfeit the war, and destroy the country.

Originality is not a fixed trait. It is a free choice. Lincoln wasn't born with an original personality. Taking on controversy wasn't programmed into his DNA; it was an act of conscious will. As the great thinker W. E. B. DuBois wrote, "He was one of you and yet he became Abraham Lincoln."

Too often that possibility of control is missing from our work and our lives. A few years ago, Google asked a brilliant Yale professor named Amy Wrzesniewski to help enrich the jobs of employees in sales and administrative positions, who didn't have the same perceived freedom, status, or moon-shot projects as the company's engineers. I joined her and another collaborator, Justin Berg, on a trip to California, New York, Dublin, and London in search of a solution.

Many employees were so committed to Google that they accepted their own jobs as defaults. Since they saw their tasks and interactions as set like plaster, they did not question whether they could adjust them.

To unlock their mindsets, we partnered with Jennifer Kurkoski and Brian Welle, two innovators behind Google's people analytics work. We designed a workshop introducing hundreds of employees to the notion that jobs are not static sculptures, but flexible building blocks. We gave them examples of people becoming the architects of their own jobs, customizing their tasks and relationships to better align with their interests, skills, and values—like an artistic salesperson volunteering to design a new logo and an outgoing financial analyst communicating with clients using video chat instead of email. Then, they looked at their familiar jobs in an unfamiliar way: **vuja de**. They set out to create a new vision of their roles that was more ideal but still realistic.

Managers and coworkers rated each employee's happiness and performance before the workshop and after several weeks and months had passed. The whole experience lasted only ninety minutes, so we weren't sure that it would be enough to make a difference. But six weeks later, Googlers who were randomly assigned to think about their jobs as malleable showed a spike in happiness and performance. Having considered how their jobs could be modified, they had taken action to improve them. Employees in a control group who didn't attend the same workshop didn't show any changes in happiness or performance. When we added a feature to encourage employees to see both their skills and jobs as flexible, the gains lasted for at least six months. Instead of using only their existing talents, they took the initiative to develop new capabilities that enabled them to create an original, personalized job. As a result, they were 70 percent more likely than their peers to land a promotion or a transition to a coveted role. By refusing to stick with their default jobs and default skills, they became happier and more effective—and qualified themselves for roles that were a better fit. Many of their limits, they came to realize, were of their own making.

———

Having revealed that successful originals often begin by questioning defaults and balancing risk portfolios, the rest of this book is about closing the gap between insight and action. Once you have a new idea, how do you champion it effectively? As an organizational psychologist at Wharton, I've spent more than a decade studying originality in a wide range of settings, from technology companies and banks to schools, hospitals, and governments. I've also sought out some of the most prominent originals of our time, and I want to share their wisdom about how we can all be more original without jeopardizing our relationships, reputations, and careers. I hope my findings will help people develop the courage and strategies to pursue originality, and give leaders the knowledge necessary to create cultures of originality in their teams and organizations.

Using studies and stories spanning business, politics, sports, and entertainment, I'll look at the seeds of creative, moral, and organizational change—and the barriers that hinder progress. The first section of this book focuses on managing the risks involved in generating, recognizing, and voicing original ideas. By definition, new ideas are fraught with uncertainty, and powerful evidence illuminates how we can hone our skills in separating the wheat from the chaff, to avoid the risks of betting on bad ideas and passing on good ones. After you spot a promising idea, the next step is to communicate it effectively. I'll share some best practices for speaking up, shedding light on how to select the messages and audiences to get heard more and punished less. Along the way, you'll find out why the most popular television show of all time narrowly escaped the cutting-room floor, why an entrepreneur pitches his startups by highlighting the reasons *not* to invest in them, how a CIA analyst convinced the intelligence community to stop being so secretive, and how a woman at Apple challenged Steve Jobs from three levels below—and won.

The second section of the book deals with the choices that we make to scale originality. I'll start with the dilemma of timing: It turns out that you should be wary of being the first mover, because it's often riskier to act early than late. Unexpectedly, some of the greatest creative achievements and change initiatives in history have their roots in procrastination, and the tendency to delay and postpone can help entrepreneurs build companies that last, leaders guide transformation efforts, and innovators maintain their originality. I'll then turn to the challenges of coalition building, investigating how to grow support for an original idea and reduce the risks of rejection. The unsung hero of the women's suffrage movement will illustrate why enemies make better allies than frenemies, and shared values can divide rather than unite. A founder who hid her firm's mission from employees and a Hollywood director who shifted Disney's direction for animated films will demonstrate how to recruit collaborators by balancing idealism with pragmatism and blending the familiar with the new.

The third section of the book concerns unleashing and sustaining originality, both at home and in work. I'll examine how to nurture originality in children, explaining how parents, siblings, and role models shape our tendencies to rebel. You'll see why the number of bases that professional baseball players steal can be traced to their birth order, the most original comedians in America come from similar family backgrounds, the people who risked their lives to perform heroic rescues during the Holocaust received a particular kind of discipline from their parents, and the innovation and economic growth rates of entire countries can be traced to the books we read to our children. From there, I'll consider why some cultures become cults, and how leaders can encourage dissenting opinions that allow originality to flourish. You'll learn from a billionaire financial wizard who fires employees for failing to criticize him, an inventor who struggled to spread his ingenuity, and an expert who helped change the norm of silence at NASA after the space shuttle *Columbia* exploded.

I'll close with reflections on the emotions that hold us back from pursuing originality. You'll gain insight on overcoming fear and apathy from a group of twentysomethings who toppled a tyrant and a lawyer who fought climate change by swimming the North Pole. Their examples underscore evidence that calming down isn't the best way to manage anxiety, that venting backfires when we're angry, and that pessimism is sometimes more energizing than optimism.

Ultimately, the people who choose to champion originality are the ones who propel us forward. After spending years studying them and interacting with them, I am struck that their inner experiences are not any different from our own. They feel the same fear, the same doubt, as the rest of us. What sets them apart is that they take action anyway. They know in their hearts that failing would yield less regret than failing to try.

2

Blind Inventors and
One-Eyed Investors

The Art and Science of Recognizing Original Ideas

"Creativity is allowing yourself to make mistakes.
Art is knowing which ones to keep."

Scott Adams

A t the turn of the century, an invention took Silicon Valley by storm. Steve Jobs called it the most amazing piece of technology since the personal computer. Enamored with the prototype, Jobs offered the inventor $63 million for 10 percent of the company. When the inventor turned it down, Jobs did something out of character: he offered to advise the inventor for the next six months—for free. Amazon founder Jeff Bezos took one look at the product and immediately got involved, telling the inventor, "You have a product so revolutionary, you'll have no problem selling it." John Doerr, the legendary investor who bet successfully on Google and many other blue-chip startups, pumped $80 million into the business, predicting that it would be the fastest company ever to reach $1 billion and "would become more important than the internet."

The inventor himself was described as a modern Thomas Edison— he already had a track record of remarkable breakthroughs. His portable dialysis machine had been named the medical product of the year, his portable drug infusion pump reduced the time that patients were stuck in hospitals, and his vascular stent is connected to Vice President Dick Cheney's heart. He had accumulated hundreds of patents and received America's highest honor for invention, the National Medal of Technology and Innovation, from President Bill Clinton.

The inventor projected that within a year, sales of his newest product would reach 10,000 units a week. But six years later, they had sold only about 30,000 units in total. After more than a decade, the company still hadn't become profitable. It was supposed to transform lives and cities, but today it is used only in niche markets.

That product was the Segway, the self-balancing personal transporter. *Time* called it one of the ten biggest technology flops of the decade. "Segway as an investment was a failure, no question about it," Doerr admitted in 2013. "I made some pretty bold predictions about Segway that were wrong." Why did such savvy business minds all miss the mark?

Some years earlier, two entertainers got together to create a 90-minute television special. They had no experience writing for the medium and quickly ran out of material, so they shifted their concept to a half-hour weekly show. When they submitted their script, most of the network executives didn't like it or didn't get it. One of the actors involved in the program described it as a "glorious mess."

After filming the pilot, it was time for an audience test. The one hundred viewers who were assembled in Los Angeles to discuss the strengths and weaknesses of the show dismissed it as a dismal failure. One put it bluntly: "He's just a loser, who'd want to watch this guy?" After about six hundred additional people were shown the pilot in four different cities, the summary report concluded: "No segment of the audience was eager to watch the show again." The performance was rated weak.

The pilot episode squeaked onto the airwaves, and as expected, it wasn't a hit. Between that and the negative audience tests, the show should have been toast. But one executive campaigned to have four more episodes made. They didn't go live until nearly a year after the pilot, and again, they failed to gain a devoted following. With the clock winding down, the network ordered half a season as replacement for a canceled show, but by then one of the writers was ready to walk away: he didn't have any more ideas.

It's a good thing he changed his mind. Over the next decade, the show dominated the Nielsen ratings and brought in over $1 billion in revenues. It became the most popular TV series in America, and *TV Guide* named it the greatest program of all time.

If you've ever complained about a close talker, accused a partygoer of double-dipping a chip, uttered the disclaimer "Not that there's anything wrong with that," or rejected someone by saying "No soup for you," you're using phrases coined on the show. Why did network executives have so little faith in *Seinfeld*?

When we bemoan the lack of originality in the world, we blame it on the absence of creativity. If only people could generate more novel ideas, we'd all be better off. But in reality, the biggest barrier to originality is not idea generation—it's idea *selection*. In one analysis, when over two hundred people dreamed up more than a thousand ideas for new ventures and products, 87 percent were completely unique. Our companies, communities, and countries don't necessarily suffer from a shortage of novel ideas. They're constrained by a shortage of people who excel at choosing the right novel ideas. The Segway was a false positive: it was forecast as a hit but turned out to be a miss. *Seinfeld* was a false negative: it was expected to fail but ultimately flourished.

This chapter is about the hurdles and best practices in idea selection. To figure out how we can make fewer bad bets, I sought out skilled forecasters who have learned to avoid the risks of false positives and false negatives. You'll meet two venture capitalists who anticipated the failure of the Segway, and the NBC executive who didn't even work in comedy but was so enthusiastic about the *Seinfeld* pilot that he went out on a limb to fund it. Their methods question conventional wisdom about the relative importance of intuition and analysis in assessing ideas, and about how we should weigh passion in evaluating the people behind those ideas. You'll see why it's so difficult for managers and test audiences to accurately evaluate new ideas, and how we can get better at deciding when to roll the dice.

A Random Walk on the Creative Tightrope

The inventor of the Segway is a technological whiz named Dean Kamen, whose closet is stocked with one outfit: a denim shirt, jeans, and work boots. When I asked venture capitalists to describe Kamen, the most common response was "Batman." At sixteen, he took it upon himself to redesign a museum's lighting system—and only then sought the chairman's permission to implement it. In the 1970s, he invented the drug infusion pump, which was profitable enough that he bought a jet and a helicopter and built a mansion in New Hampshire, complete with a machine shop, an electronics lab, and a baseball field. In the 1980s, his portable dialysis machine was a massive success.

In the 1990s, Kamen designed the iBOT, a wheelchair that could climb stairs. Recognizing broader applications for the technology, he brought in a team to help create the Segway. The goal was to build a safe, fuel-efficient vehicle that would prevent pollution and help individuals navigate congested cities. Because it was small, lightweight, and balanced on its own, it would be a natural fit for mail carriers, police officers, and golfers, but also had the potential to fundamentally alter everyday transportation. The Segway was the most extraordinary technology he had ever created, and Kamen predicted that it would "be to the car what the car was to the horse and buggy."

But can creators ever be objective in judging their own ideas? One of my former students, Justin Berg, is now a wunderkind professor at Stanford who has spent years investigating this question. Berg specializes in creative forecasting, the art of predicting the success of novel ideas. In one study, he showed different groups of people videos of circus performances and asked them to make projections about how well each would do. Circus artists from Cirque du Soleil and other organizations submitted predictions about how popular their videos would be. Circus managers watched the videos and registered their predictions, too.

To test the accuracy of their forecasts, Berg then measured the actual success of each performance by tracking how much general audience members liked, shared, and funded the videos. He invited over thirteen thousand people to rate the videos; they also had a chance to share them via Facebook, Twitter, Google+, and email, and received a ten-cent bonus that they could donate to the performers.

The creators proved to be terrible at judging how their performances would do with the test audiences. On average, when ranking their videos against the performances of nine other circus artists, they put their own work two slots too high. The managers were more realistic: they had some distance from the performances, which put them in a more neutral position.

Social scientists have long known that we tend to be overconfident when we evaluate ourselves. Here are some highlights of their findings:

• High school seniors: 70 percent report that they have "above average" leadership skills, compared with 2 percent "below average"; in the ability to get along with others, 25 percent rate themselves in the top 1 percent, and 60 percent put themselves in the top 10 percent.

• College professors: 94 percent rate themselves as doing above-average work.

• Engineers: In two different companies, 32 percent and 42 percent rated themselves among the top 5 percent of performers.

• Entrepreneurs: When 3,000 small-business owners rated the probability that different companies would succeed, on average they rated the prospects of their own businesses as 8.1 out of 10 but gave similar enterprises odds of only 5.9 out of 10.

———

Overconfidence may be a particularly difficult bias to overcome in the creative domain. When you're generating a new idea, by definition it's unique, so you can ignore all the feedback you've received in the past about earlier inventions. Even if your previous ideas have bombed, this one is different.

When we've developed an idea, we're typically too close to our own tastes—and too far from the audience's taste—to evaluate it accurately. We're giddy from the thrill of the eureka moment or the triumph of overcoming an obstacle. As Brandon Tartikoff, NBC's longtime entertainment president, frequently reminded his producers, "Nobody walks in here with what they think is a bad idea." To some degree, entrepreneurs and inventors have to be overconfident about the odds of their ideas succeeding, or they wouldn't have the motivational fuel to pursue them. But even when they do learn about their audience's preferences, it's too easy for them to fall victim to what psychologists call confirmation bias: they focus on the strengths of their ideas while ignoring or discounting their limitations.

After spending his career studying creative productivity, psychologist Dean Simonton has found that even geniuses have trouble recognizing when they have a hit on their hands. In music, Beethoven was known as a perceptive self-critic, yet as Simonton observes, "Beethoven's own favorites among his symphonies, sonatas, and quartets are not those most frequently performed and recorded by posterity." In one analysis, psychologist Aaron Kozbelt pored over letters in which Beethoven evaluated seventy of his compositions, comparing those appraisals to expert judgments of Beethoven's works. In that set of seventy, Beethoven committed fifteen false positives, expecting pieces to be major that turned out to be minor, and only eight false negatives, criticizing pieces that ended up becoming highly valued.

This 33 percent error rate occurred despite the fact that Beethoven made many of his assessments *after* receiving audience feedback.

If creators knew when they were on their way to fashioning a masterpiece, their work would progress only forward: they would halt their idea-generation efforts as they struck gold. But time and again, Simonton finds that they backtrack, returning to iterations that they had earlier discarded as inadequate. In Beethoven's most celebrated work, the Fifth Symphony, he scrapped the conclusion of the first movement because it felt too short, only to come back to it later. Had Beethoven been able to distinguish an extraordinary from an ordinary work, he would have accepted his composition immediately as a hit. When Picasso was painting his famous *Guernica* in protest of fascism, he produced seventy-nine different drawings. Many of the images in the painting were based on his early sketches, not the later variations. "The subsequent sketches proved to constitute 'blind alleys' in which the artist did not know in advance that he was taking the wrong track," Simonton explains. If Picasso could judge his creations as he produced them, he would get consistently "warmer" and use the later drawings. But in reality, it was just as common that he got "colder."

Kissing Frogs

If originals aren't reliable judges of the quality of their ideas, how do they maximize their odds of creating a masterpiece? They come up with a large number of ideas. Simonton finds that on average, creative geniuses weren't qualitatively better in their fields than their peers. They simply produced a greater volume of work, which gave them more variation and a higher chance of originality. "The odds of producing an influential or successful idea," Simonton notes, are "a positive function of the total number of ideas generated."

Consider Shakespeare: we're most familiar with a small number of his classics, forgetting that in the span of two decades, he produced 37 plays and 154 sonnets. Simonton tracked the popularity of Shakespeare's plays, measuring how often they're performed and how widely they're praised by experts and critics. In the same five-year window that Shakespeare produced three of his five most popular works—*Macbeth*, *King Lear*, and *Othello*—he also churned out the comparatively average *Timon of Athens* and *All's Well That Ends Well*, both of which rank among the worst of his plays and have been consistently slammed for unpolished prose and incomplete plot and character development.

In every field, even the most eminent creators typically produce a large quantity of work that's technically sound but considered unremarkable by experts and audiences. When the London Philharmonic Orchestra chose the 50 greatest pieces of classical music, the list included six pieces by Mozart, five by Beethoven, and three by Bach. To generate a handful of masterworks, Mozart composed more than 600 pieces before his death at thirty-five, Beethoven produced 650 in his lifetime, and Bach wrote over a thousand. In a study of over 15,000 classical music compositions, the more pieces a composer produced in a given five-year window, the greater the spike in the odds of a hit.

Picasso's oeuvre includes more than 1,800 paintings, 1,200 sculptures, 2,800 ceramics, and 12,000 drawings, not to mention prints, rugs, and tapestries—only a fraction of which have garnered acclaim. In poetry, when we recite Maya Angelou's classic poem "Still I Rise," we tend to forget that she wrote 165 others; we remember her moving memoir *I Know Why the Caged Bird Sings* and pay less attention to her other 6 autobiographies. In science, Einstein wrote papers on general and special relativity that transformed physics, but many of his 248 publications had minimal impact. If you want to be original, "the most important possible thing you could do," says Ira Glass, the producer of

This American Life and the podcast *Serial*, "is do a lot of work. Do a huge volume of work."

Across fields, Simonton reports that the most prolific people not only have the highest originality; they also generate their most original output during the periods in which they produce the largest volume.* Between the ages of thirty and thirty-five, Edison pioneered the lightbulb, the phonograph, and the carbon telephone. But during that period, he filed well over one hundred patents for other inventions as diverse as stencil pens, a fruit preservation technique, and a way of using magnets to mine iron ore—and designed a creepy talking doll. "Those periods in which the most minor products appear tend to be the same periods in which the most major works appear," Simonton notes. Edison's "1,093 patents notwithstanding, the number of truly superlative creative achievements can probably be counted on the fingers of one hand."

It's widely assumed that there's a tradeoff between quantity and quality—if you want to do better work, you have to do less of it—but this turns out to be false. In fact, when it comes to idea generation, quantity is the most predictable path to quality. "Original thinkers," Stanford professor Robert Sutton notes, "will come up with many ideas that are strange mutations, dead ends, and utter failures. The cost is worthwhile because they also generate a larger pool of ideas—especially novel ideas."

Many people fail to achieve originality because they generate a few ideas and then obsess about refining them to perfection. At Upworthy,

---

* This is one reason why men seemed to have more influential creative accomplishments than women. Historically, the doors to many creative careers were closed to women. Those who managed to get their feet in the door were often full-time caregivers for children. As a result, men simply produced more output than women, giving them a higher chance of originality. With greater equality of opportunity today, these gender differences in creative output ought to disappear, and may even reverse. Berg finds that on average, women make better creative forecasts than men: They're more open to novel ideas, which leaves them less prone to false negatives.

the company that makes good content go viral, two different staff members wrote headlines for a video of monkeys reacting to receiving cucumbers or grapes as rewards. Eight thousand people watched it when the headline was "Remember *Planet of the Apes*? It's Closer to Reality than You Think." A different headline led to fifty-nine times more views, enticing nearly half a million people to watch the same video: "2 Monkeys Were Paid Unequally; See What Happens Next." Upworthy's rule is that you need to generate at least twenty-five headline ideas to strike gold. Backtracking studies show that wizards do sometimes come up with novel ideas early in the creative process. But for the rest of us, our first ideas are often the most conventional—the closest to the default that already exists. It's only after we've ruled out the obvious that we have the greatest freedom to consider the more remote possibilities. "Once you start getting desperate, you start thinking outside the box," the Upworthy team writes. "#24 will suck. Then #25 will be a gift from the headline gods and will make you a legend."

While working on the Segway, Dean Kamen was aware of the blind variations that mark the creative process. With more than 440 patents to his name, he had plenty of misses as well as hits. "You gotta kiss a lot of frogs," he often told his team, "before you find a prince." In fact, frog kissing was one of his mantras: he encouraged his engineers to try out many variations to increase their chances of stumbling on the right one. But he settled on the Segway before considering other ideas for solving transportation problems, losing sight of the fact that inventors will necessarily struggle mightily in gauging whether their creations are ultimately frogs or princes.

The best way to get better at judging our ideas is to gather feedback. Put a lot of ideas out there and see which ones are praised and adopted by your target audience. After spending decades creating comedy, *The Daily Show* cocreator Lizz Winstead still doesn't know what will make people laugh. She recalls that she was "desperately trying to figure out jokes, writing them out, and trying them on stage." Some of them sizzled; others popped. Now, with social media, she has a more rapid feedback mechanism. When she thinks of a joke, she tweets it; when she comes up with a longer bit, she posts it on Facebook. When she receives at least twenty-five retweets in less than a minute, or a high number of Facebook shares, she saves the idea. At the end of the day, she develops the material that proved most popular with her audience. "Twitter and Facebook have tremendously helped me decide what people care about," Winstead explains.

When developing the Segway, Dean Kamen didn't open the door to this kind of feedback. Concerned that someone would steal his idea, or that the fundamental concept would become public too soon, he maintained strict secrecy rules. Many of his own employees weren't allowed access to the area where the Segway was being developed; only an elite group of potential investors had a chance to try it out. When building the Segway, his team generated a wide number of ideas, but didn't have enough critical input from customers to make the right choices for the final product. The device went through three or four iterations before a customer ever saw it.* Conviction in our ideas is dangerous not only because it leaves us vulnerable to false positives, but also because it stops us from generating the requisite variety to reach our creative potential.

But Kamen and his team weren't the only ones who were too bullish on the Segway. Where did virtuosos like Steve Jobs, Jeff Bezos, and John Doerr misstep in their judgments about the device? To find out, let's first take a look at why many executives and test audiences failed to see the potential in *Seinfeld*.

---

* The lesson here isn't to ask customers what they want. As the famous line often attributed to Henry Ford goes: "If I had asked my customers what they wanted, they would have said a faster horse." Instead, creators ought to build a car and see if customers will drive it. That means identifying a potential need, designing what *The Lean Startup* author Eric Ries calls a minimum viable product, testing different versions, and gathering feedback.

Prisoners of Prototypes and Parochial Preferences

When the first *Seinfeld* script was submitted, executives didn't know what to do with it. It was "totally unconventional," NBC executive Warren Littlefield said. "It didn't sound like anything else on television. There was no historical precedent."

In Justin Berg's study of circus performances, although circus managers made more accurate forecasts than artists, they still weren't very good, especially regarding the most novel acts. Managers tend to be too risk averse: they focus on the costs of investing in bad ideas rather than the benefits of piloting good ones, which leads them to commit a large number of false negatives. The author of the initial report on the *Seinfeld* pilot felt it was on the border between "weak" and "moderate." He was leaning toward moderate, but his boss overruled him and rated it weak.

These types of false negatives are common in the entertainment industry. Studio executives passed on hits ranging from *Star Wars* to *E.T.* to *Pulp Fiction.* In publishing, managers rejected *The Chronicles of Narnia, The Diary of Anne Frank, Gone with the Wind, Lord of the Flies,* and *Harry Potter*—as of 2015, J. K. Rowling's books alone had brought in over $25 billion and sold more copies than any book series, ever. The annals of corporate innovation are filled with tales of managers ordering employees to stop working on projects that turned out to be big hits, from Nichia's invention of LED lighting to Pontiac's Fiero car to HP's electrostatic displays. The Xbox was almost buried at Microsoft; the laser printer was nearly canceled at Xerox for being expensive and impractical.

In the face of uncertainty, our first instinct is often to reject novelty, looking for reasons why unfamiliar concepts might fail. When managers vet novel ideas, they're in an evaluative mindset. To protect themselves against the risks of a bad bet, they compare the new notion on the table to templates of ideas that have succeeded in the past. When publishing executives passed on *Harry Potter*, they said it was too long for a children's book; when Brandon Tartikoff saw the *Seinfeld* pilot, he felt it was "too Jewish" and "too New York" to appeal to a wide audience.

Rice professor Erik Dane finds that the more expertise and experience people gain, the more entrenched they become in a particular way of viewing the world. He points to studies showing that expert bridge players struggled more than novices to adapt when the rules were changed, and that expert accountants were worse than novices at applying a new tax law. As we gain knowledge about a domain, we become prisoners of our prototypes.

In principle, audiences should be more open to novelty than managers. They don't have the blinders associated with expertise, and they have little to lose by considering a fresh format and expressing enthusiasm for an unusual idea. In practice, though, Justin Berg finds that test audiences are no better than managers at predicting the success of new ideas: focus groups are effectively set up to make the same mistakes as managers.

When you watch a show in your living room, you get absorbed in the plot. If you find yourself laughing throughout, you'll end up pronouncing it funny. When you watch it in a focus group, however, you don't engage with the program in the same way. You're conscious of the fact that you're there to evaluate it, not experience it, so you're judging it from the start. Because you're trying to figure out whether people will watch it, you naturally assess it against established ideas of how such a show ought to work. When test audiences viewed the *Seinfeld* pilot, they thought it lacked the community of *Cheers*, the family dynamics of *The Cosby Show*, and the relatability of *ALF*. It was all too easy to find flaws in a show that was ostensibly about nothing.

"The truth is, most pilots don't test well," Warren Littlefield observes, because "audiences do not respond well to things that are new or different." Audiences don't have enough experience: they simply haven't seen a lot of the novel ideas that landed on the cutting-room floor. "The *Seinfeld* testing should put an end to all conversations about testing, ever. Please don't tell me my show is going to come down to twenty people in Sherman Oaks," comedian Paul Reiser says. "I've never been to any testing that's any good."

So neither test audiences nor managers are ideal judges of creative ideas. They're too prone to false negatives; they focus too much on reasons to reject an idea and stick too closely to existing prototypes. And we've seen that creators struggle as well, because they're too positive about their own ideas. But there is one group of forecasters that does come close to attaining mastery: fellow creators evaluating one another's ideas. In Berg's study of circus acts, the most accurate predictors of whether a video would get liked, shared, and funded were peers evaluating one another.

When artists assessed one another's performances, they were about twice as accurate as managers and test audiences in predicting how often the videos would be shared. Compared to creators, managers and test audiences were 56 percent and 55 percent more prone to major false negatives, undervaluing a strong, novel performance by five ranks or more in the set of ten they viewed.

We often speak of the wisdom of crowds, but we need to be careful about which crowds we're considering. On average, the combined forecasts of all 120 circus managers were no better than a typical single creator's predictions. Managers and test audiences tended to fixate on a particular category of favored acts and reject the rest. Creators were more open to different kinds of performances—they saw potential in peers who did aerial and ground acrobatics, but also in skilled jugglers and mimes.*

Instead of attempting to assess our own originality or seeking feedback from managers, we ought to turn more often to our colleagues.

---

* One category of circus acts was universally disliked by managers, test audiences, and creators: clowns. It's not a coincidence that one *Seinfeld* episode revolves around clowns striking fear into the hearts of adults as well as children.

They lack the risk-aversion of managers and test audiences; they're open to seeing the potential in unusual possibilities, which guards against false negatives. At the same time, they have no particular investment in our ideas, which gives them enough distance to offer an honest appraisal and protects against false positives.

This evidence helps to explain why many performers enjoy the approval of audiences but covet the admiration of their peers. Comedians often say that the highest badge of honor is to make a fellow comic laugh; magicians like fooling audiences but live to baffle their brethren. The usual explanation for this preference is status striving: we crave acceptance by our peer group, those similar to us. But Berg's research suggests that we're also drawn to peer evaluations because they provide the most reliable judgments.

When we evaluate new ideas, we can become better at avoiding false negatives by thinking more like creators. In a series of experiments, Berg asked over a thousand adults to make forecasts about the success of novel products in the marketplace. Some were ideas that might be useful—a 3-D image projector, a flooring system that simulates natural ground, and an automatic bed-maker. Others were less practical, like an electrified tablecloth to prevent ants from ruining a picnic. The rest were conventional ideas that varied in usefulness, from a portable container for steaming food in a microwave to a hands-free system for carrying towels.

Berg wanted to boost the chances that people would correctly rank a novel, useful idea first, as opposed to favoring conventional ideas. He randomly assigned half of the participants to think like managers by spending six minutes making a list of three criteria for evaluating the success of new products. This group then made the right bet on a novel, useful idea 51 percent of the time. But the other group of participants was much more accurate, choosing the most promising new idea over 77 percent of the time. All it took was having them spend their initial six minutes a little differently: instead of adopting a managerial mindset for evaluating ideas, they got into a creative mindset by generating ideas themselves. Just spending six minutes developing original ideas made them more open to novelty, improving their ability to see the potential in something unusual.

From these findings you might think that we can improve idea selection simply by making sure that managers have some experience as creators. But in Berg's circus data, former artists who become managers aren't significantly better in their evaluations than regular managers; pure artists are still the best forecasters. Once you take on a managerial role, it's hard to avoid letting an evaluative mindset creep in to cause false negatives. Berg demonstrated this in an experiment by asking people to generate product ideas and then come up with a list of evaluation criteria, and subsequently measured the success of the ideas with an actual audience. Thinking like creators and then donning the manager hat dropped their forecasting accuracy to 41 percent.

When Berg reversed the order, so that they made a list of evaluation criteria first and then generated ideas, their accuracy climbed to 65 percent. If we want to increase our odds of betting on the best original ideas, we have to generate our own ideas immediately before we screen others' suggestions. And this, it turns out, helps to explain why *Seinfeld* saw the light of day.

The Double-Edged Sword of Experience

When the test audience panned the *Seinfeld* pilot, "it was a dagger to the heart," Warren Littlefield reflected. "We were afraid to go forward with something that was so strongly rejected by research." Although the ideal people to give the show a chance might have been fellow comedy writers, there weren't any pure writers in positions of power. But Rick Ludwin, the man who ultimately made the show happen, was the next best thing.

Ludwin would later make his mark by standing up for Jay Leno, going to bat for Conan O'Brien, and fighting to renew a show that didn't have a big enough following early on: *The Office*. But his greatest contribution to television was commissioning the pilot for *Seinfeld*.

At that point in his career, Rick Ludwin didn't even work in the comedy department, but handled variety and specials. When the *Seinfeld* pilot didn't take off, he went on a mission to give it another chance. He found a few hours in his lineup that hadn't been assigned, divided them into half-hour slots, and took the money from his specials budget to fund more episodes. "As far as we know, that was the smallest order of episodes ever for a television show," Ludwin says. Jerry Seinfeld would go on to remark that an order of six episodes "is like a slap in the face." NBC ordered just four.

"If you're gonna make connections which are innovative," Steve Jobs said back in 1982, "you have to not have the same bag of experience as everyone else does." Working outside the sitcom department may have been Rick Ludwin's greatest advantage. "Larry [David] and Jerry had never written a sitcom, and my department had never developed one," Ludwin recalls. "We were a good match, because we didn't know what rules we weren't supposed to break." His outsider status gave him enough detachment from the standard format of sitcoms to consider something different. Most sitcoms shot a few continuous scenes in a tidy 22-minute episode; *Seinfeld* often left conflicts unresolved and had as many as twenty different scenes packed in. This was bothersome if you lived exclusively in the sitcom world, but perfectly comfortable for a guy who used a different arrangement in every special.

At the same time, Ludwin did have the requisite experience in creating comedy. While working as a producer in the 1970s, he wrote jokes and sold them to Bob Hope, and then produced segments for a daytime variety show that featured comedy sketches. "Being around comedy writers is like going to a baseball fantasy camp. You think you're really good, until you get up to bat," he reminisces. "Not only can't you hit the ball; you can't even see the ball. I knew I was not in their league, but I at least spoke the same language."

It is when people have moderate expertise in a particular domain that they're the most open to radically creative ideas. Ludwin's deep experience in comedy gave him the necessary expertise in humor; his broad experience outside sitcoms prevented him from getting blinded to alternative ways of delivering it. Instead of narrowly scrutinizing what made a sitcom a hit, he had cast a wider net in studying what made comedy in general succeed:

> *You never know where the next big hit is coming from. It can come from left field. If you think, "That can't possibly work because that producer doesn't have enough experience, or no idea like that has ever worked"—if you have those kinds of roadblocks in your head, you're going to miss something. One of the best things that I had going for me was the fact that I had never developed a primetime situation comedy, but I was accustomed to offbeat, off-kilter ideas. I could see what worked, and what didn't work. The time I spent reading* Saturday Night Live *scripts made me more open to the offbeat storylines that are now legendary on* Seinfeld.

This unique combination of broad and deep experience is critical for creativity. In a recent study comparing every Nobel Prize–winning scientist from 1901 to 2005 with typical scientists of the same era, both groups attained deep expertise in their respective fields of study. But the Nobel Prize winners were dramatically more likely to be involved in the arts than less accomplished scientists. Here's what a team of fifteen researchers at Michigan State University found about engagement in the arts among Nobel Prize winners relative to ordinary scientists:

Artistic hobby	Odds for Nobel Prize winners relative to typical scientists
Music: playing an instrument, composing, conducting	2x greater
Arts: drawing, painting, printmaking, sculpting	7x greater
Crafts: woodworking, mechanics, electronics, glassblowing	7.5x greater
Writing: poetry, plays, novels, short stories, essays, popular books	12x greater
Performing: amateur actor, dancer, magician	22x greater

A representative study of thousands of Americans showed similar results for entrepreneurs and inventors. People who started businesses and contributed to patent applications were more likely than their peers to have leisure time hobbies that involved drawing, painting, architecture, sculpture, and literature.

Interest in the arts among entrepreneurs, inventors, and eminent scientists obviously reflects their curiosity and aptitude. People who are open to new ways of looking at science and business also tend to be fascinated by the expression of ideas and emotions through images, sounds, and words.* But it's not just that a certain kind of original

---

* The personality trait most associated with an interest in the arts is called openness, the tendency to seek out novelty and variety in intellectual, aesthetic, and emotional pursuits. When

person seeks out exposure to the arts. The arts also serve in turn as a powerful source of creative insight.

When Galileo made his astonishing discovery of mountains on the moon, his telescope didn't actually have enough magnifying power to support that finding. Instead, he recognized the zigzag pattern separating the light and dark areas of the moon. Other astronomers were looking through similar telescopes, but only Galileo "was able to appreciate the implications of the dark and light regions," Simonton notes. He had the necessary depth of experience in physics and astronomy, but also breadth of experience in painting and drawing. Thanks to artistic training in a technique called chiaroscuro, which focuses on representations of light and shade, Galileo was able to detect mountains where others did not.

Just as scientists, entrepreneurs, and inventors often discover novel ideas through broadening their knowledge to include the arts, we can likewise gain breadth by widening our cultural repertoires. Research on highly creative adults shows that they tended to move to new cities much more frequently than their peers in childhood, which gave them exposure to different cultures and values, and encouraged flexibility and adaptability. In a recent study, a team of researchers led by strategy professor Frédéric Godart explored whether creativity might be influenced by time spent abroad. They focused on the fashion industry, tracking ratings from buyers and fashion critics of the creativity of collections produced by hundreds of fashion houses over the course of twenty-one seasons.

---

psychologist Robert McCrae analyzed four dozen questions across fifty-one different cultures, one of the best indicators of openness was agreeing with the statement: "Sometimes when I am reading poetry or looking at a work of art, I feel a chill or wave of excitement." Around the world, from the U.S. to Japan and Brazil to Norway, the most open-minded people experience aesthetic chills—shivers and goose bumps—when appreciating art or hearing beautiful music. "I acquired a strong taste for music," Charles Darwin once wrote, so that when listening to an anthem, "my backbone would sometimes shiver."

The researchers studied the creative directors' biographies, tracking the international experiences of industry icons like Giorgio Armani, Donna Karan, Karl Lagerfeld, Donatella Versace, and Vera Wang.

The most creative fashion collections came from houses where directors had the greatest experience abroad, but there were three twists. First, time *living* abroad didn't matter: it was time *working* abroad, being actively engaged in design in a foreign country, that predicted whether their new collections were hits. The most original collections came from directors who had worked in two or three different countries.

Second, the more the foreign culture differed from that of their native land, the more that experience contributed to the directors' creativity. An American gained little from working in Canada, compared to the originality dividends of a project in Korea or Japan.

But working in multiple countries with different cultures wasn't enough. The third and most important factor was depth—the amount of time spent working abroad. A short stint did little good, because directors weren't there long enough to internalize the new ideas from the foreign culture and synthesize them with their old perspectives. The highest originality occurred when directors had spent thirty-five years working abroad.

Rick Ludwin's experience lines up with this model. He had depth from spending well over a decade working on different comedy sketches. He had breadth from living in the television equivalents of several very different foreign countries: variety and specials, and daytime and late-night talk shows. Having become fluent in multiple television languages, he saw promise where others had doubts. Once he got *Seinfeld* approved, Ludwin continued to oversee the show for the entire series, and he bet on writers who had the same insider-outsider status that he did. Almost all came from late night, and most had never worked on a sitcom before *Seinfeld,* which meant "there was never a problem with offbeat ideas."*

The Hazards of Intuition: Where Steve Jobs Went Wrong

The first time Steve Jobs stepped on a Segway, he refused to climb off. When Dean Kamen gave other potential investors a turn, Jobs begrudgingly handed it over, but soon cut in. Jobs invited Kamen over for dinner, and as journalist Steve Kemper tells it, Jobs "thought the machine was as original and enthralling as the PC, and felt he *had* to be involved."

Steve Jobs was famous for making big bets based on intuition rather than systematic analysis. Why was he right so often in software and hardware, but wrong this time? Three major forces left him over-confident about the Segway's potential: domain inexperience, hubris, and enthusiasm.

Let's start with experience. Whereas many NBC executives were too experienced in traditional sitcoms to appreciate the unorthodox genius of *Seinfeld,* the Segway's early investors had the opposite problem: they didn't know enough about transportation. Jobs specialized in the digital world, Jeff Bezos was the king of internet retail, and John Doerr had made his fortune investing in software and internet companies like Sun Microsystems, Netscape, Amazon, and Google. They

---

* Do diverse experiences really generate originality, or do original people seek out diverse experiences? In fashion houses, perhaps the most creative directors would choose to immerse themselves in new cultures for the longest periods of time. This might be part of the story, but there is evidence that variety of experience can foster creativity. When we diversify our knowledge base, we're more likely to sample original ideas and retrieve unconventional knowledge. Studies show that people become more creative when reminded of time they spent living in a foreign culture, and bilinguals tend to be more creative than people who speak only a single language. And in one experiment, when European Americans watched a 45-minute slide show about American-Chinese fusion culture, they wrote more creative Cinderella stories for Turkish children than peers who learned only about American or Chinese culture.

had all been originals in their respective arenas, but being a creator in one particular area doesn't make you a great forecaster in others. To accurately predict the success of a novel idea, it's best to be a creator in the domain you're judging.

New research led by Erik Dane shows us why: our intuitions are only accurate in domains where we have a lot of experience. In one experiment, people looked at ten designer handbags and judged whether they were real or fake. Half the participants had only five seconds to guess, which forced them to rely on their gut feelings. The other half had thirty seconds, which allowed them to inspect and analyze the features. Dane's team also measured their handbag experience—some had a lot, owning more than three handbags made by Coach or Louis Vuitton, whereas others had never touched a designer bag.

If you're the proud owner of several designer handbags, the less time you have to inspect them, the more accurate your judgments. Experienced handbag owners were 22 percent more accurate when they had just five seconds than when they had thirty seconds. When you've spent years studying handbags, intuition can beat analysis, because your unconscious mind excels at pattern recognition. If you stop and take the time to think, it's easy to lose the forest in the trees.

If you don't know anything about handbags, however, your intuition isn't going to help you. In dealing with unfamiliar products, you need to take a step back and assess them. Non-experts make sounder judgments when they conduct a thorough analysis. When Steve Jobs had a gut feeling that the Segway would change the world, he was seduced by an impulsive attraction to its novelty rather than a careful examination of its usefulness. Harvard psychologist Teresa Amabile, one of the world's foremost authorities on creativity, reminds us that to be successfully original, an invention needs to be new—but it also has to be practical. In a digital world dominated by invisible bits and bytes, Jobs was enamored with the possibility that the next breakthrough innovation would be in transportation. The Segway was an engineering marvel, and riding it was a thrill. "It was like a magic carpet. It was transformational as a product," says Bill Sahlman, the Harvard entrepreneurship professor who introduced Kamen to Doerr. "But products don't create value. Customers do."

For a group of people with no transportation experience, a lot of homework was required to figure out whether the Segway was actually practical. One of the few investors to raise concerns in that area was Aileen Lee, then an associate partner working for Doerr at Kleiner Perkins. In board meetings, Lee asked questions about how the Segway would be used. How would you lock it? Where would you store groceries? She had another big practical concern: the price tag, since "five or eight thousand dollars is a lot of money for a normal person." Looking back, she says, "I should have stood up more and said, 'We aren't getting this right.'"

Another early skeptic was Randy Komisar, who had been an entrepreneur, senior counsel at Apple, CEO at LucasArts Entertainment, and a founding board member at TiVo. "I think about it as if I was in that seat with the entrepreneur. I don't think I'm smarter than those guys, but I saw something differently than they did. I think they saw a brilliant technology in an application that seemed extremely novel. When we got on the machines that day, it was a magical experience to be on two wheels, self-balancing, moving around," Komisar recalls. "That first impression was a 'wow' experience. Now, why did I not get convinced by that?"

When Komisar scrutinized the market, he saw that the Segway wasn't likely to replace the car but would be a substitute for walking or riding a bike. He didn't view it as a product for ordinary consumers. "It's a huge change of behavior at a very high expense with limited value beyond the wow factor for anybody with two feet," he explains. Even if it was approved for use on sidewalks (which was still an open question), and the price point became affordable, it would take years to get people on board. He suggested instead focusing on the device's usefulness for golf courses, postal services, police departments, and Disney parks. "You could see that there was a cost-value tradeoff in those applications, where this might have some advantages." But Komisar continued to have serious reservations:

> *I still looked at it as a very significant change of behavior at a very significant cost. It wasn't clear to me that this would improve a mail carrier's productivity, or that that was the goal for the postal service, which was pretty much hamstrung by labor-union contracts. On the golf course, people drive electric carts around all day long. Why will they use this instead?*

Jobs, meanwhile, stuck to his intuition about novelty: "If enough people see the machine, you won't have to convince them to architect cities around it. People are smart, and it'll happen."

As Nobel Prize–winning psychologist Daniel Kahneman and decision expert Gary Klein explain, intuitions are only trustworthy when people build up experience making judgments in a predictable environment. If you're confronting a patient's symptoms as a doctor or entering a burning building as a firefighter, experience will make your intuitions more accurate. There's a stable, robust relationship between the patterns you've seen before and what you encounter today. But if you're a stockbroker or political forecaster, the events of the past don't have reliable implications for the present. Kahneman and Klein review evidence that experience helps physicists, accountants, insurance analysts, and chess masters—they all work in fields where cause-and-effect relationships are fairly consistent. But admissions officers, court judges, intelligence analysts, psychiatrists, and stockbrokers didn't benefit much from experience. In a rapidly changing world, the lessons of experience can easily point us in the wrong direction. And because the pace of change is accelerating, our environments are becoming ever more unpredictable. This makes intuition less reliable as a source of insight about new ideas and places a growing premium on analysis.

Given that Jobs hadn't accumulated the relevant experience in transportation, why was he so trusting of his intuition? This brings us to the second factor: "There's a hubris that comes with success," Komisar explains. Had he pushed back harder about his concerns, "Steve Jobs would've probably said, 'You just don't get it.'" Research in the transportation and airline industries backs Komisar up. The more successful people have been in the past, the worse they perform when they enter a new environment. They become overconfident, and they're less likely to seek critical feedback even though the context is radically different. Jobs was in one of these success traps: with his track record and his history of proving naysayers wrong, he didn't bother to check his intuition by gathering input from enough creators with relevant domain knowledge. And his intuition led him further astray when he encountered Dean Kamen's presentation style.

The Perils of Passion

When Kamen pitched the Segway, he spoke passionately about how developing nations like China and India were building cities the size of New York every year. These urban centers were going to become clogged with cars, which are bad for our environment; the Segway could solve this problem. "He's a force of nature," Aileen Lee remembers. "He's technical, experienced, and superpassionate about these issues, so he is transfixing."

In a study led by Northeastern University entrepreneurship professor Cheryl Mitteness, more than five dozen angel investors made over 3,500 evaluations of entrepreneurs' pitches and decided whether or not to fund them. The investors filled out a survey about whether their own styles were more intuitive or analytical, rated each entrepreneur's passion and enthusiasm, and then evaluated the funding potential of each startup. The results showed that the more intuitive investors were, the greater their odds of being swayed by an entrepreneur's passion.

As Daniel Kahneman explains in *Thinking, Fast and Slow*, intuition operates rapidly, based on hot emotions, whereas reason is a slower, cooler process. Intuitive investors are susceptible to getting caught up in an entrepreneur's enthusiasm; analytical investors are more likely to focus on the facts and make cold judgments about the viability of the business. Jobs's intuitive style predisposed him to get swept away by Kamen's passion and the inherent novelty of the technology. And his hubris and inexperience with transportation left him vulnerable to trusting what would eventually be revealed as a false positive.

When assessing the prospects of a novel idea, it's all too easy to be seduced by the enthusiasm of the people behind it. In the words of Google executives Eric Schmidt and Jonathan Rosenberg, "Passionate people don't wear their passion on their sleeves; they have it in their hearts." The passion to see an idea to fruition isn't visible in the emotion people express. The enthusiasm we inject into our words, tone of voice, and body language isn't a clue to the internal passion we experience, but merely a reflection of our presentation skills and our personalities. For example, research shows that extraverts tend to be more expressive than introverts, which means that they display more passion. But whether we tend to be more extraverted or introverted has essentially no bearing on whether we'll succeed as entrepreneurs. You can love an idea and be determined to succeed, but still communicate it in a reserved manner.

This isn't to say that passion is irrelevant to entrepreneurial success. There's plenty of evidence that passionate entrepreneurs are able to grow their ventures faster and more successfully. For his part, Kamen was lacking the element of passion that helps ideas grow from invention to impact. Instead of being enticed by his passion for creating the Segway, the early investors should have assessed his passion for building a company and bringing the product successfully to market. And to do that, they shouldn't have only paid attention to what he *said*. They should have also examined what he *did*.

After studying his history, Randy Komisar concluded that Kamen was a more impressive inventor than entrepreneur. In the past, Kamen's most successful inventions were a response to customers coming to him with a problem to solve. In the 1970s, he came up with the idea for the portable drug infusion pump when his brother, a doctor, lamented that nurses were constantly delivering medications by hand that should be automated, and many patients were stuck in hospitals when they could be receiving medication at home. In the 1980s, Kamen developed the portable dialysis machine after Baxter Healthcare hired his company to refine its kidney dialysis for diabetic patients. He excelled at creating brilliant solutions to problems identified by others, not in finding the right problems to solve. In the case of the Segway, he started with a solution and then went hunting for a problem. Rather than responding to market pull, he made the mistake of initiating a technology push.

Although Kamen was passionate about the Segway, he wasn't prepared to execute it successfully. If we want to improve our idea selection skills, we shouldn't look at *whether* people have been successful. We need to track *how* they've been successful. "When we looked at Dean, we saw a credible founder who had a history of inventing successful medical devices, and the people he'd partnered with to make those products were still with him," Aileen Lee says. "But when it came down to actually making the product, the day-to-day execution and making the product cost-effective was important." Kamen didn't have that experience. Bill Sahlman adds: "It's never the idea; it's always the execution."

If we want to forecast whether the originators of a novel idea will make it successful, we need to look beyond the enthusiasm they express about their ideas and focus on the enthusiasm for execution that they reveal through their actions. Rick Ludwin didn't bet on Jerry Seinfeld and Larry David because they looked or sounded passionate when they pitched their script—or even because they were genuinely excited about their concept for a show. He gave them a chance because he watched them revise their concept and observed their ability to get the execution right. "They were the kinds of guys who would be in the writer's room trying to figure out how to fix the second act at midnight. You saw how meticulous Jerry was in his work. That's the passion you're looking for."

Corrective Lenses for Idea Selection

My personal failure to invest in Warby Parker was a major false negative. After reading the research on idea selection, I recognized one of my limitations: I wasn't a fellow creator in the domain, nor was I a customer. At first, I blamed my poor creative forecasting on my 20/20 vision. When you've never owned a pair of glasses, it's awfully hard to gauge the preferences of people who do. But upon reflection, I realized that what I truly lacked was breadth. I had spent two years doing research and consulting for an eye-care company whose primary source of revenue was selling glasses in-store after optometrists provided prescriptions and customers tried them on. I was stuck in the default mindset of how glasses were traditionally bought and sold. Had I spent time generating ideas before hearing the pitch, or reading up on how other clothing and accessory products were sold online, I might have been more open to the idea.

The four founders weren't hindered by these blinders: they had the right depth and breadth of experience. Three of them wore glasses and brought combined experience in bioengineering, health care, consulting, and banking. One of them, Dave, had lost his glasses while spending several months traveling abroad with no phone. When he came back to the United States, the need to buy a phone and glasses at the same time gave him a fresh perspective. Neil Blumenthal didn't wear glasses, but he had spent the past five years working at a nonprofit that trained women to start businesses in Asia, Africa, and Latin America. The product that he taught women to sell was eyeglasses. That gave him the necessary depth of knowledge in the optical industry: he knew that glasses could be manufactured, designed, and sold at a lower cost. And having spent time outside the conventional eyeglass channels, he had the breadth to adopt a fresh approach. "It's rare that originality comes from insiders," Neil tells me, "especially when they're as entrenched and comfortable as the optical industry."

Because of the diversity of their experience, the Warby Parker entrepreneurs weren't hampered by existing prototypes or limited by evaluative mindsets. Instead of assuming that their idea would work and going into full-on enthusiastic sales mode like Kamen did, they first sought extensive feedback from fellow creators and potential customers. By cutting out the middleman of the retailer, they had determined that they could sell pairs of glasses that normally cost $500 for $45. After a marketing expert warned them that their costs would increase—and that price was viewed as a sign of quality—they created a survey with mock product pages, randomly assigning customers to different price points. They found that the likelihood of purchase increased up to prices around $100, then plateaued and dropped in higher ranges. They tested different website designs with friends to see what would generate not only the most clicks, but also the strongest trust.

Since other companies could sell glasses online, the founders realized that branding would be critical to their success. To name the company, they spent six months generating ideas, building a spreadsheet with more than two thousand potential names. They tested their favorites in surveys and focus groups, finding that the Kerouac-inspired name of Warby Parker sounded sophisticated and unique, and evoked no negative associations. Then they brought passion for execution in spades.

Much of Warby Parker's recent success is due to the way they involved peers in evaluating ideas. In 2014, they created a program called Warbles, inviting everyone in the company to submit suggestions and requests for new technology features at any time. Before Warbles was introduced, they had received ten to twenty idea submissions per quarter. With the new program, the number of submissions jumped to nearly four hundred as employees trusted that the idea selection process was meritocratic. One of the suggestions led to the company's overhauling how they conducted retail sales; another led to a new booking system for appointments. "Neil and Dave are really brilliant," says Warby Parker's chief technology officer, Lon Binder, "but there's no way they can be as brilliant as two hundred people combined."

Instead of limiting access to the ideas and leaving it up to managers to decide which ones to pursue and implement, Warby Parker made the suggestions completely transparent in a Google document. Everyone in the company could read them, comment on them online, and discuss them in a biweekly meeting. This means that, just as Justin Berg recommends, the ideas are evaluated not only by managers, but also by fellow creators—who tend to be more open to radically novel ideas. The time employees spend generating ideas makes them better at discerning which suggestions from their colleagues are worthwhile.

The technology teams have full discretion to sort through the requests and start working on the ones that interest them. It sounds like a democracy, but there's one twist: to give employees some guidance on which suggestions represent strategic priorities for the company, managers vote the promising ones up and the bad ones down. To avoid false positives and false negatives, the votes aren't binding. Technology teams can overrule managers by selecting a request that didn't receive a lot of votes and work to prove its value. "They don't wait for permission to start building something," says applied psychology expert Reb Rebele, who has worked on a study at Warby Parker. "But they gather feedback from peers before rolling things out to customers. They start fast and then slow down."

Had the Segway been submitted to the Warbles process, a lot more critical feedback might have rolled in to prevent it from being made—or to generate a more useful design. Before it was too late, Dean Kamen would have learned to make it practical or licensed the technology to someone who could.

The Segway may have failed, but Kamen is still a brilliant inventor, Jeff Bezos is still a visionary entrepreneur, and John Doerr is still a shrewd investor. Whether you're generating or evaluating new ideas, the best you can do is measure success on the kind of yardstick that batters use in baseball. As Randy Komisar puts it, "If I'm hitting .300, I'm a genius. That's because the future cannot be predicted. The sooner you learn it, the sooner you can be good at it."

Dean Kamen has moved on to unveil a series of new inventions, back in the health-care space where he made his original mark. There's a prosthetic arm with advanced robotics technology that makes it possible for a soldier or amputee to pick up a grape and operate a hand drill—nicknamed "Luke" after a *Star Wars* scene in which Skywalker gets a bionic arm. There's a new Stirling engine, a quiet, fuel-efficient machine for generating power and heating water. That engine powers the Slingshot water purifier, which can distill drinking water from any source, needs no filter, and can run on cow dung as a source of fuel. Kamen came full circle when he pitched the Slingshot to Komisar. Once again, though, Komisar is skeptical. Having traipsed around the developing world with a backpack himself, he thinks the machinery is too complicated for off-the-grid installations; when it stops working, it will wind up in a garbage heap. Whether this is an accurate forecast or a false negative remains to be seen.

As an inventor, Kamen's best bet is to blindly generate novel ideas and gather more feedback from fellow creators to hone his vision about which ones might prove useful. As an investor, you'll be able to see more clearly, but you'll still be making one-eyed gambles. Instead of banking on a single idea, your wisest move might be to bet on a whole portfolio of Kamen's creations.

In 2013 alone, over three hundred thousand patents were granted in the United States. The chances that any one of these inventions will change the world are tiny. Individual creators have far better odds over a lifetime of ideas. When we judge their greatness, we focus not on their averages, but on their peaks.

3

Out on a Limb

Speaking Truth to Power

"Great spirits have always encountered opposition
from mediocre minds."

Albert Einstein

In the early 1990s, a high-flying CIA analyst named Carmen Medina went to Western Europe on a three-year assignment. When she returned to the United States, she found that leaving the country had set her career back. After getting stuck with one job after another that didn't fit her skills and aspirations, she searched for another way to contribute. She began attending working groups about the future of intelligence.

During the course of her career at the CIA, Medina recognized a fundamental problem with communication in the intelligence community. The default system for sharing information was through "finished intelligence reports," which were released once a day and difficult to coordinate across agencies. Analysts had no way of sharing insights as they emerged. Since knowledge was evolving constantly, it took too long for critical information to land in the right hands. With lives at stake and national security on the line, every second mattered. Each agency was effectively producing its own daily newspaper, and Medina saw a need for a dramatically different system that would allow for real-time updates to be shared between agencies. To break down the silos and speed up communication, she proposed something wildly countercultural: instead of printing reports on sheets of paper, intelligence agencies ought to begin publishing their findings instantaneously and transmitting them over Intelink, the intelligence community's classified internet.

Her colleagues quickly shot down her suggestion. Nothing like Medina's plan had ever been attempted before. The internet, they argued, was a threat to national security. Intelligence was a clandestine service for good reason. Under the current system they could ensure that printed documents reached the designated recipient with the need to know; electronic communications didn't seem secure in that way. If knowledge landed in the wrong hands, we would all be in jeopardy.

Medina refused to back down. If the whole point of these groups was to explore the future, and she couldn't speak truth to power there, where could she? Having witnessed how the fax machine enabled more efficient information sharing, she was convinced that the digital revolution would ultimately shake up the intelligence world. She continued advocating for an internet platform that would allow the CIA to transmit intelligence back and forth with other agencies like the FBI and NSA.

Medina kept voicing her opinions, but no one listened. A senior colleague warned her: "Be careful what you're saying in these groups. If you're too honest, and say what you really think, it will ruin your career." Soon, even her good friends started isolating themselves from her. Finally, fed up with the lack of respect she was receiving, Medina blew up and got into a shouting match that forced her to take three sick days and then start hunting for a new job.

When she couldn't find outside work, she ended up in a staff position that took her away from the action—pretty much the only CIA job she could get. She stayed quiet for a while, but three years after her flameout, she decided to speak up again in support of an online system for real-time, continuous reporting across agencies.

Less than a decade later, Carmen Medina played an indispensable role in creating a platform called Intellipedia, an internal Wikipedia for intelligence agencies to access one another's knowledge. It was so radically at odds with CIA norms that, in the words of one observer, "it was like being asked to promote vegetarianism in Texas."

By 2008, Intellipedia was a key resource that intelligence agencies used for such wide-ranging challenges as protecting the Beijing Olympics and identifying the terrorists behind the Mumbai attacks. Within a few years, the site accrued over half a million registered users in the intelligence community, over a million pages, and 630 million page views—and won the Service to America Homeland Security Medal. "It's hard to overstate what they did," said one senior leader. "They made a major transformation almost overnight with no money after other programs failed to achieve these results with millions of dollars in funding."

Why did Medina fail in her first efforts at speaking up, and what enabled her to be heard the second time? In between, the world changed: the internet gained widespread acceptance and the September 11 terrorist attacks sounded an alarm for better coordination between intelligence agencies. But there was no online solution until Medina rose to become the deputy director of intelligence at the CIA, which gave her the authority to back Intellipedia. To land that position, she needed to learn to communicate differently—to speak up in ways that won credibility instead of losing it.

At some point, we've all considered voicing a minority opinion, protesting a policy that doesn't make sense, championing a novel way of doing things, or standing up for a disadvantaged group of people. This chapter is about when to speak up and how to do it effectively without jeopardizing our careers and relationships. What are the right times to raise our voices, and what steps can we take to get heard? Along with unpacking Carmen Medina's discoveries, you'll learn from an entrepreneur who pitches his companies upside down and a manager who took on Steve Jobs. You'll see why the most supportive managers sometimes provide the least support, how gender and race influence voice, and why the photos we like of ourselves are the opposite of the ones we prefer of our friends. The goal is to explain how we can all reduce the risks of speaking up—and gain the potential benefits of doing so.

Power Without Status

Leaders and managers appreciate it when employees take the initiative to offer help, build networks, gather new knowledge, and seek feedback. But there's one form of initiative that gets penalized: speaking up with suggestions. In one study across manufacturing, service, retail, and nonprofit settings, the more frequently employees voiced ideas and concerns upward, the less likely they were to receive raises and promotions over a two-year period. And in an experiment, when individuals voiced their objections to racism, they were criticized as self-righteous by those who failed to speak out against it. When we climb up the moral ladder, it can be rather lonely at the top.

To understand the barriers that Carmen Medina encountered, we need to tease apart two major dimensions of social hierarchy that are often lumped together: power and status. Power involves exercising control or authority over others; status is being respected and admired. In an experiment led by University of North Carolina professor Alison Fragale, people were punished for trying to exercise power without status. When people sought to exert influence but lacked respect, others perceived them as difficult, coercive, and self-serving. Since they haven't earned our admiration, we don't feel they have the right to tell us what to do, and we push back. This is what happened to Carmen Medina; her years overseas left her with little status. She hadn't had the opportunity to prove her worth to her colleagues, so they didn't give her ideas any credence. As people dismissed her concerns, she felt her frustration mounting.

When we're trying to influence others and we discover that they don't respect us, it fuels a vicious cycle of resentment. In an effort to assert our own authority, we respond by resorting to increasingly disrespectful behaviors. The most shocking demonstration of this vicious cycle occurred when researchers asked people to work on a task in pairs, and gave one person power over what tasks the other would have to carry out to earn a shot at a $50 bonus. When the power holders were randomly assigned to learn that their peers admired and respected them, they chose mostly reasonable assignments: for the $50 bonus, their peers would have to tell a funny joke or write about their experiences the previous day. But when power holders learned that their peers looked down on them, they retaliated by setting up some humiliating tasks, such as telling their partners to bark like a dog three times, say "I am filthy" five times, or count backward from five hundred in increments of seven. Just being told that they weren't respected nearly doubled their chances of using their power in ways that degraded others.

Carmen Medina didn't go nearly that far. But as she continued speaking up, her effort to exercise power without status elicited increasingly negative reactions. Status cannot be claimed; it has to be earned or granted.

During her second effort years later, Medina didn't put her career on the line by attempting to attack the system from below. Instead, she aimed to earn status by becoming part of the system and then changing it from within. As iconic filmmaker Francis Ford Coppola observed, "The way to come to power is not always to merely challenge the Establishment, but first make a place in it and then challenge and double-cross the Establishment." When Medina made the risky choice to present her idea again, she stabilized her risk portfolio by applying for a job that focused on information security. Her primary role was to keep knowledge safe. "That's not something I would have normally gone for—it was a very conservative thing," she remembers.

The other things I had to do with the security of our publications didn't excite me. But I could eventually use this in a smaller way to do the things I wanted to get done. Way down at the bottom of the list of responsibilities was to begin to explore digital publication options for the things that we were trying to keep secure. I had this very conservative top cover. It was a balanced risk portfolio.

Earlier, her case for sharing information over the internet sounded like a security threat. Now, she was able to frame it as part of her mission to protect security. "People saw that I stood *for* something, not just against the status quo. I thought that if I proved myself in that position, I would get a chance to start planting the seeds for even bigger change."

As Medina gained respect for these efforts, she accumulated what psychologist Edwin Hollander called idiosyncrasy credits—the latitude to deviate from the group's expectations. Idiosyncrasy credits accrue through respect, not rank: they're based on contributions. We squash a low-status member who tries to challenge the status quo, but tolerate and sometimes even applaud the originality of a high-status star.

In a recent experiment led by Silvia Bellezza, people rated male professors at top universities as having 14 percent more status and competence when they donned a T-shirt and a beard than when they wore a tie and were clean shaven. Most professors dress formally, and refusing to follow the norm usually carries a cost. Those who successfully buck convention signal that they've earned the idiosyncrasy credits to do as they please.

After Carmen Medina took the job in security, she spent the next few years making major progress in the digital arena. By doing work that advanced the CIA's mission, she earned the idiosyncrasy credits to champion her vision for knowledge sharing. She was promoted to the executive level. In 2005, Sean Dennehy and Don Burke, two CIA analysts from different parts of the agency, joined forces to help create Intellipedia, a classified variation on Wikipedia that would be accessible across the intelligence community. Many managers were skeptical of the value of a wiki for cross-agency information sharing. "Trying to implement these tools in the intelligence community is basically like telling people their parents raised them wrong," Dennehy admitted. They were turned down at every stage until they found Carmen Medina, who had quietly been building a network of rebels within the CIA. She provided the senior-level support that their fledgling effort needed, securing a space for them to introduce the concept of open source to a culture built upon secrecy.

Since Medina had power, she no longer had to worry as much about how she voiced her ideas. But along the way, to earn the status that eventually gave her power, she did have to alter the way she spoke. Her shift in strategy shares something with the most bizarre startup pitch you might ever encounter.

Putting Your Worst Foot Forward: The Sarick Effect

After having their first child, Rufus Griscom and Alisa Volkman were appalled by the amount of false advertising and bad advice being offered about parenting. They started an online magazine and blog network called Babble to challenge the dominant parenting clichés and tackle the cold, hard truth with humor. In 2009, when Griscom pitched Babble to venture capitalists, he did the exact opposite of what every entrepreneur has been taught to do: he presented a slide listing the top five reasons *not* to invest in his business.

This should have killed his pitch. Investors are looking for reasons to say yes, and here he was, hand delivering a list of reasons to say no. Entrepreneurs are supposed to talk about the upsides of their companies, not the downsides. But his counterintuitive approach worked: that year, Babble brought in $3.3 million in funding.

Two years later, Griscom made a sales visit to Disney to see if they might be interested in acquiring Babble. For this pitch, it would logically have been unthinkable to lead with the downsides. It's one thing to admit that your startup has problems; you can promise to fix the flaws. But when you're selling an established company, you have every incentive to emphasize the silver linings—and you're not going to stick around long enough to do anything about the clouds.

Strangely, though, Griscom did it again. One of his slides read: "Here's Why You Should Not Buy Babble."

Presenting to the family division of digital at Disney, he explained that user engagement, at less than three page views per visit, was lower than expected. Babble was supposed to be a parenting website, but 40 percent of the posts were about celebrities. And the back end of the website was in sore need of retooling.

Disney ended up buying the company for $40 million.

This is called the Sarick Effect, named after the social scientist Leslie Sarick.

In both situations, Griscom was presenting ideas to people who had more power than he had, and trying to convince them to commit their resources. Most of us assume that to be persuasive, we ought to emphasize our strengths and minimize our weaknesses. That kind of powerful communication makes sense if the audience is supportive.

But when you're pitching a novel idea or speaking up with a suggestion for change, your audience is likely to be skeptical. Investors are looking to poke holes in your arguments; managers are hunting for reasons why your suggestion won't work. Under those circumstances, for at least four reasons, it's actually more effective to adopt Griscom's form of powerless communication by accentuating the flaws in your idea.

The first advantage is that leading with weaknesses disarms the audience. Marketing professors Marian Friestad and Peter Wright find that when we're aware that someone is trying to persuade us, we naturally raise our mental shields. Rampant confidence is a red flag— a signal that we need to defend ourselves against weapons of influence. In the early days of Babble, when Griscom presented at the first two board meetings, he talked about everything that was going right with the business, hoping to excite the board about the company's momentum and potential. "Every time I would say something emphasizing the upside, I would get skeptical responses," he recalls. "Unbridled optimism comes across as salesmanship; it seems dishonest somehow, and as a consequence it's met with skepticism. Everyone is allergic to the feeling, or suspicious of being sold."

At the third meeting of the board, Griscom reversed his approach, opening with a candid discussion of everything that was going wrong with the company and what was keeping him up at night. Although this tactic might be familiar in a debate, it was highly unconventional for an entrepreneur. Board members, though, responded much more favorably than they had in previous meetings, shifting their attention away from self-defense and toward problem solving. Griscom decided to try the same approach with investors, and noticed a similar reaction: they let their guard down. "When I put up a slide that says 'Here's why you shouldn't buy this company,' the first response was laughter. Then you could see them physically relax. It's sincere; it doesn't smell, feel, or look anything like sales. They're no longer being sold."

In her first attempts at speaking up, Carmen Medina failed to acknowledge the limitations of her ideas. She stated it as a fact that the intelligence community needed to share information more openly, making a dangerous argument that solely stressed the benefits of transparency. One friend confided, "Carmen, you talk as if you won't be happy until everyone accepts what you say as the truth." In the second round of speaking up a few years later, she became much more balanced in her presentations, aiming to express "that little bit of doubt by saying, 'Maybe I'm wrong.'"

After Medina advanced to a leadership position, she found herself on the receiving end of pitches. When people only touted the pluses of their ideas, she quickly concluded that "this idea is full of holes; they really haven't thought it through, and they've constructed their slide deck to keep me from figuring it out. When people presented drawbacks or disadvantages, I would become an ally. Instead of selling me, they've given me a problem to solve."

Along with changing the frame of the interaction, being forthright about faults alters how audiences evaluate us. In a fascinating experiment, Teresa Amabile asked people to gauge the intelligence and expertise of book reviewers. She wondered whether adjusting the tone of reviews would change people's judgments of the critics. She took actual book reviews from the *New York Times* and edited them so the content was identical, but the evaluations were either flattering or scathing. Half of the participants were randomly assigned to read a positive review:

> *In 128 inspired pages, Alvin Harter, with his first work of fiction, shows himself to be an extremely capable young American author.* A Longer Dawn *is a novella—a prose poem, if you will— of tremendous impact. It deals with elemental things: life, love, and death, and does so with such great intensity that it achieves new heights of superior writing on every page.*

The other half read a harsh version of the same review, in which Amabile left the language intact but substituted some adjectives that were critical rather than complimentary:

> *In 128 uninspired pages, Alvin Harter, with his first work of fiction, shows himself to be an extremely incapable young American*

author. A Longer Dawn is a novella—a prose poem, if you will— of negligible impact. It deals with elemental things: life, love, and death, but does so with such little intensity that it achieves new depths of inferior writing on every page.

Which version makes the reviewer sound smarter? They should be equal. The quality of the reviewer's prose hasn't changed. The vocabulary is comparable, and so is the grammatical structure. It took the same level of ability to write both versions. But people rated the critical reviewer as 14 percent more intelligent, and having 16 percent greater literary expertise, than the complimentary reviewer.

People think an amateur can appreciate art, but it takes a professional to critique it. Merely changing a handful of words from positive to negative—*inspired* to *uninspired, capable* to *incapable, tremendous impact* to *negligible impact, great intensity* to *little intensity,* and *heights of superior writing* to *depths of inferior writing*—was sufficient to make the critical reviewer sound smarter. "Prophets of doom and gloom appear wise and insightful," Amabile writes, "while positive statements are seen as having a naïve 'Pollyanna' quality."

This is the second benefit of leading with the limitations of an idea: it makes you look smart.* Rufus Griscom first discovered this early in his career, which started in publishing. "There's nothing more shameful than writing a review that's too positive," he learned. Even if reviewers loved a book, they felt an obligation to add a paragraph at the end noting where it fell short. According to Griscom, it's their way of saying, "I'm not a chump; I was not totally snowed by this author. I am discerning." When he told investors about the problems with

---

* As you probably anticipated, this doesn't work if you're pitching a bad idea. Stanford psychologist Zak Tormala finds that audiences are more convinced when experts express doubt than certainty, due to the element of surprise. We expect an entrepreneur or a change agent to be certain. When they're not, we're intrigued, and we pay more attention to the message—which means we'll get on board if the idea is compelling. The Sarick Effect only holds if you have a persuasive message to deliver.

Babble, he demonstrated that he wasn't snowed by his own ideas or trying to snow them; he was a shrewd judge of his shortcomings. He was smart enough to do his homework and anticipate some of the problems that they would spot.

The third advantage of being up front about the downsides of your ideas is that it makes you more trustworthy. When Griscom described the hurdles he faced in his own business, he came across not only as knowledgeable, but also as honest and modest. Of course, highlighting weaknesses can backfire if the audience doesn't already recognize them; it can give them ammunition to shoot down your idea. But Griscom's audiences were already skeptical, and they were going to find out about many of the problems anyway during due diligence. "The job of the investor is to figure out what's wrong with the company. By telling them what's wrong with the business model, I'm doing some of the work for them. It established trust," Griscom explains. And speaking frankly about the weaknesses of the business in turn made him more credible when he talked about the strengths. "You need confidence to be humble, to front-run your weaknesses," Griscom says. "If I'm willing to tell them what's wrong with my business, investors think, 'There must be an awful lot that's right with it.'" Disney came to trust Griscom so much that after they bought Babble, they brought him on board to run the business unit for two years as vice president and general manager, where he played a key role in developing Disney Interactive's digital strategy. The Sarick Effect strikes again.

A fourth advantage of this approach is that it leaves audiences with a more favorable assessment of the idea itself, due to a bias in how we process information. To illustrate this bias, I often ask executives to judge how happy they are after thinking about the positive features of their lives. One group is tasked with writing three good things about their lives; another group has to list twelve good things. Everyone expects the twelve group to be happier: the more blessings you count, the better you should feel about your circumstances. But most of the time, the opposite is true. We're happier after we list three good things than twelve. Why would this be?

Psychologist Norbert Schwarz has shown that the easier it is to think of something, the more common and important we assume it is. We use ease of retrieval as information. It's a cinch for executives to come up with three good things about their lives. They immediately list their love of their children, their spouses, and their jobs. Since it was a breeze to generate a few positives, they infer that their lives are pretty darn good. It's noticeably harder to name twelve good things about their lives. After covering family and work, executives often mention their friends and then ask if they can count each one separately. Having struggled to come up with a dozen good things, they draw the conclusion that their lives aren't quite so good after all.*

This is what happened to investors when Rufus Griscom cited Babble's weaknesses. By acknowledging its most serious problems, he made it harder for investors to generate their own ideas about what was wrong with the company. And as they found themselves thinking hard to identify other concerns, they decided Babble's problems weren't actually that severe. Griscom saw this happen in the early Babble board meeting when he first tested his upside-down pitch. "When I led with the factors that could kill the company, the response from the board was the exact opposite: oh, these things aren't so bad. Newton's third law can be true in human dynamics as well: every action has an equal and opposite reaction."

Just as presenting negatives can ironically make it more difficult

---

* Since I feel guilty about skewing their life satisfaction judgments, I counterbalance the exercise by asking the executives to name three or twelve bad things about their lives. Naming three bad things is easy; it leaves us thinking that life isn't so great. But it's actually pretty challenging to come up with a dozen things that are wrong, which leads to the realization that life could be a whole lot worse. Another way to make the point is to ask people to judge someone famous. In an experiment by psychologist Geoffrey Haddock, people generated a list of two or five negative attributes of Tony Blair. After coming up with more reasons to dislike him, they actually liked him more. It was more difficult to think of many negative attributes, so they assumed he must not be that bad.

for audiences to think of them, speaking up effectively depends on making the positive features easier to process.

Unfamiliarity Breeds Contempt

Take a look at this list of familiar songs. Pick one of them and tap the rhythm to it on a table:

- "Happy Birthday"
- "Mary Had a Little Lamb"
- "Jingle Bells"
- "Rock Around the Clock"
- "Twinkle, Twinkle Little Star"
- "Row, Row, Row Your Boat"
- "The Star-Spangled Banner"

Now, what do you think the odds are that one of your friends would recognize the song you're tapping?

I've been running this exercise for years with leaders and students, and it's as fun at a dinner party as it is educational. What was your estimate? If you said zero, you're either questioning your own tapping skills or seriously doubting the ear of your friend. In the original study at Stanford, after tapping a song, people thought it would be easy for a listener to guess it: they predicted that their peers had a 50 percent chance of naming it accurately. But when they went ahead and tapped the songs, only 2.5 percent actually guessed correctly. Of the 120 songs tapped in total, people expected 60 of them to be recognized. In reality, only three were recognized. I've found the same results at numerous organizations. At a senior leadership event at JPMorgan Chase, CEO Jamie Dimon predicted that the executive sitting next to him would have a 100 percent chance of guessing it. He turned out to be right—but most of the time, we're overconfident in our predictions. Why?

It's humanly impossible to tap out the rhythm of a song without hearing the tune in your head. That makes it impossible to imagine what your disjointed knocks sound like to an audience that is not hearing the accompanying tune. As Chip and Dan Heath write in *Made to Stick*, "The listeners can't hear that tune—all they can hear is a bunch of disconnected taps, like a kind of bizarre Morse Code."

This is the core challenge of speaking up with an original idea. When you present a new suggestion, you're not only hearing the tune in your head.

You wrote the song.

You've spent hours, days, weeks, months, or maybe even years thinking about the idea. You've contemplated the problem, formulated the solution, and rehearsed the vision. You know the lyrics and the melody of your idea by heart. By that point, it's no longer possible to imagine what it sounds like to an audience that's listening to it for the first time.

This explains why we often undercommunicate our ideas. They're already so familiar to us that we underestimate how much exposure an audience needs to comprehend and buy into them. When Harvard professor John Kotter studied change agents years ago, he found that they typically undercommunicated their visions by a factor of ten. On average, they spoke about the direction of the change ten times less often than their stakeholders needed to hear it. In one three-month period, employees might be exposed to 2.3 million words and numbers. On average during that period, the vision for change was expressed in only 13,400 words and numbers: a 30-minute speech, an hour-long meeting, a briefing, and a memo. Since more than 99 percent of the communication that employees encounter during those three months does not concern the vision, how can they be expected to understand it, let alone internalize it? The change agents don't realize this, because they're up to their ears in information about their vision.

If we want people to accept our original ideas, we need to speak up about them, then rinse and repeat. To illustrate, which of these two words do you like better?

iktitaf   *sarick*

If you're like most people, you'll choose *sarick* over *iktitaf*. But it has nothing to do with the word itself.

Eminent psychologist Robert Zajonc called it the mere exposure effect: the more often we encounter something, the more we like it. When he showed people the nonsense words *iktitaf* and *sarick* for the first time, the two words tested as equally appealing. But when Zajonc presented either one of those words twice before the comparative test, people developed a preference for it—and liking increased further after five, ten, and twenty-five views.

To enhance your liking of *sarick*, I embedded it five times in the previous section about Rufus Griscom.

There is no such thing as the Sarick Effect, and there was no social scientist named Leslie Sarick. I made them up to demonstrate the mere exposure effect. (For the record, Rufus Griscom is a real person, as is every other person in this book.)

The mere exposure effect has been replicated many times—the more familiar a face, letter, number, sound, flavor, brand, or Chinese character becomes, the more we like it. It's true across different cultures and species; even baby chickens prefer the familiar. My favorite test was when people looked at photographs of themselves and their friends that were either regular or inverted, as if seen in a mirror. We prefer the regular photos of our friends, because that's how we're used to seeing them, but we like the inverted photos of ourselves, because that's how we see ourselves when we look in the mirror. "Familiarity doesn't breed contempt," says serial entrepreneur Howard Tullman. "It breeds comfort."

One explanation for this effect is that exposure increases the ease of processing. An unfamiliar idea requires more effort to understand. The more we see, hear, and touch it, the more comfortable we become with it, and the less threatening it is.

Just as film is ruined when it's overexposed, and songs we hear too often become irritatingly stuck in our heads, too much familiarity with an idea can lead to boredom. But in the context of speaking up, people rarely oversaturate their audiences. Overall, the evidence suggests that liking continues to increase as people are exposed to an idea between ten and twenty times, with additional exposure still useful for more complex ideas. Interestingly, exposures are more effective when they're short and mixed in with other ideas, to help maintain the audience's curiosity. It's also best to introduce a delay between the presentation of the idea and the evaluation of it, which provides time for it to sink in. If you're making a suggestion to a boss, you might start with a 30-second elevator pitch during a conversation on Tuesday, revisit it briefly the following Monday, and then ask for feedback at the end of the week.

When Carmen Medina became the deputy director of intelligence at the CIA, she knew that if she wanted intelligence analysts to share information more openly, she would have to give them regular exposure to the idea. So she started a blog on the classified intranet in an effort to model the transparency she was advocating. Twice a week, she wrote short commentaries, expressing her views about the need for less secrecy and for sharing news, and suggesting that this would be the wave of the future. At first, many leaders reflexively dismissed the concept. But just as exposure research would suggest, the brief presentations interspersed between other communications—and the delays between them—caused leaders to warm up to Medina's ideas.

Soon, the CIA's technology experts developed a platform on the intranet that allowed individual employees to set up their own blogs, and familiarity spread further. People began crediting Medina for their courage to blog.* Due in no small part to her efforts, the intelligence community gained a vibrant blogging scene where analysts across different agencies informally share knowledge.

Quitting Before Leaving

When I learned about Carmen Medina's story, I was puzzled about why she chose to continue speaking up after it sank her career. Building on a classic book by economist Albert Hirschman, there are four different options for handling a dissatisfying situation. Whether you're unhappy with your job, your marriage, or your government, decades of research show that you have a choice between exit, voice, persistence, and neglect. Exit means removing yourself from the situation altogether: quitting a miserable job, ending an abusive marriage, or leaving an oppressive country. Voice involves actively trying to improve the situation: approaching your boss with ideas for enriching your job, encouraging your spouse to seek counseling, or becoming a political activist to elect a less corrupt government. Persistence is gritting your teeth and bearing it: working hard even though your job is stifling, sticking by your spouse, or supporting your government even though you disagree with it. Neglect entails staying in the current situation but reducing your effort: doing just enough at work not to get

---

* When Dennehy and Burke started to encourage people to contribute to the wiki, many managers refused to let employees use it. They worried about security breaches, quality dilution, and inefficiencies related to posting and accessing information between agencies. But as they gained exposure, they became more accustomed to the idea that they didn't have to get changes approved up their chains of command—and that it was actually more efficient to share information by topic than by agency. Within three years, Intellipedia was averaging over four thousand edits a day.

fired, choosing new hobbies that keep you away from your spouse, or refusing to vote.

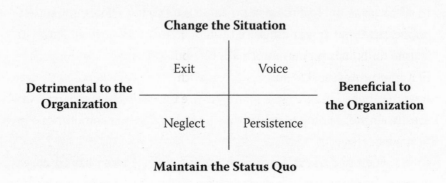

Change the Situation

Exit | Voice

Detrimental to the Organization   **Beneficial to the Organization**

Neglect | Persistence

Maintain the Status Quo

Fundamentally, these choices are based on feelings of control and commitment. Do you believe you can effect change, and do you care enough to try? If you believe you're stuck with the status quo, you'll choose neglect when you're not committed, and persistence when you are. If you do feel you can make a difference, but you aren't committed to the person, country, or organization, you'll leave. Only when you believe your actions matter *and* care deeply will you consider speaking up.

After Carmen Medina was silenced in her early attempts to voice her ideas, she no longer believed she could make a difference. She wasn't the kind of person to shirk her responsibilities, but some of her commitment had been shattered: "I was like a refugee on a boat, somewhere in between neglect and loyalty." Even after a few years, she couldn't shake the feeling that speaking up had torpedoed her career. "I was very hesitant to go back in there. I wasn't sure enough time had passed," she recalls, mulling it over. "You know why I was crazy enough to do it again? Because I was working for Mike, my favorite boss that I've had in my career."

At work, our sense of commitment and control depends more on our direct boss than on anyone else. When we have a supportive boss, our bond with the organization strengthens and we feel a greater span of influence. As I envisioned the boss who gave Medina the confidence to speak up again, I pictured someone agreeable—warm, trusting, and cooperative—so I was surprised when Medina described Mike as "prone to cynicism and mercurial." Her portrait of him fit the profile of a more disagreeable manager, one with a critical, skeptical stance toward others. Disagreeable managers are typically the last people we seek when we're going to go out on a limb, but they are sometimes our best advocates.

As much as agreeable people may love us, they often hate conflict even more. Their desire to please others and preserve harmony makes them prone to backing down instead of sticking up for us. "Because agreeable people value cooperation and conform to norms, they should not be inclined to make waves and upset interpersonal relationships," management researchers Jeff LePine and Linn Van Dyne wrote after studying voice. It is often the prickly people who are more comfortable taking a stand against others and against convention. As a Google employee put it, disagreeable managers may have a bad user interface but a great operating system.

In one study led by psychologist Stéphane Côté, adults filled out a personality survey measuring their tendencies toward agreeableness and disagreeableness. For the next three weeks, six times a day, they reported what they were doing and how they were feeling. Agreeable people were happiest in the moments when they doled out compliments and praise, smiled and laughed with others, expressed affection, reassured others, and compromised or made concessions to please others. Disagreeable people, in contrast, experienced the greatest joy when they were criticizing, confronting, or challenging others.

In the decision to speak up, whom we choose as our audience matters as much as how we deliver our message. When we speak up to agreeable audiences, their instinct is to nod and smile. In their effort to be accommodating and avoid conflict, they often shy away from offering critical feedback. Disagreeable managers are more inclined to challenge us, improving our ability to speak up effectively. "A lot can be said for cynicism, as long as it doesn't go too far," Medina notes. "I don't think Mike ever fully believed this was the way the organization had to go, but he had respect for diversity of thought. Even though he didn't necessarily agree—and we often did disagree on things—I felt I could be honest with him, and he would give me enough rope, but he would actually stop me before I hung myself."

Instead of speaking up to audiences who are highly agreeable, we're better off targeting suggestions to people with a history of originality. Research shows that when managers have a track record of challenging the status quo, they tend to be more open to new ideas and less threatened by contributions from others. They care more about making the organization better than about defending it as it stands. They're motivated to advance the organization's mission, which means they're not so loyal that they turn a blind eye to its shortcomings. "Mike loved the agency, but he was willing to be critical of it. He would get tears in his eyes talking about the mission," Medina says. "He had a much higher tolerance for misfits, for eccentrics, than a lot of managers in the agency did."

With the support of a tough boss whose top priority was to strengthen the CIA, Medina regained her sense of control and commitment. Knowing that her boss had her back, she was ready to resume her effort to promote more open information sharing.

As she climbed up the CIA ladder, Medina noticed that her colleagues became more receptive to her suggestions, though it was mostly middle managers who dismissed them. Social scientists have long demonstrated this middle-status conformity effect. If you're perched at the top, you're expected to be different and therefore have the license to deviate. Likewise, if you're still at the bottom of a status hierarchy, you have little to lose and everything to gain by being original. But the middle segment of that hierarchy—where the majority of people in an organization are found—is dominated by insecurity. Now that you have a bit of respect, you value your standing in the group and don't want to jeopardize it. To maintain and then gain status, you play a game of follow-the-leader, conforming to prove your worth as a group member. As sociologist George Homans observed, "Middle-status conservatism reflects the anxiety experienced by one who aspires to a social station but fears disenfranchisement." The fall from low to lower hardly hurts; the fall from middle to low is devastating.

Not long ago, I was asked to interview Google CEO Larry Page on stage. At dinner the night before the event, I asked him why he and Sergey Brin had been so hesitant to drop out of Stanford and make a full-time commitment to Google early in the company's history. His answer focused on their career stage. Had they already established themselves as academic superstars, they could have devoted themselves to Google without the risk of sacrificing anything professionally. Earlier in their careers, when they had no status, they were perfectly content to take risks: Page kept himself busy in college working on solar cars and building a printer out of Legos. But once they had made significant progress toward their doctorates, they had more to lose by quitting.

Middle-status conformity leads us to choose the safety of the tried-and-true over the danger of the original. Sociologists Damon Phillips of Columbia and Ezra Zuckerman of MIT found that security analysts were significantly less likely to issue negative stock ratings when they or the banks that employed them had middle status. Making a recommendation to sell a stock can anger corporate executives and investors who value the stock. Analysts with poor track records at minor banks have nowhere to fall by taking this risk, and star analysts at elite banks have a safety net. But for moderately successful analysts at average

banks who are trying to advance themselves, a negative recommendation could be a career-limiting move.*

As Carmen Medina moved up the ranks, she learned that it was
more effective to voice ideas upward and downward, and spent less
time attempting to make suggestions to middle managers. Senior
leaders saw her as one of the rare employees who believed there were
things wrong with the agency, and also believed it could change. Her
credibility was further bolstered by a growing following of junior colleagues. As she shared her views with rising stars in the CIA, they
grew excited about her vision and granted her status. "Younger
employees appreciated her fresh ideas and looked to her as a real role
model, which made it more difficult for others not to listen," Medina's
colleague Susan Benjamin notes. "It cemented her reputation and
helped her get heard."

Speaking While Female, and the Double Jeopardy of Double Minorities

Speaking up to an audience of risk-averse middle managers is challenging for anyone, but it was especially so for Carmen Medina as a
woman in a male-dominated organization. When I first heard her
story, I naively assumed that the days when women were undervalued
in professional settings were long gone, and she would ultimately be

---

* Does middle status really cause us to choose conformity over originality? Perhaps conventional
people simply choose to occupy middle-status roles—or have enough ambition to get to the
middle, but lack the originality to get to the top. Not so. There's new evidence that landing in the
middle of the status hierarchy actually makes us less original. When psychologists Michelle
Duguid and Jack Goncalo asked people to generate ideas, their output was 34 percent less original after being randomly assigned to a middle-manager role than a president or assistant role. In
another experiment, merely thinking about a time that they were in a middle-status role caused
participants to generate 20–25 percent fewer ideas and 16 percent less original ideas than thinking about being in a high-status or low-status role. With the most to lose in the middle, they were
more hesitant to take the task in an original direction.

evaluated on the quality of her ideas rather than her gender. But when I looked at the evidence, I was dismayed to discover that even today, speaking while female remains notoriously difficult. Across cultures, there's a rich body of evidence showing that people continue to hold strong gender-role stereotypes, expecting men to be assertive and women to be communal. When women speak up, they run the risk of violating that gender stereotype, which leads audiences to judge them as aggressive. Voice is an act of leadership, and as Sheryl Sandberg writes in *Lean In*, "When a girl tries to lead, she is often labeled bossy."

When I analyzed my own data, the results were deeply disconcerting. In an international bank and a health-care company, I found that voicing new revenue-generating ideas led to higher performance evaluations for men, but not for women. Other studies show that male executives who talk more than their peers are rewarded, but female executives who engage in the same behavior are devalued by both men *and* women. Similarly, when women offer suggestions for improvement, managers judge them as less loyal than men and are less likely to implement their proposals. Especially in male-dominated organizations, women pay a price for exercising voice.*

During her first attempt to speak up, Carmen Medina paid a price for speaking out. "The range of acceptable behavior for women was narrower than for men," she says. During her second tour, she had a different experience. Because it was part of her job to put information online, she no longer needed to worry about appearing too aggressive as she voiced her ideas for transparency. "In the early nineties when it all blew up, my commitment to this change was confused with my

---

* This helps to explain patterns of sexual harassment. In three studies, gender expert Jennifer Berdahl found that sexual harassment isn't primarily motivated by sexual desire: Women who meet feminine standards of beauty don't experience the most harassment. Instead, "it is motivated primarily by a desire to punish gender-role deviants and, therefore, is directed at women who violate feminine ideals." Women who were "assertive, dominant, and independent" faced the most harassment, particularly in male-dominated organizations. Sexual harassment, she concludes, is mostly targeted toward "uppity women."

personal frustration at not advancing in my career. It was always me-focused," Medina tells me. "The whole second chapter of this journey was really very different from the first chapter. I was mission focused." Extensive research shows that when women speak up on behalf of others, they avoid backlash, because they're being communal.

There's little doubt that the road was bumpier for Medina because she was a woman in a male-dominated CIA. But as a Puerto Rican woman, she belonged to not one but two minority groups. New research suggests that her double minority status may have amplified the costs and the benefits of speaking up. Management researcher Ashleigh Rosette, who is African American, noticed that she was treated differently when she led assertively than were both white women and black men. Working with colleagues, she found that double minority group members faced double jeopardy. When black women failed, they were evaluated much more harshly than black men and white leaders of both sexes. They didn't fit the stereotype of leaders as black or as female, and they shouldered an unfair share of the blame for mistakes. For double minorities, Rosette's team pointed out, failure is not an option.

Interestingly, though, Rosette and her colleagues found that when black women acted dominantly, they didn't face the same penalties as white women and black men. As double minorities, black women defy categories. Because people don't know which stereotypes to apply to them, they have greater flexibility to act "black" or "female" without violating stereotypes.

But this only holds true when there's clear evidence of their competence. For minority-group members, it's particularly important to earn status before exercising power. By quietly advancing the agenda of putting intelligence online as part of her job, Carmen Medina was able to build up successes without attracting too much attention. "I was able to fly under the radar," she says. "Nobody really noticed what

I was doing, and I was making headway by iterating to make us more of a publish-when-ready organization. It was almost like a backyard experiment. I pretty much proceeded unfettered."

Once Medina had accumulated enough wins, she started speaking up again—and this time, people were ready to listen. Rosette has discovered that when women climb to the top and it's clear that they're in the driver's seat, people recognize that since they've overcome prejudice and double standards, they must be unusually motivated and talented. But what happens when voice falls on deaf ears?

The Road Not Taken

Donna Dubinsky was just shy of thirty, and it was the most hectic time of her life. As Apple's distribution and sales manager in 1985, she was working virtually nonstop from morning until bedtime, maniacally focused on shipping computers to keep up with explosive demand. Suddenly, Steve Jobs proposed eliminating all six U.S. warehouses, dropping their inventory, and moving to a just-in-time production system in which computers would be assembled upon order and overnighted by FedEx.

Dubinsky thought this was a colossal mistake, one that could put the company's entire future in jeopardy. "In my mind, Apple being successful depended on distribution being successful," she says. For a while, she ignored the issue, thinking it would go away. When it didn't, she started making her case. Distribution was working just fine, she insisted: her team was coming off a record quarter, and complaints were virtually nonexistent.

Even though she was the master of the distribution domain, her objections were overruled. Eventually, she was assigned to a task force that spent several months reviewing Jobs's proposal. At the final task-force meeting, her boss's boss asked if everyone agreed to the just-in-time system. Jobs had the power and the majority following; Dubinsky was in the minority. Should she speak up and challenge the famously mercurial founder and chairman of the board, or should she stay quiet and keep Jobs happy?

Although Dubinsky was one of the few women in a management position at Apple in the 1980s, "it never crossed my mind that gender was an issue for me." She was committed—she had put her heart and soul into the company. She had control—she was in charge of part of the distribution division. She decided to stand her ground and restated her objection to Jobs's proposal. Knowing that she needed more time to prove her case, she met with her boss's boss and delivered an ultimatum: if she didn't get thirty days to create her own counterproposal, she would leave Apple.

Drawing such a stark line in the sand was a precarious move, but her request was granted. Dubinsky developed a novel proposal for consolidating customer service centers rather than moving to just-in-time production, which would gain some of the desired benefits without the risks. Her proposal was accepted.

"What got me heard," Dubinsky explains, "was output and impact. People saw me as somebody who could make things happen. If you become known as someone who delivers, you do your job and do it well, you build respect." She had earned status before exercising power, so she had idiosyncrasy credits to cash in.

From the outside, the prospect of speaking up against Steve Jobs might seem a losing battle. But given his disagreeable tendencies, Jobs was exactly the kind of person who could be confronted. Dubinsky knew that Jobs respected those who stood up to him and was open to new ways of doing things. And she wasn't speaking up for herself; she was advocating for Apple.

By virtue of her willingness to challenge an idea she viewed as wrong, Dubinsky landed a promotion. She was not alone. Starting in 1981, the Macintosh team had begun granting an annual award to one person who challenged Jobs—and Jobs promoted every one of them to run a major division of Apple.

Comparing Carmen Medina's and Donna Dubinsky's experiences raises fundamental questions about the best way to handle dissatisfaction. In the quest for originality, neglect isn't an option. Persistence is a temporary route to earning the right to speak up. But in the long run, like neglect, persistence maintains the status quo and falls short of resolving your dissatisfaction. To change the situation, exit and voice are the only viable alternatives.

Years ago, Hirschman alerted us to a major drawback of exit. Although it has the advantage of altering your own circumstances, it doesn't make them better for anyone else, as it enables the status quo to endure. "Voice feeds," Hirschman argued, "on the lack of opportunity for exit."

In recent years, the world has changed in ways that make exit dramatically easier than it was when Carmen Medina couldn't find an outside position after her blowup in 1995 at the CIA. Spending your career in one organization is a thing of the past: the dynamic labor market has made it possible for many people to land new positions with other employers. Thanks to globalization, social media, and rapid transportation and communication technologies, we have more mobility than ever before. Given these advantages, if you're unhappy in your job and it's easy to move, why pay the price of speaking up?

In Hirschman's view, exit is bad for originality. But Donna Dubinsky's experience casts exit in a different light. After winning the distribution battle at Apple, she landed a senior position in international sales and marketing at Claris, one of Apple's software subsidiaries. Within a few years, her group accounted for half of all of Claris's sales. When Apple refused to spin Claris off as an independent company in 1991, Dubinsky was so frustrated with the lack of opportunity for impact that she quit. She jetted to Paris for a yearlong sabbatical and took up painting, contemplating ways to contribute to a bigger mission.

When she met an entrepreneur named Jeff Hawkins, she decided that his startup, Palm Computing, was the next big wave of technology, and accepted a position as CEO.

Under Dubinsky's leadership, the startup developed the PalmPilot, the first runaway success in the fledgling market for personal digital devices. The PalmPilot was released in 1996 and, within a year and a half, sold over a million units. But in 1997, when Palm was acquired by 3Com, Dubinsky did not agree with some strategic decisions. For example, when the finance group wanted to require all departments to cut budgets by 10 percent, Dubinsky spoke up in protest, urging the company to invest in areas that were succeeding and apply cuts to those that weren't. In response, she was told, "You are not a very good corporate citizen. You need to go back and do your share."

Frustrated, Dubinsky and Hawkins left Palm to found a new company, Handspring, in 1998. After merely a year, Handspring launched the Visor handheld computer, rapidly capturing a quarter of its market. After the development of the successful Treo smartphone, Handspring merged with Palm in 2003. And a few years later, Steve Jobs launched the iPhone.

Years earlier, Dubinsky remembers "sitting in a room with Steve Jobs. He said, 'There's no way I'm ever building a phone.' Would he admit that he was influenced by us—that we made a great phone, and he changed his mind? No. He would never admit it. But despite his stubbornness, he evolved."

It was the impossibility of exit that led Carmen Medina to move national security forward; it was the possibility of exit that enabled Donna Dubinsky to pioneer the smartphone revolution. The lesson here is that voice isn't inherently superior to exit. In some circumstances, leaving a stifling organization can be a better path to originality. The best we can do is voice our opinions and secure our risk portfolios, preparing for exit if necessary. If our bosses evolve, as Jobs did, there's a case to be made for sticking around and speaking up. But if they don't, and our audiences lack the openness to consider a shift in direction, we may find better opportunities elsewhere.

Questions may linger about what might have been. Had Medina left the CIA, would she have been able to champion transparency from the outside? Had Dubinsky stayed at Apple, would the company have developed the iPhone or spawned a different set of innovations?

We'll never have answers to these counterfactual scenarios, but we can learn something from the decisions that Medina and Dubinsky made. Although one ultimately chose voice and the other opted to exit, there's one way in which their choices were the same: they chose to speak up rather than stay silent. And in the long run, research shows that the mistakes we regret are not errors of commission, but errors of omission. If we could do things over, most of us would censor ourselves less and express our ideas more. That's exactly what Carmen Medina and Donna Dubinsky did, and it left them with few regrets.

4

Fools Rush In

*Timing, Strategic Procrastination,
and the First-Mover Disadvantage*

"Never put off till tomorrow what you can do
the day after tomorrow."

Mark Twain

Late at night in his hotel room, a young man stared at a blank piece of paper on the desk. Dripping with anxiety, he reached for the telephone and pitched some ideas to an adviser in a room several floors below, who then raced up the stairs to discuss a speech that would change history. At 3:00 A.M., the man was still working feverishly, "bone weary, almost in collapse from exhaustion." It was August 1963, and though the March on Washington for Jobs and Freedom was scheduled for the following morning, Martin Luther King, Jr., had not yet prepared his closing speech.

"He worked on it all night, not sleeping a wink," King's wife, Coretta, recalled. "He was to be the final speaker, and his words would be carried on television and radio to millions of people in America and throughout the world, so it was vitally important that his speech be both inspiring and wise."

The march had been announced to the press two months earlier; King knew it would be a monumental event. Along with the media coverage, a crowd of at least a hundred thousand was expected, and King had a hand in recruiting a number of famous figures to attend in support. The audience included civil rights pioneers Rosa Parks and Jackie Robinson, actors Marlon Brando and Sidney Poitier, and singers Harry Belafonte and Bob Dylan.

With relatively little time to prepare for his closing speech, it would have been natural for King to begin drafting it immediately. Since each speaker was initially given a time limit of five minutes, he needed to be particularly careful in choosing his words. Great thinkers throughout history—from Benjamin Franklin to Henry David Thoreau to King's namesake Martin Luther—have observed that it takes longer to write a short speech than a long one. "If it is a ten-minute speech it takes me all of two weeks to prepare it," said President Woodrow Wilson; "if I can talk as long as I want to it requires no preparation at all." But King did not begin writing out his speech until after 10:00 P.M. the night before the march.

Parents and teachers are constantly imploring children to begin their assignments earlier instead of waiting until the last minute. In the self-help world, an entire cottage industry of resources is devoted to fighting procrastination. But what if the very act of procrastinating was the reason that King gave the best speech of his life?

In work and in life, we are constantly taught that acting early is the key to success, because "he who hesitates is lost." When we have a meaningful task, we're advised to get it done well ahead of schedule. When we have an original idea to invent a product or start a company, we're encouraged to be the first mover. There are, of course, clear advantages to speed: we can be sure to finish what we start and beat competitors to market. But surprisingly, as I've studied originals, I've learned that the advantages of acting quickly and being first are often outweighed by the disadvantages. It's true that the early bird gets the worm, but we can't forget that the early worm gets caught.

This chapter considers the question of when to take original action. When you're preparing to row against the tide, you have choices about whether to start at the crack of dawn, wait until midday, or hold off until twilight. My goal here is to overturn common assumptions about timing by examining the unexpected benefits of delaying when we start and finish a task, as well as when we unleash our ideas into the world. I'll discuss why procrastination can be as much of a virtue as a vice, how first-mover entrepreneurs frequently face an uphill battle, why older innovators sometimes outdo younger ones, and why the leaders who drive change effectively are those who wait patiently for the right moment. Although it can be risky to delay, you'll see that waiting can also reduce risk by preventing you from putting all your eggs in one basket. You don't have to be first to be an original, and the most successful originals don't always arrive on schedule. They are fashionably late to the party.

The Other da Vinci Code

Recently, an unusually creative doctoral student named Jihae Shin approached me with a counterintuitive idea: procrastination might be conducive to originality. When you procrastinate, you're intentionally delaying work that needs to be done. You might be thinking about the task, but you postpone making real progress on it or finishing it to do something less productive. Shin proposed that when you put off a task, you buy yourself time to engage in divergent thinking rather than foreclosing on one particular idea. As a result, you consider a wider range of original concepts and ultimately choose a more novel direction. I challenged her to test it.

Shin asked college students to write proposals for a business on a university campus to fill a lot vacated by a convenience store. When they started the task immediately, they tended to propose conventional ideas—like another convenience store. When Shin randomly assigned some of the participants to procrastinate, putting off the task to play computer games like Minesweeper, FreeCell, and Solitaire, they produced more novel business ideas, like a tutoring center and a storage facility. Independent raters evaluated the final proposals, without knowing who procrastinated and who started immediately. The proposals from the procrastinators were 28 percent more creative.

Although we were excited by these results, we were concerned that procrastination wasn't the real cause of creativity. Perhaps it was playing the games that provided mental stimulation, giving people the energy to think more creatively—or that simply gave them a break away from the task to think. But the experiment showed that neither playing games nor taking a break boosted creativity. When people played the games first, before learning about the task, they didn't submit more novel proposals. To do that, they needed to actually be procrastinating while playing the games, keeping the business proposal task in the back of their minds. And when they started the task immediately and then took a break before returning to it, they had already made too much progress to start over afresh. It was only when they began thinking about the task and then deliberately procrastinated that they considered more remote possibilities and generated more creative ideas. Delaying progress enabled them to spend more time considering different ways to accomplish it, rather than "seizing and freezing" on one particular strategy.

Would Shin's findings hold true in the real world? To find out, she gathered data from a Korean furniture company. Employees who procrastinated regularly spent more time engaging in divergent thinking and were rated as significantly more creative by their supervisors. Procrastination didn't always fuel creativity: if the employees weren't intrinsically motivated to solve a major problem, stalling just set them behind. But when they were passionate about coming up with new ideas, putting off the task led them to more creative solutions.

Procrastination may be the enemy of productivity, but it can be a resource for creativity. Long before the modern obsession with efficiency precipitated by the Industrial Revolution and the Protestant work ethic, civilizations recognized the benefits of procrastination. In ancient Egypt, there were two different verbs for *procrastination*: one denoted laziness; the other meant waiting for the right time.

It may not be a coincidence that some of the most original thinkers and inventors in history have been procrastinators. A prime example is Leonardo da Vinci, whose original accomplishments spanned painting and sculpting, architecture and music, math and engineering, geology and cartography, and anatomy and botany. Scholars estimate that da Vinci painted the *Mona Lisa* on and off for a few years starting in 1503, left it unfinished, and didn't complete it until close to his death in 1519. His critics believed he was wasting his time dabbling with optical experiments and other distractions that kept him from completing his paintings. These distractions, though, turned out to be vital to his originality. As historian William Pannapacker explains:

> Leonardo's studies of how light strikes a sphere, for example, enable the continuous modeling of the "Mona Lisa" and "St. John the Baptist." His work in optics might have delayed a project, but his final achievements in painting depended on the experiments.... Far from being a distraction—like many of his contemporaries thought—they represent a lifetime of productive brainstorming, a private working out of the ideas on which his more public work depended.... If creative procrastination, selectively applied, prevented Leonardo from finishing a few commissions—of minor importance when one is struggling with the inner workings of the cosmos—then only someone who is a complete captive of the modern cult of productive mediocrity ... could fault him for it. Productive mediocrity requires discipline of an ordinary kind. It is safe and threatens no one. Nothing will be changed by mediocrity.... But genius is uncontrolled and uncontrollable. You cannot produce a work of genius according to a schedule or an outline.

Da Vinci spent about fifteen years developing the ideas for *The Last Supper* while working on a variety of other projects. The painting began as a sketch of figures sitting on a bench. A dozen years later, it became the foundation of the novel horizontal arrangement of thirteen seated at a table in the famous painting. Although he was often exasperated by his procrastination, da Vinci realized that originality could not be rushed. He noted that people of "genius sometimes accomplish most when they work the least, for they are thinking out inventions and forming in their minds the perfect idea."*

The Discipline to Delay

Procrastination turns out to be a common habit of creative thinkers and great problem solvers. Consider winners of the Science Talent Search, which is known as the "Super Bowl of Science" for high school seniors in the United States. A team led by psychologist Rena Subotnik interviewed these elite performers more than a decade after their victories, when they were in their early thirties, asking whether they procrastinated on routine and creative tasks, as well as in social life and health behavior. More than 68 percent admitted procrastinating in at least two of the four domains. Procrastination proved especially

---

* Procrastination may be particularly conducive to creativity when it leaves us solving problems at moments where we're unfocused. Psychologists Mareike Wieth and Rose Zacks surveyed students on whether they were morning people or night owls, and then gave them analytical and insight problems to solve at 8 A.M. or 4:30 P.M. They were equally good at solving the analytical problems regardless of the time. But with the insight problems, the night owls did better early in the morning, and the morning people did better in the late afternoon. One of the insight problems asked students to explain how an antique dealer recognized a bronze coin as a fake. The coin had an emperor's head on one side and the date 544 B.C. on the other. When they were wide awake, they were more likely to engage in overly structured linear thinking that prevented them from stumbling upon novel ideas. When they were sleepy, they were more open to random thoughts and had about 20 percent higher odds of suddenly remembering that B.C. stands for "Before Christ." Since Jesus hadn't been born yet, the coin could only have been stamped more than half a millennium later. If you're feeling pressured to start working on a creative task when you're wide awake, it might be worth delaying it until you're a little sleepier.

fruitful for creative work. The science stars "used procrastination as a form of incubation to stave off a premature choice of a scientific problem or solution." As one explained: "Often when I am procrastinating, I really have something on the back burner and I need the time to work it through." Another said: "In scientific work, ideas need time to mature," and procrastination is one way to "restrain that urge to respond prematurely." After poring over the interviews with these precocious thinkers and doers, Subotnik's team drew a curious conclusion. "Paradoxically," they wrote, those with "the most and least at stake . . . were the most likely to procrastinate in the creative domain."

In American history, there may be just one speech as famous as King's: Abraham Lincoln's Gettysburg Address. In just 272 words, Lincoln reframed the Civil War as a quest for the freedom and equality promised in the Declaration of Independence. The formal invitation to deliver the speech reached Lincoln about two weeks in advance. By the day before his departure for Gettysburg, the president had only composed about half of the address. His secretary, John Nicolay, wrote that Lincoln "probably followed his usual habit in such matters, using great deliberation in arranging his thoughts, and molding his phrases mentally, waiting to reduce them to writing until they had taken satisfactory form." Lincoln ultimately didn't write the closing paragraph until the night before the speech, and it was the morning of the speech before he finalized it. He waited because he wanted to develop the most compelling theme.

Early in the summer before the "I have a dream" speech, King sought advice from three close advisers about the appropriate content and tone. Then King had an extended dialogue about the address with Clarence Jones, his lawyer and speechwriter. King later asked Jones and another activist to start working on a draft.

In the subsequent weeks, King resisted the temptation to foreclose on a theme or direction. He waited until four days before the march to actively begin working on the address. The night before, he gathered a group of advisers to go back to the drawing board. As Jones recalls, King "said that this was such 'an important milestone in our civil rights struggle,' we should make every effort to get the best ideas" from key players in the movement. King opened the meeting by explaining that he "wanted to review the ideas again and get the best approaches."

By delaying the task of fleshing out and firming up the speech, King allowed Jones to benefit from the Zeigarnik effect. In 1927, Russian psychologist Bluma Zeigarnik demonstrated that people have a better memory for incomplete than complete tasks. Once a task is finished, we stop thinking about it. But when it is interrupted and left undone, it stays active in our minds. As Jones was comparing his early draft to the topic of that evening's discussion, "something worked its way up from the depths of my subconscious."*

Four months earlier, Jones had met with Governor Nelson Rockefeller, a noted philanthropist whose family was supportive of civil rights, seeking funds to bail King out of the Birmingham jail. Rockefeller opened a bank on a Saturday and gave Jones a briefcase with $100,000. Banking regulations required Jones to sign a promissory note; Rockefeller paid for the note. Reminiscing about that experience the night before King's speech, Jones realized that the promissory note could be a powerful metaphor. The next day, King used it early in the speech: "When the architects of our republic wrote the magnificent words of the Constitution and the Declaration of Independence, they were signing a promissory note. . . . It is obvious today that America has defaulted on this promissory note, insofar as her citizens of color are concerned."

---

* I deliberately procrastinated while writing this chapter. Instead of completing this section the day I had planned, I left it hanging, literally stopping in midsentence to answer emails. The next morning, it dawned on me that the Zeigarnik effect was relevant. Zeigarnik might have been pleased that I remembered her research on memory for unfinished tasks after leaving a task unfinished. Of course, delaying can go too far. "I love deadlines," Douglas Adams said. "I like the whooshing sound they make when they go by."

When King finally sent Jones to create a complete draft, it was with the broadest set of ideas at his disposal. But that wasn't the only upside of procrastinating.

On a Wing and a Prayer

Half a century after King delivered his momentous speech, four words are etched into the stone tablets of our collective memory: "I have a dream." It remains one of the most recognizable phrases in the history of human rhetoric, as it painted a vivid portrait of a better future. But I was stunned to find that the "dream" idea was not written into the speech at all. It didn't appear in the draft by Jones, nor did King include it in his script.

During the address, King's favorite gospel singer, Mahalia Jackson, shouted from behind him, "Tell 'em about the dream, Martin!" He continued with his script, and she encouraged him again. Before a live crowd of 250,000, and millions more watching on TV, King improvised, pushing his notes aside and launching into his inspiring vision of the future. "In front of all those people, cameras, and microphones," Clarence Jones reflects, "Martin winged it."

Along with providing time to generate novel ideas, procrastination has another benefit: it keeps us open to improvisation. When we plan well in advance, we often stick to the structure we've created, closing the door to creative possibilities that might spring into our fields of vision. Years ago, Berkeley psychologist Donald MacKinnon discovered that the most creative architects in America tended to be more spontaneous than their technically skilled but unoriginal peers, who rated themselves higher in self-control and conscientiousness. In a study of pizza chains that I conducted with Francesca Gino and David Hofmann, the most profitable stores were run by leaders who rated themselves as the least efficient and prompt. Similarly, when strategy researchers Sucheta Nadkarni and Pol Herrmann studied nearly two hundred companies in India, the firms with the highest financial returns were the ones whose CEOs rated themselves the lowest on efficiency and promptness.

In both cases, the most successful organizations were run by executives who admitted that they often wasted time before settling down to work and sometimes failed to pace themselves to get things done on time. Although these habits could impede progress on tasks, they opened leaders up to being more strategically flexible. In the Indian companies, multiple members of each company's top management teams rated their CEOs on strategic flexibility. The CEOs who planned carefully, acted early, and worked diligently scored as more rigid: once they formulated a strategy, they stuck to it. The CEOs who tended to delay work were more flexible and versatile—they were able to change their strategies to capitalize on new opportunities and defend against threats.*

As King walked to the podium to deliver his speech, even as he approached the microphone, he was still revising it. "Just before King spoke," politician Drew Hansen writes in *The Dream,* he was "crossing out lines and scribbling new ones as he awaited his turn," and "it

---

* When new leaders take over a team or organization, they're often eager to institute changes. But there's value in being patient. In one experiment, Carnegie Mellon professor Anita Woolley gave teams fifty minutes to build a residential structure out of Legos, scored on dimensions like size, sturdiness, and aesthetics. She randomly assigned teams to discuss their strategies either at the beginning of the task or after twenty-five minutes. Teams that evaluated their strategies at the midpoint were 80 percent more effective than teams that had the conversation at the start. The beginning of the task was too early for the conversation to be useful. The task was unfamiliar, so they didn't know enough to set an effective strategy. There was something special about pausing at the midpoint that enabled the teams to construct tall, pleasing Lego buildings that had lots of rooms but could be lifted, flipped, and dropped without breaking. Yale researcher Connie Gersick finds that the midpoint of a task is often the best time for a leader to institute change, as it's when groups become most open to originality. They still have plenty of time to try new things, which makes them receptive to radically different approaches. And since they've used up half of their time, they're highly motivated to choose a good strategy. This is one of the reasons that halftimes can be so influential in basketball and football: They allow coaches to intervene when teams are most amenable to new strategies.

looked like King was still editing the speech until he walked to the podium to deliver it." In the Pulitzer Prize–winning book *Bearing the Cross*, historian David Garrow observes that King improvised "like some sort of jazz musician." King acted spontaneously, beginning with small ad-libs. One of the early portions of the written speech called the Constitution and the Declaration of Independence "a promise that all men would be guaranteed the unalienable rights of life, liberty, and the pursuit of happiness." At the podium, King expanded the line to emphasize racial equality: "a promise that all men—*yes, black men as well as white men*—would be guaranteed the unalienable rights."

It was eleven minutes into the speech that Mahalia Jackson called for King to share his dream. It is unclear whether he heard her, but "just all of a sudden, I decided," King recalled. He followed the emotion of the moment and unfolded his dream. By the time the speech was done, Hansen notes, "King added so much new material to his prepared speech that the length of his address nearly doubled."

Great originals are great procrastinators, but they don't skip planning altogether. They procrastinate strategically, making gradual progress by testing and refining different possibilities. Although the memorable lines about the dream were improvised, King had rehearsed variations of them in earlier speeches. He had spoken of his dream nearly a year earlier, in November 1962 in Albany, and in the ensuing months he referred to it frequently, from Birmingham to Detroit. During the year of his "dream" speech alone, it is estimated that he traveled over 275,000 miles and delivered over 350 speeches.

While King may have deferred writing the "dream" speech, he had a wealth of material at his disposal that he could draw upon extemporaneously, which made his delivery more authentic. "King had collected a repertoire of oratorical fragments—successful passages from his own sermons, sections from other preachers' work, anecdotes, Bible verses, lines from favorite poets," Hansen explains. "King did not so much write his speeches as assemble them, by rearranging and adapting material he had used many times before. . . . It gave King the flexibility to alter his addresses as he was speaking. . . . Had King not decided to leave his written text, it is doubtful that his speech at the march would be remembered at all."

Pioneers and Settlers

After being involved in starting over one hundred companies, Idealab founder Bill Gross ran an analysis to figure out what drove success versus failure. The most important factor was not the uniqueness of the idea, the capabilities and execution of the team, the quality of the business model, or the availability of funding. "The number one thing was timing," Gross reveals. "Timing accounted for forty-two percent of the difference between success and failure."

Research shows that in American culture, people believe strongly in a first-mover advantage. We want to be leaders, not followers. Scientists rush to make discoveries ahead of their rivals; inventors hurry to apply for patents before their adversaries; entrepreneurs aspire to launch before their competitors. If you're the first out of the gate with a new product, service, or technology, you can move up the learning curve earlier, gobble up prime space, and monopolize customers. These edges create barriers to entry for your competitors: their own efforts to innovate will be stifled by your patents and superior capabilities, and their growth will be stymied by the fact that it's expensive to convince customers to make a switch.

In a classic study, marketing researchers Peter Golder and Gerard Tellis compared the success of companies that were either pioneers or settlers. The pioneers were first movers: the initial company to develop or sell a product. The settlers were slower to launch, waiting until the pioneers had created a market before entering it. When Golder and Tellis analyzed hundreds of brands in three dozen different product categories, they found a staggering difference in failure rates: 47 percent for pioneers, compared with just 8 percent for settlers. Pioneers were about six times more likely to fail than settlers. Even when the pioneers did survive, they only captured an average of 10 percent of the market, compared with 28 percent for settlers.

Surprisingly, the downsides of being the first mover are frequently bigger than the upsides. On balance, studies suggest that pioneers may sometimes capture greater market share, but end up not only with lower chances of survival but lower profits as well. As marketing researcher Lisa Bolton summarizes, "Although first movers face some advantages in particular industries, the academic research remains mixed and does not support an overall first-mover advantage."

If you're someone who's tempted to rush into a new domain, this knowledge should stop you cold and leave you thinking carefully about the ideal timing. But Bolton finds something frightening: even when people learn that evidence doesn't support the first-mover advantage, they still believe in it. It's easier to think of pioneers that succeeded; the failed ones are long forgotten, so we assume they're rare. The best way to shatter the myth of the first-mover advantage is to ask people to generate reasons for first-mover *dis*advantage. In your experience, what are the four biggest drawbacks of being a pioneer?

Settlers are often branded as copycats, but this stereotype misses the mark. Instead of conforming to the existing demand, they bide their time until they're ready to introduce something new. They're often slow to enter because they're working on revolutionary products, services, or technologies within the category. In home video-game consoles, the pioneer was Magnavox Odyssey in 1972, which mostly featured rudimentary sports games. A settler, Nintendo, acquired the Odyssey's distribution rights for Japan in 1975, and then blew Magnavox out of the water in the following decade by creating an original Nintendo Entertainment System that featured games like

Super Mario Bros. and *The Legend of Zelda.* Nintendo transformed gaming with a user-friendly controller, sophisticated characters, and interactive role-playing. Being original doesn't require being first. It just means being different and better.

When originals rush to be pioneers, they're prone to overstep; that's the first disadvantage. Before the internet bubble burst, a young Goldman Sachs banker named Joseph Park was sitting in his apartment, frustrated at the effort required to get access to entertainment. Why should he trek all the way to Blockbuster to rent a movie? He should just be able to open a website, pick out a movie, and have it delivered to his door.

Despite raising around $250 million, Kozmo, the company Park founded, went bankrupt in 2001. His biggest mistake was making a brash promise for one-hour delivery of virtually anything, and investing in building national operations to support growth that never happened. One study of over three thousand startups indicates that roughly three out of every four fail because of premature scaling— making investments that the market isn't yet ready to support.

Had Park proceeded more slowly, he might have noticed that with the current technology available, one-hour delivery was an impractical and low-margin business. There was, however, a tremendous demand for online movie rentals. Netflix was just then getting off the ground, and Kozmo might have been able to compete in the area of mail-order rentals and then online movie streaming. Later, he might have been able to capitalize on technological changes that made it possible for Instacart to build a logistics operation that made one-hour grocery delivery scalable and profitable. Since the market is more defined when settlers enter, they can focus on providing superior quality instead of deliberating about what to offer in the first place. "Wouldn't you rather be second or third and see how the guy in first did, and then . . . improve it?" Malcolm Gladwell asked in an interview. "When ideas get really complicated, and when the world gets complicated, it's foolish to think the person who's first can work it all out," Gladwell remarked. "Most good things, it takes a long time to figure them out."*

Second, there's reason to believe that the kinds of people who choose to be late movers may be better suited to succeed. Risk seekers are drawn to being first, and they're prone to making impulsive decisions. Meanwhile, more risk-averse entrepreneurs watch from the sidelines, waiting for the right opportunity and balancing their risk portfolios before entering. In a study of software startups, strategy researchers Elizabeth Pontikes and William Barnett find that when entrepreneurs rush to follow the crowd into hyped markets, their startups are less likely to survive and grow. When entrepreneurs wait for the market to cool down, they have higher odds of success: "Nonconformists . . . that buck the trend are most likely to stay in the market, receive funding, and ultimately go public."

Third, along with being less recklessly ambitious, settlers can improve upon competitors' technology to make products better. When you're the first to market, you have to make all the mistakes yourself. Meanwhile, settlers can watch and learn from your errors. "Moving first is a tactic, not a goal," Peter Thiel writes in *Zero to One*; "being the first mover doesn't do you any good if someone else comes along and unseats you."

Fourth, whereas pioneers tend to get stuck in their early offerings, settlers can observe market changes and shifting consumer tastes and

---

* Moving too fast was one of the forces behind the flop of the Segway. Randy Komisar "counseled patience," journalist Steve Kemper writes in *Reinventing the Wheel*, advising Dean Kamen's team to "go slow and build a track record." Before the launch, Steve Jobs urged the team to do a complete redesign. Then, they should run safety and usability studies on some university campuses and at Disney, so that people could see it in action and begin craving it before it was available. Instead of heeding this advice, Kamen's team rushed the Segway to market without working out the customer, safety, legal, pricing, and design issues. Harvard entrepreneurship professor Bill Sahlman was involved from the beginning, and to this day he wonders what might have happened if the Segway team had worked more slowly to prove the product's safety, improve the design, reduce costs, and obtain approvals to ride it on sidewalks in major cities. "If it didn't look dorky, if it weighed 25 pounds and cost $700, it would sell," he says wistfully.

adjust accordingly. In a study of the U.S. automobile industry over nearly a century, pioneers had lower survival rates because they struggled to establish legitimacy, developed routines that didn't fit the market, and became obsolete as consumer needs clarified. Settlers also have the luxury of waiting for the market to be ready. When Warby Parker launched, e-commerce companies had been thriving for more than a decade, though other companies had tried selling glasses online with little success. "There's no way it would have worked before," Neil Blumenthal tells me. "We had to wait for Amazon, Zappos, and Blue Nile to get people comfortable buying products they typically wouldn't order online."

This holds true beyond the world of business, where many original people, ideas, and movements have failed because they were ahead of their time. At the CIA in the early 1990s, when Carmen Medina initially voiced her idea to share digital information online more rapidly, the agency wasn't ready to consider the concept. As electronic communication became more secure and more familiar, people became more receptive to the idea. After the terrorist attacks of September 11 and the misidentification of weapons of mass destruction in Iraq, it became increasingly clear that the costs of failing to share information among agencies effectively were too consequential to bear. "Timing is everything," Medina's colleague Susan Benjamin notes. "In that intervening period, it became obvious to even people who were real Luddites that we had to do things differently; the times called for it. It became difficult for anyone who had half a brain in their head not to listen to her, and agree that that was the direction in which to move."

In the 1840s, when Hungarian physician Ignaz Semmelweis discovered that having medical students wash their hands dramatically reduced death rates during childbirth, he was scorned by his colleagues and ended up in an asylum. It would be two decades before his ideas gained scientific legitimacy as Louis Pasteur and Robert Koch laid the foundations of germ theory. As physicist Max Planck once observed, "A new scientific truth does not triumph by convincing its opponents and making them see the light, but rather because its opponents eventually die."

I don't mean to imply that it's *never* wise to be first. If we all wait for others to act, nothing original will ever be created. Someone has to be the pioneer, and sometimes that will pay off. First-mover advantages tend to prevail when patented technology is involved, or when there are strong network effects (the product or service becomes more valuable when there are a greater number of users, as with telephones or social media). But in the majority of circumstances, your odds of success aren't higher if you go first. And when the market is uncertain, unknown, or underdeveloped, being a pioneer has pronounced disadvantages. The key lesson here is that if you have an original idea, it's a mistake to rush with the sole purpose of beating your competitors to the finish line. Just as procrastinating can give us flexibility on a task, delaying market entry can open us up to learning and adaptability, reducing the risks associated with originality.

But what happens when we broaden the lens beyond task timetables and product life cycles? Over the course of a person's lifetime, is there a risk of waiting too long to act?

The Two Life Cycles of Creativity: Young Geniuses and Old Masters

It's commonly believed that originality flows from the fountain of youth. In the words of famed venture capitalist Vinod Khosla, "People under 35 are the people who make change happen. People over 45 basically die in terms of new ideas." After publishing his first revolutionary paper on relativity in his midtwenties, Albert Einstein made a similar observation: "A person who has not made his great contribution to science before the age of 30 will never do so." Tragically, innovators often do lose their originality over time. After Einstein transformed physics with two papers on relativity, he opposed quantum mechanics, which became the next major revolution in the field. "To punish me for my contempt for authority, fate made me an authority myself," Einstein lamented.

But this decline isn't inevitable. When companies run suggestion boxes, there is evidence that older employees tend to submit more ideas and higher-quality ideas than their younger colleagues, with the most valuable suggestions coming from employees older than fifty-five. And in technology startups that have raised venture capital funding, the average founder is thirty-eight.

In the arts and sciences, Chicago economist David Galenson shows that although we're quick to remember the young geniuses who peak early, there are plenty of old masters who soar much later. In medicine, for every James Watson, who helped to discover the double helix structure of DNA at age twenty-five, there is a Roger Sperry, who identified different specializations between the right and left hemispheres of the brain at age forty-nine. In film, for every Orson Welles, whose masterpiece *Citizen Kane* was his very first feature film at age twenty-five, there is an Alfred Hitchcock, who made his three most popular films three decades into his career, at ages fifty-nine (*Vertigo*), sixty (*North by Northwest*), and sixty-one (*Psycho*). In poetry, for every E. E. Cummings, who penned his first influential poem at twenty-two and more than half of his best work before turning forty, there is a Robert Frost, who wrote 92 percent of his most reprinted poems after forty. What explains these dramatically different life cycles of creativity? Why do some peak early and others bloom late?

The time at which we reach our heights of originality, and how long they last, depends on our styles of thinking. When Galenson studied creators, he discovered two radically different styles of innovation: conceptual and experimental. Conceptual innovators formulate a big idea and set out to execute it. Experimental innovators solve problems through trial and error, learning and evolving as they go along. They are at work on a particular problem, but they don't have a specific solution in mind at the outset. Instead of planning in advance, they figure it out as they go. To paraphrase writer E. M. Forster, how can I know what I think until I see what I say?

According to Galenson, conceptual innovators are sprinters, and experimental innovators are marathoners. When he studied economists who won the Nobel Prize, on average the conceptual innovators did their most influential work at forty-three, whereas the experimental innovators did theirs at sixty-one. When he analyzed the most often reproduced poems by famous poets, conceptual innovators authored their best works at twenty-eight, compared with age thirty-nine for experimental innovators. And in an independent study of every physicist who has ever won the Nobel Prize, of the young geniuses under thirty, exactly half were conceptual innovators who did theoretical work. Among the old masters forty-five and above, 92 percent did experimental work.

These fundamental differences between conceptual and experimental innovators explain why some originals peak early and others bloom late. Conceptual innovation can be done quickly, because it doesn't require years of methodical investigation. When Watson and Crick discovered the double helix structure of DNA, they didn't need to wait for data to amass. They had built a three-dimensional theoretical model and examined X-ray images provided by Rosalind Franklin. In addition, conceptual breakthroughs tend to occur early, because it is easiest to come up with a strikingly original insight when we approach a problem with a fresh perspective. "Conceptual innovators normally make their most important contributions to a discipline not long after their first exposure to it," Galenson finds. For this reason, conceptual innovators become less original once they're entrenched in conventional ways of approaching problems. As Galenson explains:

The inability of... aging conceptual innovators to match the brilliant achievements of their youth is not a product of their depletion of a stock of some magical elixir of artistry. Instead, it is caused by the impact of accumulating experience. . . . The real enemies of conceptual innovators are the establishment of fixed habits of thought. . . . Conceptual innovators may become the captives of an important early achievement.

As a conceptual innovator, this was Einstein's problem. When he developed his theory of special relativity, he wasn't conducting scientific studies, but thought experiments: he was imagining himself chasing a beam of light. His major contributions to science were ideas and theories that explained the results of other people's experiments. Once Einstein had internalized his principles of relativity, he struggled to accommodate the departures from those principles that quantum physics demanded. In poetry, Galenson points out that E. E. Cummings faced a similar hurdle. After imagining his own rules of language, grammar, and punctuation in his early twenties, by age fifty, as one critic remarked, "Cummings is still the experimentalist of one experiment. The fascinating thing about Cummings is that he is always talking about growth, and always remains the same." Later, when Cummings was sixty-five, another reviewer commented that "Cummings is a daringly original poet," but "his books are all exactly alike." As psychologist Abraham Maslow noted, when you have a hammer, everything looks like a nail.

Conversely, while experimental innovation can require years or decades to accumulate the requisite knowledge and skill, it becomes a more sustainable source of originality. It took Roger Sperry years to conduct experiments with split-brain cats and human patients to determine how the brain hemispheres worked. Robert Frost wrote none of his most reproduced poems in his twenties and just 8 percent in his thirties, finally blossoming in his forties and again in his sixties.

"Step by step," poet Robert Lowell observed, Frost "tested his observation of places and people until his best poems had the ... richness of great novels." Like an explorer, Frost gathered material by venturing out into the world, listening carefully to real conversations. "I would never use a word or combination of words that I hadn't *heard* used in running speech," Frost acknowledged. Each poem was an experiment in mixing different elements: "No surprise for the writer, no surprise for the reader," he was fond of saying. "When I begin a poem I don't know—I don't want a poem that I can tell was written toward a good ending. . . . You've got to be the happy discoverer of your ends."

Conceptual innovators tend to generate original ideas early but risk copying themselves. The experimental approach takes longer, but proves more renewable: instead of reproducing our past ideas, experiments enable us to continue discovering new ones. Mark Twain published *Adventures of Huckleberry Finn* at age forty-nine using a "trial-and-error method," scholars note, and "discovered his pliable plot as he went along, writing without a definite resolution or plan in mind." Twain himself commented, "As the short tale grows into the long tale, the original intention (or motif) is apt to get abolished and find itself superseded by a quite different one."

To sustain our originality as we age and accumulate expertise, our best bet is to adopt an experimental approach. We can make fewer plans in advance for what we want to create, and start testing out different kinds of tentative ideas and solutions. Eventually, if we're patient enough, we may stumble onto something that's novel and useful. The experimental approach served Leonardo da Vinci well: he was forty-six when he finished painting *The Last Supper* and in his early fifties when he started working on the *Mona Lisa*. "Only by drawing did he truly come to understand, was his vision clarified," one scholar wrote; another observed that "Leonardo works like a sculptor modelling in clay who never accepts any form as final but goes on creating, even at the risk of obscuring his original intentions."

Martin Luther King, Jr., too, was an experimental innovator. Despite being just thirty-four when he gave his "dream" speech, it was his twentieth year of speaking publicly about civil rights. At fifteen, he made the state finals for delivering an original speech on civil rights. He spent the intervening decades testing out a range of possible lyrics to articulate his vision. In the thousands of speeches that he delivered, he was constantly rehearsing different melodies and refrains. Having gained the experience of an old master, he achieved originality, as management scholar Karl Weick describes it, by "putting old things in new combinations and new things in old combinations."

Good things come to those who wait, and for experimentalists, it's never too late to become original. After Frank Lloyd Wright received the contract for Fallingwater, his most celebrated architectural work, he procrastinated for nearly a year while making sporadic drawings before finally completing the design at age sixty-eight. Raymond Davis shared the Nobel Prize in physics for research that he started at fifty-one and finished at the tender age of eighty. The more experiments you run, the less constrained you become by your ideas from the past. You learn from what you discover in your audience, on the canvas, or in the data. Instead of getting mired in the tunnel vision of your imagination, by looking out into the world you improve the acuity of your peripheral vision.

Sprinting is a fine strategy for a young genius, but becoming an old master requires the patience of experimentation to run a marathon. Both are paths to creativity. Yet for those of us who aren't struck by a bolt of insight, slow and steady experimentation can light the way to a longer stretch of originality. "Of course, not every unaccomplished 65-year-old is some undiscovered experimental innovator," author Daniel Pink reflects. "But it might bolster the resolve of the relentlessly curious, the constantly tinkering, the dedicated tortoises undaunted by the blur of the hares."

5

Goldilocks and the Trojan Horse

Creating and Maintaining Coalitions

"Now, the Star-Belly Sneetches

Had bellies with stars.

The Plain-Belly Sneetches

Had none upon thars.

Those stars weren't so big. They were really so small

You might think such a thing wouldn't matter at all.

But, because they had stars, all the Star-Belly Sneetches

Would brag, 'We're the best kind of Sneetch on the beaches.'

With their snoots in the air, they would sniff and they'd snort

'We'll have nothing to do with the Plain-Belly sort!'"

Dr. Seuss

Memories of her greatness have faded, but no one did more for women's suffrage in America than Lucy Stone. In 1855, she took a stand for women's rights that moved thousands to follow in her footsteps, calling themselves Lucy Stoners in homage. Over the next century, the Lucy Stone League included aviator Amelia Earhart, poet Edna St. Vincent Millay, and artist Georgia O'Keeffe. Among today's women who qualify as Lucy Stoners are Beyoncé, Sheryl Sandberg, Sarah Jessica Parker, and Spanx founder Sara Blakely.

Lucy Stone was the first woman in America to keep her own name after getting married. It was one of her many firsts: she was the first woman from Massachusetts to earn a bachelor's degree. She was the first American to become a full-time lecturer for women's rights, mobilizing countless supporters and converting numerous adversaries to join the movement. She became one of only a handful of women who spoke in public at all, let alone on women's rights. She led national conventions, and she launched the country's foremost women's newspaper, the *Woman's Journal,* which ran for half a century. In the words of Carrie Chapman Catt, the suffragist who campaigned successfully for the Nineteenth Amendment, which gave women the right to vote: "The suffrage success of today is not conceivable without the *Woman's Journal*'s part in it."

In 1851, Stone organized a women's rights convention, but didn't take the podium until she was coaxed into speaking on the last day. "We want to be something more than the appendages of society," Stone pronounced, calling for women to petition state legislatures for the rights to vote and hold property. Her remarks became known as the speech that set the women's rights movement on fire. Her words made their way across the Atlantic Ocean, where they inspired British philosophers John Stuart Mill and Harriet Taylor Mill to publish a famous essay on the enfranchisement of women, which helped to mobilize women's suffrage activists in England.

In America, perhaps the most significant effect was on a Rochester teacher named Susan B. Anthony—Stone's speech inspired her to join the suffrage movement. Two years later, the other great suffragist of the era, Elizabeth Cady Stanton, wrote a glowing note to Anthony about Stone: "We have no woman who compares with her."

For the next decade and a half, Stone, Anthony, and Stanton collaborated as the renowned leaders of the women's suffrage crusade. But long before they could realize their shared goal of equal voting rights for women, their coalition crumbled.

In 1869, Anthony and Stanton severed their collaboration with Stone, splitting off to form their own women's suffrage organization. The former allies fought bitterly as rivals, publishing their own

newspapers, petitioning and fund-raising separately, and lobbying legislatures independently. "The division," historian Jean Baker laments,
"led to a duplication of energies in a movement that was numerically
small and organizationally limited." It also reinforced stereotypes that
women were unfit for political life, encouraging newspapers to focus
on the "hens at war" story rather than on that of the great cause itself.
Anthony masterminded a plot to poach leaders from Stone's organization, and the animosity that Anthony and Stanton harbored toward
Stone was so intense that they wrote her organization out of their
history of the suffrage movement. This act appalled even Stanton's
own daughter, who rectified the omission by writing a chapter on
Stone's efforts herself. Since the three leaders shared a deep commitment to the same cause, why did they end up in such a heated, destructive conflict?

This chapter examines how originals form alliances to advance
their goals, and how to overcome the barriers that prevent coalitions
from succeeding. By definition, most efforts to change the status quo
involve a movement by a minority group to challenge a majority. Coalitions are powerful, but they are also inherently unstable—they
depend heavily on the relationships among individual members. Lucy
Stone's conflict with Susan B. Anthony and Elizabeth Cady Stanton
shattered the most important alliance in the suffrage movement, nearly
causing its demise. Through an analysis of their challenges—along
with a talented entrepreneur's struggle to convince people to give her
idea a chance, a hit Disney movie that almost didn't get made, and the
collapse of the Occupy Wall Street movement—you'll see how building effective coalitions involves striking a delicate balance between
venerable virtues and pragmatic policies. In doing so, you'll find out
why singing "O Canada" can help us form alliances, why common tactics can be more influential than common values, why Western states
won suffrage sooner than states in the East and the South, and why it's
often wiser to partner with enemies than frenemies.

The key insight is a Goldilocks theory of coalition formation. The originals who start a movement will often be its most radical members, whose ideas and ideals will prove too hot for those who follow their lead. To form alliances with opposing groups, it's best to temper the cause, cooling it as much as possible. Yet to draw allies into joining the cause itself, what's needed is a moderately tempered message that is neither too hot nor too cold, but just right.

The Narcissism of Small Differences

We assume that common goals bind groups together, but the reality is that they often drive groups apart. According to Dartmouth psychologist Judith White, a lens for understanding these fractures is the concept of horizontal hostility. Even though they share a fundamental objective, radical groups often disparage more mainstream groups as impostors and sellouts. As Sigmund Freud wrote a century ago, "It is precisely the minor differences in people who are otherwise alike that form the basis of feelings of strangeness and hostility between them."

White noticed horizontal hostility everywhere. When a deaf woman won the Miss America crown, instead of cheering her on as a trailblazer, deaf activists protested. Since she spoke orally rather than using sign language, she wasn't "deaf enough." When a light-skinned black woman was appointed as a law professor at one university, its Black Students Association objected on the grounds that she wasn't black enough. A radical environmental activist dismissed the more mainstream Greenpeace as a "mindless monster motivated by eco-buck profits" and "a dynamic threat to the integrity of the green movement." To explain why this kind of animosity happened, White led fascinating research on horizontal hostility in different movements and minority groups.

In one study, vegans and vegetarians evaluated members of their own groups and one another's groups, relative to members of the general public. Vegans showed nearly three times as much prejudice toward vegetarians as vegetarians did toward vegans. In the eyes of the more extreme vegans, the mainstream vegetarians were wannabes: if they really cared about the cause, they wouldn't eat animal products like eggs. In another study in Greece, members of the most conservative party judged the most similar party more unfavorably than they did a progressive party, and members of the most liberal party were much harsher toward the progressive party than toward even the most conservative party. Orthodox Jews evaluated conservative Jewish women more negatively than Jewish women who didn't practice or observe religious holidays at all. The message was clear: if you were a true believer, you'd be all in. The more strongly you identify with an extreme group, the harder you seek to differentiate yourself from more moderate groups that threaten your values.

It was this kind of horizontal hostility that caused Susan B. Anthony and Elizabeth Cady Stanton to split off from Lucy Stone. Anthony and Stanton were relatively radical; Stone was more mainstream. The earth between them cracked in 1866, when Anthony and Stanton partnered with a known racist, George Francis Train, who supported women's suffrage because he believed women could help to curtail the political influence of African Americans. Stone was outraged to see them campaigning with Train and allowing him to bankroll their efforts.

The fault line only grew wider when Anthony and Stanton opposed the Fifteenth Amendment proposal to grant African-American men the right to vote. They drew a hard line: if women weren't given the right to vote, other minority groups shouldn't be allowed it, either. Their position was radical not only because it was inflexible, but also because they were trying to reach liberal constituents who favored the amendment. Stone was more sympathetic to the abolitionist cause. At an equal rights convention, she attempted to build a bridge between black activists and Anthony and Stanton, announcing her support for a continued alliance:

Both are perhaps right. . . . Woman has an ocean of wrongs too deep for any plummet, and the negro too has an ocean of wrongs that cannot be fathomed. . . . I thank God for the Fifteenth Amendment, and hope that it will be adopted in every state. I will be thankful in my soul if any body can get out of that terrible pit.

Anthony and Stanton viewed Stone's support of voting rights for black men as a betrayal of the women's cause. They reneged on their commitment to a joint organization and announced the formation of their own national women's suffrage organization the following week, in May 1869. Stone and a group of colleagues published a letter calling for a more comprehensive organization, but it was to no avail. By the fall, they had little choice but to form their own group. For more than two decades, they maintained their distance, working independently in some cases and at cross-purposes in others.

With the women's suffrage movement splintered, Lucy Stone needed new allies, as did Anthony and Stanton. They all found support in an unexpected place—the Woman's Christian Temperance Union (WCTU), which had been formed to fight alcohol abuse, as drunken men often abused their wives and left their families in poverty. In contrast to the suffrage groups, the WCTU was heavily conservative. Its members tended to be middle- and upper-class women with strong religious beliefs and traditional values. Yet somehow, coalitions between the WCTU and suffragists sprang up in almost every state in the nation. The reasons for suffragists to partner with the WCTU were clear: the suffrage movement had stalled in influencing legislation, a surge of antisuffrage organizations was forming to work against them, and suffrage membership was dwindling. By the early 1880s, Stanton and Anthony's organization was down to just a hundred members. The

WCTU, meanwhile, was experiencing a membership explosion, growing from a few thousand in 1874 to thirteen thousand in 1876 and well over a hundred thousand by 1890. With the support of the country's largest women's organization, suffragists could make meaningful progress. The puzzle is why the WCTU agreed to partner with suffragists.

In a clever experiment, Stanford researchers Scott Wiltermuth and Chip Heath randomly assigned people in groups of three to listen to the national anthem "O Canada" under different conditions of synchrony. In the control condition, participants read the words silently while the song played. In the synchronous condition, they sang the song out loud together. In the asynchronous condition, they all sang, but not in unison: each person heard the song at a different tempo.

The participants thought they were being tested on their singing. But there was a twist: after singing, they moved into what was supposedly a different study, where they had a chance to keep money for themselves or cooperate by sharing it with the group. The few minutes they spent singing shouldn't have affected their behavior, but it did. The group that sang together shared significantly more. They reported feeling more similar to each other and more like a team than participants in the other conditions.*

In seeking alliances with groups that share our values, we overlook the importance of sharing our strategic tactics. Recently, sociologists Wooseok Jung and Brayden King of Northwestern University and Sarah Soule of Stanford University tracked the emergence of unusual alliances between social movements—like coalitions between environmental and gay-rights activists, the women's movement and the peace

---

* In an experiment led by Yale psychologist Erica Boothby, people liked chocolate better when they tasted it at the same time as another person. I hate chocolate, so this experiment would not have worked with me—but their follow-up study showed that eating disgustingly bitter chocolate was even more unpleasant when tasted simultaneously with someone else. Apparently, both positive and negative experiences are amplified when we share them, leading to even greater feelings of similarity.

movement, and a marine base and a Native American tribe. They found that shared tactics were an important predictor of alliances. Even if they care about different causes, groups find affinity when they use the same methods of engagement. If you've spent the past decade taking part in protests and marches, it's easy to feel a sense of shared identity and community with another organization that operates the same way.

Lucy Stone recognized that common goals weren't sufficient for a coalition to prosper, noting, "People will differ as to what they consider the best methods & means." Stanton, for her part, "pointed to the difference in methods as the 'essential issue' dividing the two associations." Stone was committed to campaigning at the state level; Anthony and Stanton wanted a federal constitutional amendment. Stone involved men in her organization; Anthony and Stanton favored an exclusively female membership. Stone sought to inspire change through speaking and meetings; Anthony and Stanton were more confrontational, with Anthony voting illegally and encouraging other women to follow suit.

The suffragists who formed alliances with the temperance activists were more moderate in their methods, which helped the two groups find common ground. At the same time that women were organizing local WCTU clubs, Lucy Stone introduced suffrage clubs. Both groups had extensive histories with lobbying and publishing. They began to work together to lobby and speak in front of state legislatures, publish articles and distribute literature, and hold public suffrage meetings, rallies, and debates.* Together, suffragists and temperance activists

---

* Shared tactics only facilitate alliances up to a point. When the overlap in tactics between groups was more than 61 percent, coalitions became less likely. When their methods are pretty much the same, groups simply have less to learn and gain from one another; their efforts are more likely to be redundant. Although the WCTU and suffrage groups shared a number of tactics, they also had some unique methods to teach one another. The suffragists began to march in parades and set up booths at fairs; the WCTU increasingly used petitions. Also, status differences mattered: Movements were more likely to align when one had moderately higher status than the other, as opposed to when there was no status difference or an extreme status difference. It's obvious that a lower-status movement would pursue the visibility associated with a

persuaded several states to allow women to vote. And in doing so, the suffragists discovered a profound principle about gaining allies. That principle is best illuminated by a young, visionary entrepreneur who found a surprising way to get naysayers to give her idea a chance.

Tempered Radicals

In 2011, a college senior named Meredith Perry noticed that something very basic was wrong with technology. She didn't need a cord to make phone calls or connect to the internet. Everything that used to be wired was now wireless . . . except for one thing. Sitting in her dorm room, she was still tethered to the wall by the most ancient component of her devices: the power that charged them. To use her phone and her computer, she had to plug them in. She wanted wireless power.

She started thinking of things that could beam energy through the air. The signal in a TV remote was too weak, radio waves were too inefficient, and X-rays were too dangerous. Then she came across a device that could convert physical vibration into energy. If you put it under a train, for example, you could collect the energy the train generated. Although it wasn't practical to have people gathering near trains to capture their energy, she realized that sound travels through the air by vibration. What if she could use ultrasound, which is invisible and silent, to generate air vibrations and convert them into wireless power?

Her physics professors said it was impossible. Ultrasonic engineers agreed; it couldn't be done. Some of the world's most respected scientists told her she was wasting her time on the effort. But then she won

---

higher-status partner, but there are benefits to the higher-status group, too. Sociologists Jung, King, and Soule explain: "As challengers to the established social order, movements need to refresh and update their agenda continuously in order to be seen as cutting-edge, authentic, and relevant. If they fail to innovate their movement agenda and engage with new ideas, a movement can become obsolete and lose touch with its original constituency. For this reason, high-status movements may seek to absorb newly emerging or previously ignored vintage issues."

an invention competition, and a journalist challenged her to demo the technology at a digital conference just four weeks later. With a proof of concept, but no working prototype, she had a chicken-and-egg problem: she needed funding to build a prototype, but her idea was so radical that investors wanted to see a prototype first. As the solo founder of a technology startup, with no engineering background, she needed allies to move forward.

Three years later, I met Perry at a Google event. After landing $750,000 in seed money from Mark Cuban, Marissa Mayer, and Peter Thiel's Founders Fund, her team had just finished its first functional prototype. It could power devices faster than a wire, at longer distances, and would be ready for consumers in two years. By the end of 2014, her company, uBeam, had accumulated eighteen patents and $10 million in venture funding.

Perry took her place onstage in a lineup that included Snoop Dogg, a Nobel Prize winner, and former President Bill Clinton. She was the only one to get a standing ovation. Debate continued about how well the product would work, but she had overcome the fundamental barrier to proving the viability of the technology. "Every single person that is now working for the company didn't think it was possible or was extremely skeptical," Perry said.

Perry faced an extreme version of every original's struggle in challenging the status quo: overcoming the skepticism of potential key stakeholders. Her initial efforts fell flat. She reached out to scores of technical experts, who were so quick to point out the flaws in the math and physics that they wouldn't even consider working with her. It probably didn't help that she was offering to hire them as contractors on deferred payment—they might never see a check.

Finally, Perry made a move that flew in the face of every piece of wisdom she had heard about influence; she simply stopped telling experts what it was she was trying to create. Instead of explaining her plan to generate wireless power, she merely provided the specifications of the technology she wanted. Her old message had been: "I'm trying to build a transducer to send power over the air." Her new pitch disguised the purpose: "I'm looking for someone to design a transducer with these parameters. Can you make this part?"

The approach worked. She persuaded two acoustics experts to design a transmitter, another to design a receiver, and an electrical engineer to construct the electronics. "In my head it all came together. Worst comes to worst, somebody would sue me," Perry admits. "There was no other way, given my knowledge and skill set." Soon she had collaborators on board with doctorates from Oxford and Stanford, with math and simulations confirming the idea was viable in theory. It was enough to attract a first round of funding and a talented chief technology officer who had initially been highly skeptical. "Once I showed him all the patents, he said, 'Oh sh*t, this actually can work.'"

In a popular TED talk and book, Simon Sinek argues that if we want to inspire people, we should start with *why*. If we communicate the vision behind our ideas, the purpose guiding our products, people will flock to us. This is excellent advice—unless you're doing something original that challenges the status quo. When people championing moral change explain their why, it runs the risk of clashing with deep-seated convictions. When creative non-conformists explain their why, it may violate common notions of what's possible.

Researchers Debra Meyerson and Maureen Scully have found that to succeed, originals must often become tempered radicals. They believe in values that depart from traditions and ideas that go against the grain, yet they learn to tone down their radicalism by presenting their beliefs and ideas in ways that are less shocking and more appealing to mainstream audiences. Meredith Perry is a tempered radical: she made an implausible idea plausible by obscuring its most extreme feature. When she couldn't persuade technical experts to take a leap with her, she convinced them to take a few steps by masking her purpose.

Shifting the focus from why to how can help people become less radical. In a series of experiments, when people with extreme political views were asked to explain the reasons behind their policy preferences, they stuck to their guns. Explaining why gave them a chance to affirm their convictions. But when asked to explain how their preferred policies work, they became more moderate. Considering how led them to confront the gaps in their knowledge and realize that some of their extreme views were impractical.

To form alliances, originals can temper their radicalism by smuggling their real vision inside a Trojan horse. U.S. Navy lieutenant Josh Steinman had a grand vision to open the military up to outside technology by creating a Silicon Valley hub. Steinman knew he would face resistance if he presented a radical, sweeping proposal for rethinking the navy's entire approach to innovation, so he led with a more tempered pitch. He presented some new technology for doing real-time updates in the air to Admiral Jonathan Greenert, the chief of naval operations. Intrigued, Admiral Greenert asked what would come next, and Rear Admiral Scott Stearney threw a softball question at Steinman, inquiring about how the military should think about the technical future. "That's when we threw the strike," Steinman recalls. "Sir, the future is going to be about software, not hardware, and we need an entity of the U.S. Navy in Silicon Valley."

A few months later, after other junior officers made similar cases about the importance of software, the CNO gave a speech advocating for the idea, which also circulated around the Pentagon. Not long afterward, the secretary of defense announced an embassy in Silicon Valley. Steinman leveraged what psychologist Robert Cialdini calls the foot-in-the-door technique, where you lead with a small request to secure an initial commitment before revealing the larger one. By opening with a moderate ask instead of a radical one, Steinman gained allies.

Coalitions often fall apart when people refuse to moderate their radicalism. That was one of the major failures of the Occupy Wall

Street movement, a protest against economic and social inequality that began in 2011. That year, polls showed that the majority of Americans supported the movement, but it soon fell apart. Activist Srdja Popovic marvels that its extreme positioning alienated most of its potential allies. Its fatal error, he argues, was naming the movement after the radical tactic of camping out, which few people find attractive. He believes that had the group simply relabeled itself "The 99 Percent," it might still exist. The Occupy name "implied that the only way you could belong was if you dropped everything you were doing and started occupying something," Popovic writes. "Occupying is still just a single weapon in the enormous arsenal of peaceful protest—and, more to the point, one that tends to invite only a certain type of dedicated person. . . . Movements, which are always fighting uphill battles, need to draw in more casual participants if they are to succeed." "The 99 Percent" is inclusive: it invites everyone to get involved and to use their own preferred tactics. By tempering the brand of the movement and broadening its methods, it might have been possible to gain the support of more mainstream citizens.

In the women's suffrage movement, this is where the narcissism of small differences reared its ugly head. When Anthony and Stanton partnered with the racist George Francis Train in 1867, Stone wrote that Train's support of suffrage was "enough to condemn it in the minds of all persons not already convinced," and her husband warned Anthony that the alliance would mean "irreparable harm to the cause of votes for women *and* blacks."*

---

* A longtime ally, William Lloyd Garrison, begged Anthony to back away: "In all friendliness, and with the highest regard for the woman's rights movement, I cannot refrain from expressing my regret and astonishment that you and Mrs. Stanton should have taken such leave of good sense as to be traveling companions and associate lecturers with that crack-brained harlequin and semi-lunatic, George Francis Train. . . . You will only subject yourselves to merited ridicule and condemnation, and turn the movement which you aim to promote into unnecessary contempt. . . . He may be of use in drawing an audience, but so would a kangaroo, a gorilla or a hippopotamus."

But Anthony would not budge from her radical conviction that if women couldn't gain the right to vote, blacks shouldn't, either. She campaigned with Train throughout Kansas and accepted his funding to create a suffrage newspaper. When Stone confronted her about tarnishing the reputation of their equal rights association by linking it to Train, Anthony became defensive: "I know what is the matter with you. It is envy, and spleen, and hate, because I have a paper and you have not." Stanton sided with Anthony, endorsing her decision to partner with Train: "It would be right and wise to accept aid from the devil himself," she said, "provided that he did not tempt us to lower our standard."

The alliance proved costly: Kansas had a chance to become the first state to adopt suffrage, but ended up losing the vote—and the black suffrage proposal lost as well. Many insiders held the alliance with Train accountable for both defeats. A couple years later, when Stanton and Anthony had formed their own association, instead of learning from the mistakes of the past, they refused to moderate their extreme stance that anyone who supported suffrage was a friend. Forming another alliance that cast a dark cloud over the movement, Stanton joined forces with Victoria Woodhull, an activist who became the first woman to run for the American presidency, but undermined the suffrage movement with a radical agenda. Woodhull, whose past included time as a prostitute and a charlatan healer, advocated for sexual freedom, proclaiming that she had an "inalienable, constitutional, and natural right to love whom I may, to love as long or as short a period as I can, to change that love every day if I please."

Suffrage opponents used Woodhull's position as evidence that the movement was really about sexual promiscuity rather than voting rights. Members withdrew in large numbers from Anthony and Stanton's organization, to the point that they couldn't even gather sufficient attendance for a convention. Even supportive legislators advised suffragists to put their quest for the vote aside. Suffragists remarked that Woodhull's campaign "is the most efficient agent employed to frighten people from our ranks" and "set the cause back twenty years." The alliance "precipitated a storm of criticism" so severe, Anthony's biographer would later write, that it made the prior attacks look like "a summer shower to a Missouri cyclone."

In maintaining the alliance with Woodhull, Stanton failed to recognize the value of tempered radicalism. She drove Stone and many other past and potential allies away by overlooking the dramatic differences in how insiders and outsiders judge coalitions. Her error is illuminated in a new study by management researchers Blake Ashforth and Peter Reingen, who find that insiders and outsiders have distinct ideas about who represents a coalition. For insiders, the key representative is the person who is most central and connected in the group. For the suffragists, that was clearly Stanton and Anthony. But for outsiders, the person who represents the group is the one with the most extreme views. That was Woodhull: her personal scandal overshadowed the suffrage cause and alienated many who were open to the relatively moderate idea of voting rights but not the more radical ideas of sexual independence for women. As outsiders judged the suffrage movement by the extreme company Anthony and Stanton kept, Stone had little choice but to distance her organization further from their efforts.

Enemies Make Better Allies Than Frenemies

In *The Godfather: Part II*, Michael Corleone advises, "Keep your friends close, but your enemies closer." But what should we do about people who don't fall neatly into either category?

Typically, we view our relationships on a continuum from positive to negative. Our closest friends have our backs; our greatest enemies are actively working against us. But research shows that we need to draw two independent axes: one for how positive a relationship is and a separate one for how negative the relationship is. Along with purely positive and wholly negative relationships, we can have connections that are both positive and negative. Psychologists call them ambivalent relationships. You might know them as frenemies—people who sometimes support you and sometimes undermine you.

Positivity

		Low	High
	Low	Acquaintances: indifferent	Friends: consistently supportive
Negativity	High	Enemies: consistently undermining	Frenemies: ambivalent

Stone's relationships with both Stanton and Anthony were deeply ambivalent—they had been both allies and adversaries. On the one hand, she admired Stanton's wit and Anthony's industriousness, and they had a proven record of productive collaboration. On the other hand, Stone objected to their "lunatic friends" and "wild alliances," which threatened the respectability of the women's suffrage movement. And Anthony and Stanton had a pattern of duplicity. They signed Stone's name to an ad complimenting their racist benefactor without her permission. More recently, Stone had written to Stanton in the fall of 1869, proposing the "hearty active cooperation of <u>all</u> the friends of the cause, better than either could do alone," and assuring her that Stone's organization "shall never be an enemy or antagonist of yours." Yet at the convention launching Stone's group, Anthony attempted an ill-fated coup to elect Stanton as president. Stone invited her to the podium, and Anthony concluded by accusing Stone of attempting to "nullify and crush out" her organization.

In 1872, Stanton reached out to Stone with a proposal for reconciliation, urging her to "let bygones be bygones. Let all personalities be buried in the work that is before us." Stone took some conciliatory steps, sharing Stanton's articles and speeches in her newspaper. Then came a letter from Anthony, proposing to "cooperate and make a systematic campaign," inviting Stone to Rochester to "settle the question that we are all together as one grand woman." Stone declined.

With the benefit of hindsight, it's easy to judge Stone's refusal as a stubborn mistake. Had she accepted, the organizations might have won the right to vote years earlier. But if you examine how ambivalent relationships affect our stress levels, you will find some wisdom in Stone's resistance.

To discover the most effective way to handle ambivalent relationships, Michelle Duffy, a management professor at the University of Minnesota, led a study surveying police officers on how often they were undermined and supported by their closest coworker, as well as their levels of stress and absence from work. Not surprisingly, negative relationships were stressful. When officers felt undermined by their closest coworker, they were less committed, took more unauthorized breaks, and were absent from work more often.

What happened when the undermining colleague was also supportive at times? Things didn't get better; they got worse. Being undermined and supported by the same person meant even lower commitment and more work missed.* Negative relationships are unpleasant, but they're predictable: if a colleague consistently undermines you, you can keep your distance and expect the worst. But when you're dealing with an

---

* The good news is that when officers were undermined by one person but supported by a different person, they were better off. Support from a colleague or a supervisor had a buffering effect, protecting officers against the stress and absences that undermining otherwise caused.

ambivalent relationship, you're constantly on guard, grappling with questions about when that person can actually be trusted. As Duffy's team explains, "It takes more emotional energy and coping resources to deal with individuals who are inconsistent."

In a series of groundbreaking studies, psychologist Bert Uchino found that ambivalent relationships are literally unhealthier than negative relationships. In one study, having more ambivalent relationships predicted higher rates of stress, depression, and dissatisfaction with life. In another, older adults rated their relationships with the ten most important people in their lives, and completed two anxiety-provoking tasks: delivering a speech with little preparation and taking a rapid-fire math test. The more ambivalent relationships the participants had, the more their heart rates spiked on both tasks.

Lucy Stone understood the risks of forming alliances with ambivalent ties. In 1871, she wrote that it was best "not to strike hands with those people. . . . They were our late enemies. We don't know that they are our friends." American studies expert and biographer Andrea Moore Kerr notes that Stone was "unable to predict or control the behavior of either Stanton or Anthony." In response, according to Baker, Stone "sought to keep her organization free from infection by 'the dreaded incubus' of the Stanton-Anthony forces."

Our instinct is to sever our bad relationships and salvage the ambivalent ones. But the evidence suggests we ought to do the opposite: cut our frenemies and attempt to convert our enemies.

In efforts to challenge the status quo, originals often ignore their opponents. If someone is already resisting a change, the logic goes, there's no point in wasting your time on him. Instead, focus on strengthening your ties with people who already support you.

But our best allies aren't the people who have supported us all along. They're the ones who started out against us and then came around to our side.

Half a century ago, eminent psychologist Elliot Aronson conducted a series of experiments suggesting that we're often more sensitive to gains and losses in esteem than the level of esteem itself. When someone always supports us, we take it for granted—and can discount it. But we regard someone who began as a rival and then became an enthusiastic supporter as an authentic advocate. "A person whose liking for us increases over time will be liked better than one who has always liked us," Aronson explains. "We find it more rewarding when someone's initially negative feelings toward us gradually become positive than if that person's feelings for us were entirely positive all along."

While we'll have an especially strong affinity toward our converted rivals, will they feel the same way toward us? Yes—this is the second advantage of converting resisters. To like us, they have to work especially hard to overcome their initial negative impressions, telling themselves, *I must have been wrong about that person.* Moving forward, to avoid the cognitive dissonance of changing their minds yet again, they'll be especially motivated to maintain a positive relationship.

Third, and most important, it is our former adversaries who are the most effective at persuading others to join our movements. They can marshal better arguments on our behalf, because they understand the doubts and misgivings of resisters and fence-sitters. And they're a more credible source, because they haven't just been Pollyanna followers or "yes men" all along. In one of Aronson's studies, people were most persuaded to change their opinions by those who had started out negative and then become more positive. And more recently, corporate executives were subtly influenced by board members who argued with them initially and then conformed—which signals that their "opinion appears to stand up to critical scrutiny."*

---

* Of course, not every negative relationship can be turned around. Essayist Chuck Klosterman draws an important distinction between ordinary nemeses—adversaries who might become allies—and archenemies: "You kind of like your nemesis, despite the fact that you despise him. If your nemesis invited you out for cocktails, you would accept the offer. . . . But you would never have drinks with your archenemy, unless you were attempting to spike his gin with hemlock."

Instead of avoiding her enemies, Lucy Stone sought them out and actively engaged with them. She helped convert Julia Ward Howe, a prominent poet who wrote "The Battle Hymn of the Republic." Howe had been invited to attend a suffrage meeting and came only reluctantly, "with a rebellious heart," regarding Stone as one of her "dislikes." But after listening to Stone's speech, Howe became a close ally and one of the great leaders of the movement.

In 1855, a heckler disrupted a convention by describing suffragists as unfit for marriage, disparaging the movement as "a few disappointed women." Instead of ignoring him, Lucy Stone addressed him directly in her speech, and the audience roared with applause:

The last speaker alluded to this movement as being that of a few disappointed women. From the first years to which my memory stretches, I have been a disappointed woman. . . . I was disappointed when I came to seek a profession . . . every employment was closed to me, except those of the teacher, the seamstress and the housekeeper. In education, in marriage, in religion, in everything, disappointment is the lot of women. It shall be the business of my life to deepen this disappointment in every woman's heart until she bows down to it no longer.

When Stone walked around hanging up posters announcing abolition speeches, young men often followed her and ripped them down. Stone asked them if they loved their mothers. Absolutely. Did they love their sisters? Of course. She explained that in the South, men their own age were sold as slaves, and would never see their families again. As Kerr explains, "She then invited them to attend the evening's lectures as her 'special guests.' Such street recruits proved useful allies, able to defuse other troublemakers."

In 1859, a college student named Frances Willard wrote in her journal that Lucy Stone was in town, and noted, "I don't like her views."

Given her own conservative opinions, Willard joined the temperance movement, but years later became one of the most influential suffrage leaders. She reflected that Stone was a force behind her change of heart:

I remember when I was dreadfully afraid of Susan, and of Lucy too. But now I love and honor these women, and I can not put into words my sense of what it means to have the blessings of these women who have made it possible for more timid ones like myself to come along and take our places in the world's work. If they had not blazed the trees and pioneered the way we should not have dared to come.

In 1876, Willard led the effort to align suffragists with temperance workers. Research would later show that over the next two decades, every time Willard visited a state, the odds of a suffrage-temperance alliance spiked. How did she convince the conservative WCTU members to partner with the liberal suffragists? A clue to her success can be found in Hollywood, where movies live and die based on how well writers can persuade executives to buy into their visions.

Familiar Makes the Heart Grow Fonder

In the early 1990s, a group of screenwriters proposed something that had never been done at Disney: they wanted to make an animated movie based on an original concept. Departing from a half century of hits with time-honored tales like *Cinderella* and *Snow White*, they set out to write a fresh story from scratch. Studio chief Jeffrey Katzenberg was skeptical, telling colleagues it was an experiment. "No one had any confidence in it," director Rob Minkoff recalls. "It was seen as the B movie at Disney."

The script eventually became *The Lion King*, which was the highest-grossing film of 1994, winning two Oscars and a Golden Globe. Katzenberg had said he would get down on his knees in appreciation if it brought in $50 million. By 2014, it had earned over $1 billion.

Like many original ideas, the movie almost never got off the ground. It was conceived as *"Bambi* in Africa with lions" (instead of deer as the protagonists). But after the first script failed, five of the writers gathered to rethink it. They sat together for two days, batting around ideas and weaving an epic tale about the succession of kings, and then pitched the story to a group of Disney executives. The first to respond was CEO Michael Eisner, who wasn't getting it. Grasping for a hook, he asked, "Could you make this into *King Lear*?"

Coincidentally, Minkoff had reread that Shakespeare play a few weeks earlier, and he explained why the concept didn't fit. Then, from the back of the room, a producer named Maureen Donley raised another Shakespearean suggestion: "No, this is *Hamlet*."

Suddenly, everyone got it. "There was a collective sigh of recognition," Minkoff says. "Of course it was *Hamlet*— The uncle kills the father, and the son has to avenge his father's death. So then we decided it was going to be *Hamlet* with lions." In that pivotal moment, the film got the green light.

To understand what saved the movie from the cutting-room floor, I turned to Justin Berg, the creativity expert at Stanford. The writers had to begin with lions, Berg explains. Had they started with *Hamlet*, they would have ended up with an animated knockoff of Shakespeare. Beginning with a novel template was the key to originality, but it also posed a challenge.

In an experiment, Berg asked people to design a new product to help college students succeed in job interviews. He instructed them to start with the familiar concept of a three-ring binder, and then come up with something novel. Bookstore managers and customers rated the resulting ideas as utterly conventional.

According to Berg, the starting point in generating ideas is like the first brushstroke that a painter lays down on a canvas: it shapes the path for the rest of the painting, constraining what we imagine. Beginning with a three-ring binder led Berg's participants down the path of proposing obvious products like a folder with pockets for résumés and business cards—hardly a game-changing idea. To come up with something original, we need to begin from a more unfamiliar place.

Instead of the three-ring binder, Berg gave some participants a more novel starting point: an in-line skate for roller blading. They were no longer captives of the conventional: they generated ideas that scored 37 percent higher in originality. One participant observed that during job interviews, it's often difficult to know how much time has passed, and you don't want to appear rude by looking at your watch, breaking eye contact with the interviewer. The proposed solution was to build a watch that tracks time by touch, with physical elements like the wheels on roller skates that change shape or texture as time passes.

Although a novel starting point does help foster the originality of our ideas, it doesn't necessarily make them palatable and practical to our audiences. While the Rollerblade led to a creative idea for subtly tracking time, squeezing your watch is an odd behavior. To solve this problem, Berg gave people the novel starting point of the in-line skate, but added a twist: after they developed their ideas, he showed them a picture of products that people typically use in job interviews, then asked them to spend a few additional minutes refining their concepts. For the person who wanted a polite method of timekeeping, this made all the difference. Instead of a watch that tells time by touch, after taking a look at the kinds of products that were familiar in job interviews, the same inventor designed a pen that tells time by touch:

The most promising ideas begin from novelty and then add familiarity, which capitalizes on the mere exposure effect we covered

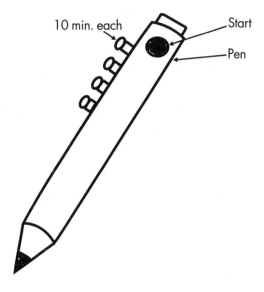

earlier. On average, a novel starting point followed by a familiarity infusion led to ideas that were judged as 14 percent more practical, without sacrificing any originality. As Berg points out, if you started the experiment with a pen rather than an in-line skate, you'd probably end up with something a lot like a conventional pen. But by starting with something unexpected in the context of job interviews, like an in-line skate, and then incorporating the familiarity of a pen, you can develop an idea that is both novel and useful.

In the case of *The Lion King*, that is what happened when Maureen Donley suggested that the script could be like *Hamlet*. The dose of familiarity helped the executives connect the novel savannah script to a classic tale. "It gives a large group of people a single point of reference," Minkoff explains. "With absolute originality, you can lose people. Executives have to sell it, so they're looking for those handles. It gives them something to hang on to." The *Lion King* team went on to take a cue from *Hamlet*. Realizing that they needed a "to be or not to be" moment, they added a scene in which the baboon, Rafiki, delivers a lesson to Simba about the importance of remembering who he is.

In the women's suffrage movement, temperance workers didn't come on board until an emerging leader offered a familiarity infusion. Vanderbilt sociologist Holly McCammon identified two main arguments that suffragists used in their quest to earn the right to vote: justice and societal reform. The justice argument focused on fairness, emphasizing that women had the unalienable right to vote. The societal reform argument focused on social good, highlighting how women's nurturing, domestic, and moral qualities would improve the country. At the time, the justice argument was considered the radical one, as it violated traditional gender-role stereotypes by proposing that women and men were equals in all domains. The societal reform argument was more moderate, as it affirmed gender-role stereotypes in suggesting that the unique qualities conservatives already valued in private life could also contribute to public life. In a form of "public motherhood," enfranchised women could benefit society by promoting education, limiting government corruption, and helping the poor.

When McCammon and colleagues coded suffrage speeches, newspaper columns, banners, and leaflets that were produced over the course of a quarter century, the justice argument appeared earliest and most frequently. Overall, suffragists wielded the justice case 30 percent of the time, compared with barely more than half that often for the societal reform argument. But justice arguments fell on deaf ears with the WCTU members, who clung to traditional gender roles and rejected the notion that women were the equals of men. The societal reform argument also failed to resonate with familiar values: conservative temperance workers were aiming for stability, not change. It was Frances Willard, now an emerging WCTU leader, who ingeniously reframed the pitch and made it widely acceptable.

How the West Was Won

Frances Willard didn't use the justice argument or the societal reform argument. She didn't even present the issue as a suffrage ballot.

Instead, she called it a "home protection ballot."

Willard saw suffrage as "a weapon of protection . . . from the tyranny of drink." Likening the ballot to "a powerful sunglass," she promised to use it to "burn and blaze on the saloon, till it shrivels up and in lurid vapors curls away like mist." Protecting the home was a familiar goal for the WCTU members. Now, suffrage could be used as a means to a desirable end: if temperance advocates wanted to fight alcohol abuse, they needed to vote. As Baker writes:

> *It was an indirect approach to suffrage made on the religious grounds of protecting the home, but it linked the two most powerful women's reform movements in the United States. Suffrage, a universal entitlement required in the minds of Anthony and Stanton on the grounds of natural rights, was a tool for Willard . . . a tactical appeal to domestic women.*

When McCammon led a study of four decades of alliances between the WCTU and suffragists, the data showed that after suffragists made the justice argument in a particular state, there was no increase in the likelihood of an alliance with the WCTU in that state the following year—in fact, an alliance became slightly less likely. But once suffragists presented the home protection framing, the odds of joining forces with the WCTU in that state increased significantly, as did the odds that a state would eventually pass suffrage.* Ultimately, Willard's

---

* Willard's home protection argument consistently moved the needle, but just how far depended on timing. She had the biggest impact when the WCTU was under threat. When she visited

leadership enabled women to gain full voting rights in several states and school board election voting rights in nineteen states. This argument was particularly effective in the West. Before the Nineteenth Amendment to the Constitution gave women full voting rights, 81 percent of the Western states and territories passed suffrage laws, compared with only two in the East and zero in the South.

It's highly unlikely that Frances Willard would have started the women's suffrage movement. Justin Berg's research suggests that if women had begun with the familiar goal of protecting their homes, they might never have considered the vote. Radical thinking is often necessary to put an original stake in the ground. But once the radical idea of voting was planted, the original suffragists needed a more tempered mediator to reach a wider audience. Frances Willard had unique credibility with the temperance activists because she drew upon comfortably familiar ideas in her speeches. She made heavy use of religious rhetoric, quoting regularly from the Bible.

Frances Willard was the quintessential tempered radical. "Under Willard, nothing seemed radical," writes Baker, even "as she was moving toward more progressive causes." Her actions offer two lessons about persuading potential partners to join forces. First, we need to think differently about values. Instead of assuming that others share our principles, or trying to convince them to adopt ours, we ought to present our values as a means of pursuing theirs. It's hard to change other people's ideals. It's much easier to link our agendas to familiar values that people already hold.

Second, just as we saw in the case of Meredith Perry's disguising

---

states after prohibition legislation failed or saloons became more widespread, WCTU coalitions with suffragists were the most likely. The conservative WCTU members felt that their mission was at risk, and began to see suffrage as a valuable weapon in their war against alcohol abuse. "Willard helped WCTU members make sense of their political defeats by interpreting them to be the result of political weakness," McCammon and a colleague explain. "By convincing WCTU members that women's voting rights could help win prohibition laws, Willard aligned WCTU thinking with that of the suffragists."

her real objective of creating wireless power, transparency isn't always the best policy. As much as they want to be straightforward with potential partners, originals occasionally need to reframe their ideas to appeal to their audience. Willard smuggled the vote inside the Trojan horse of fighting alcohol abuse.

But that argument didn't work with every group she addressed. The justice argument attracted the most radical women to the cause, as they favored equal gender roles. With the highly conservative temperance activists, the most tempered argument for home protection cemented coalitions. But for converting other allies to actually join the suffrage movement, the home protection argument was *too* tempered. McCammon's research shows that to convert more women to believe in suffrage as an end, not simply as a means to other ends, a Goldilocks pitch was necessary: the moderate societal reform argument. For movement leaders to "succeed in organizing potential recruits, they must strike the appropriate balance between resonating with the existing cultural repertoire and challenging the status quo." Membership in state suffrage organizations didn't change after suffragists framed their issue in terms of justice or home protection, but it spiked after they accentuated how women could improve society—and so did the passage of suffrage laws. "Originality is what everybody wants, but there's a sweet spot," Rob Minkoff explains. "If it's not original enough, it's boring or trite. If it's too original, it may be hard for the audience to understand. The goal is to push the envelope, not tear the envelope."

Throughout her life, Lucy Stone continued to reference justice and equality when speaking to women who were already involved in the suffrage movement. But when addressing audiences of outsiders, she was more careful to incorporate the societal reform argument and respect traditional gender roles. In 1853, when an unruly audience interrupted the proceedings of a women's rights convention, Stone took the platform. Instead of leading with justice, she affirmed the contributions of women in the domestic sphere: "I think that any woman who stands on the throne of her own house, dispensing there the virtues of love, charity, and peace, and sends out of it into the world good men, who may help to make the world better, occupies a higher position than any crowned head." She suggested that women could contribute more, and described how they were entering professions, taking care not to compare them to men. When she mentioned a woman who became a minister, the audience hissed, and Stone again reminded the audience that she supported women's domestic roles: "Some men hiss who had no mothers to teach them better."

United We Stand: Creating Coalitions Across Conflict Lines

After two decades of conflict, the two suffrage organizations finally began to converge in philosophy and tactics. Elizabeth Cady Stanton and Susan B. Anthony had avoided radical alliances for more than a decade, and they were now investing their energy in educating the public. Stanton led the writing of a history of the movement; Anthony traveled around the country to lecture and lobby, and saw eye to eye with Lucy Stone on the value of an alliance with temperance workers and a more moderate campaign focusing solely on suffrage rather than other women's issues.

Years ago, when studying the conflict between Israel and Palestine, Harvard psychologist Herbert Kelman observed that conflicts *between* two groups are often caused and intensified by conflicts *within* the groups. Although Stone's organization was aligned on the benefits of reuniting, there was strife within Anthony and Stanton's organization. Stanton objected to the alliances with temperance workers and the limited focus on suffrage; various members questioned whether suffrage should be enacted at the state or federal levels, and whether it should be full or partial.

As effective as Stone was in converting allies, she was the wrong person to negotiate with Anthony. When distrust runs as deep as it did between these two women, coalitions depend on the warring individuals serving not as leaders, but as lightning rods. As Blake Ashforth and Peter Reingen write, this could have allowed members of each organization to "blame the divisiveness of competition" on Stanton's radical stance, so that "each side could blame conflict more on the other side's firebrands," while setting the stage for them to "cooperate with other members of the rival group." To build coalitions across conflict lines, Kelman finds that it's rarely effective to send hawks to negotiate. You need the doves in each group to sit down, listen to each other's perspectives, identify their common goals and methods, and engage in joint problem solving.*

Stone and Anthony recognized the value of removing the hawks from the discussion, deciding to each designate seven members of their organizations to a joint committee that would negotiate the terms of a unification agreement. But the principles laid out by Stone and Anthony were not sufficient to create a foundation for consensus, as the committee from Anthony's organization experienced such discord that they had to appoint a separate eight-member committee to help them. When they finally reached consensus, their proposal fell so far outside the scope of the agreed-upon principles that Stone's committee lacked the authority to decide on it.

In 1890, three years into the effort to reunite, Stone recognized the challenges of solidarity and the value of passing the torch: "The younger

---

* In 1990, Kelman brought together a series of influential leaders from Israel and Palestine for a series of unofficial workshops, meeting regularly over three years. A typical workshop involved between three and six representatives from each country, along with two to four facilitators. The representatives shared their perspectives, avoiding blaming each other and justifying their own views, and focusing on analyzing the effects of their interaction on the conflict. After all participants expressed their concerns and understood and acknowledged those posed by everyone else, they embarked on joint problem solving. Shortly after the workshops ended in 1993, the Oslo Accords were signed. It was the first time the Israeli government and the Palestine Liberation Organization had reached a face-to-face agreement. The leaders won the Nobel Peace Prize for it, and insiders credited Kelman's efforts as a catalyst.

ones want to unite and the old ones who remember the causes of division will soon be gone." Her daughter and husband successfully negotiated the terms of an alliance with Anthony's committee, and their organizations merged. For her part, Anthony came to understand the value of tempered radicalism, to the point that Stanton complained, "Lucy and Susan alike see suffrage only. They do not see religious and social bondage. Neither do the young women in either association, hence they may as well combine for they have only one mind and one purpose."

Although Anthony and Stanton never mended fences with Stone, when Stone passed away, the sheer force of her contributions compelled them to speak glowingly of her. "There is none more winning than Lucy Stone," Anthony declared. "We have never had a woman in our whole fifty years of this movement who could go before an audience and melt the heart of every one in it like that woman. She stood alone."

In Stanton's eyes, "The death of no woman in America had ever called out so general a tribute of public respect and esteem." Stone was the "first who really stirred the nation's heart on the subject of women's wrongs," and their disagreement many years earlier was because Stone "felt the slaves' wrongs more deeply than her own—my philosophy was more egotistical."

"Those who cannot remember the past are condemned to repeat it," philosopher George Santayana wrote. That would prove to hold true for the American women's suffrage movement, on at least two occasions. In 1890, two members of Anthony's organization, furious at her scheming to create a national organization and the move toward tempered radicalism, split off to form a rival group that attacked the efforts to unify. Anthony and Stanton quashed it, but they were not around to warn their successors against the narcissism of small differences. At the turn of the twentieth century, in the twilight of their lives, they handed the leadership of the national suffrage organization on to Carrie Chapman Catt, then a temperance activist and WCTU member.

But a more radical woman named Alice Paul, not content to pursue suffrage with tempered tactics like lecturing, writing, and lobbying, favored bolder actions. She embarked on a hunger strike, and rejected Catt's nonpartisan position, blaming the Democratic Party for the failure to grant suffrage. Paul's actions were so radical that she was expelled from the national suffrage organization, and she formed her own in 1916. As of 1918, the national organization boasted over a million members; Paul's had only ten thousand, and like her predecessors, she avoided alliances with African Americans. Her group picketed the White House and ridiculed President Woodrow Wilson, which might have helped to move the needle. "But it was Catt's leadership—progressive but not radical—that finally led Wilson to throw his support behind the amendment," one onlooker wrote.

In her dying breath in 1893, Lucy Stone whispered four words to her daughter: "Make the world better." It would be twenty-seven more years before the Nineteenth Amendment passed. But when women gained full voting rights nationwide, Stone's footprint of tempered radicalism was powerful and visible. As Kerr sums it up: "The organizational model Stone provided would be adopted by Carrie Chapman Catt in the final, successful march to an amendment in 1920."

6

Rebel with a Cause

How Siblings, Parents, and Mentors Nurture Originality

"We are not our brother's keeper . . . in countless large and
small ways we are our brother's maker."

Harry and Bonaro Overstreet

A moment ago, he was standing calmly on third base, adjusting his
hat. Now, his feet are darting side to side, dancing away from the
bag. He is poised for a head start toward home plate.

He is one of the greatest men ever to set foot on a baseball dia-
mond, and he has been in this position before. Four previous times he
has led his team to the World Series, and all four times they have lost
to the Yankees. This time, he hopes, will be different. It's the opening
game of his fifth championship battle against the Yankees, and his
team is down 6–4 in the eighth inning. With two outs, he has a
dilemma: Should he count on his teammate to drive him in, or go for
broke and try to steal home?

Stealing a base is one of the riskiest moves in baseball. It increases
your team's odds of scoring by less than 3 percent, and to do it successfully you usually need to slide into the base, which can mean a
painful physical collision with a fielder. Stealing home is even riskier:
instead of having his back to you, as would be the case if you were
trying to steal second or third base, the pitcher is already facing the

plate, allowing for an easy throw. The pitcher has to hurl the ball only 60 feet through the air; you have to travel 90 feet by foot. In essence, you have to outrun the ball. And even if you think you can make it, your odds of getting injured are quadrupled at home plate compared to collisions at other bases.

In the entire 2012 season, only three players attempted to steal home. Although baseball's all-time steals leader, Rickey Henderson, stole more than 1,400 bases in his career, only one was a pure steal of home plate. In second place all-time for career steals is Lou Brock, whose 938 successful attempts include a grand total of zero times stealing home.

This man, though, is different. He holds the record for stealing home plate more than any player in the modern era—nineteen times. Over nearly a century, there are just two other players who have even reached double digits.

He has led the league in stolen bases twice, but if you believe his decision to steal home is about speed, think again. At thirty-six, he is well past his prime. He has missed a third of the regular season due to injuries. Six years earlier he stole thirty-seven bases in a season; in the past two seasons combined, he has barely stolen half that many. His hair is silver, and he has put on weight; sportswriters are calling him the "old gray fat man." In the past, he has batted fourth, the coveted cleanup spot. Now, he is down to seventh in the batting order. He will retire the following year.

The man's speed is a relic of the past, but he has spent his whole life taking action where others stood still, and he is not about to stop now. He waits for the right opportunity and then charges ahead. Just as he slides into home plate, the catcher reaches out to tag him. There's nothing certain about the decision. But when the umpire makes the call, he's safe.

Ultimately, it's too little, too late. His team loses the first game to the Yankees. But his effort serves a symbolic purpose. In the words of one sports historian, stealing home gives his team "a huge psychological lift." The man himself notices it, too: "Whether it was because of my stealing home or not, the team had new fire." They go on to win the series, landing the coveted championship.

Years later, reflecting on the player's legacy, one journalist wrote that his attempts to steal home plate "certainly were, collectively, the second-boldest thing he ever did in baseball."

The first was breaking the color barrier.

To become original, we have to be willing to take some risks. When we go against the grain to upend time-honored traditions, we can never be certain that we'll succeed. As journalist Robert Quillen wrote, "Progress always involves risk. You can't steal second and keep one foot on first base."

From the day that Jackie Robinson became Major League Baseball's first black player in 1947, he braved racist peers who refused to play with or against him, opponents who deliberately cut him with their spiked cleats, and hate mail and death threats. He went on to become the first black vice president of a major American company and the country's first black baseball announcer. What gave him the courage to rebel against social norms and stay resolute in the face of emotional, social, and physical risks?

We can observe some clues in an unlikely place, by examining the family backgrounds of ballplayers who have shared his penchant for stealing bases. In the modern era of baseball, since the 162-game season was introduced, only ten players have stolen at least 70 bases in two different seasons. Take a look at the list below. Do you see a pattern?

Baseball player	Steals	Birthplace	Birth Order	Children in Family
Rickey Henderson	130, 108	Chicago, Illinois	4	7
Lou Brock	118, 74	El Dorado, Arkansas	7	9
Vince Coleman	110, 109	Jacksonville, Florida	1	1
Maury Wills	104, 94	Washington, D.C.	7	13
Ron LeFlore	97, 78	Detroit, Michigan	3	4
Omar Moreno	96, 77	Puerto Armuelles, Panama	8	10
Tim Raines	90, 78	Sanford, Florida	5	7
Willie Wilson	83, 79	Montgomery, Alabama	1	1
Marquis Grissom	78, 76	Atlanta, Georgia	14	15
Kenny Lofton	75, 70	East Chicago, Indiana	1	1

Aiming to determine why some baseball players steal more bases than others, historian of science Frank Sulloway and psychologist Richard Zweigenhaft did something clever. They identified more than four hundred brothers who played professional baseball, which enabled them to compare individuals from the same families, who shared half their DNA and had similar upbringings. Their results revealed a striking fact: birth order predicted which brother tried to steal more bases.

Younger brothers were *10.6 times more likely* than their older siblings to attempt to steal a base.

The younger brothers weren't necessarily better players overall. They had no advantage when it came to batting average, for example. And comparing brothers who were pitchers, the older siblings actually had a slight edge in ball control; they tended to have more strikeouts and fewer walks. The key difference was the propensity to take risks. Along with attempting more steals, younger brothers were 4.7 times more likely to get hit by a pitch, probably because they dared more often to crowd the plate. But they didn't just take bolder action; they also succeeded more often than their older siblings. Younger brothers were 3.2 times more likely to steal a base safely.

In fact, their appetite for risk makes younger siblings less likely even to play baseball. Across twenty-four different studies of more than eight thousand people, laterborns were 1.48 times more likely to participate in sports with high injury rates, such as football, rugby, boxing, ice hockey, gymnastics, scuba diving, downhill skiing and ski jumping, bobsledding, and auto racing. Firstborns preferred safer sports: baseball, golf, tennis, track, cycling, and crew.

When laterborns do opt to play professional baseball, they tend to tear up the base path. Look at the three players who tower over their peers as the reigning home plate thieves of the modern era: all had at least three older siblings. Jackie Robinson, who has been called the "father of modern base stealing," was the youngest of five children.

The second-highest tally for stealing home in the modern era belongs to Rod Carew, the fourth of five children. Beyond having an acute sense of timing, "it also takes a certain amount of nerve," Carew noted. To steal home, he explained, "I could not have any fear within myself of getting hurt. And I didn't, because I felt in control." The third ranked, Paul Molitor, called stealing home "a courage play"; he's the fourth child of eight.

A similar pattern emerges in the base-stealing rankings listed above. Of the only ten players ever to steal at least 70 bases in two different seasons, half have at least four older siblings, and seven have at least two older siblings. These seven stealing champs are, on average, child number 6.9 in their families, and 71 percent of their siblings are older than them.

Laterborns aren't just more likely to take risks in baseball—the difference also shows up in politics and science, with serious implications for social and intellectual progress. In a landmark study, Sulloway analyzed more than two dozen major scientific revolutions and breakthroughs, from Copernican astronomy to Darwinian evolution and from Newton's mechanics to Einstein's relativity. He enlisted over a hundred historians of science to evaluate the stances of nearly four thousand scientists on a spectrum from extreme support of prevailing views to extreme advocacy of new ideas. Then, he tracked the role of birth order in predicting whether the scientists would defend the status quo or champion a revolutionary new theory. In each case, he controlled for the fact that there are more laterborns than firstborns in the population, as well as for social class, family size, and other factors that might influence the results.

Compared to firstborns, laterborn scientists had more than triple the odds of endorsing Newton's laws of gravity and motion and Einstein's theory of special relativity when these ideas were considered radical. During the half century after Copernicus published his model of the earth revolving around the sun, laterborn scientists were 5.4

times more likely to endorse the Copernican model than firstborns. After Galileo invented the telescope and published his discoveries supporting the model, the ratio dropped to 1:1. Since the theory was no longer radical, firstborns accepted it at equal rates.

The most telling evidence that later children may be born to rebel comes from Sulloway's analysis of reactions to the theory of evolution. He assessed how hundreds of scientists responded to the notion of evolution from 1700 to 1859, before Darwin released his famous findings. Prior to Darwin, 56 of 117 laterborns believed in evolution, compared with only 9 of 103 firstborns. In the sixteen years after Darwin published his discoveries, the laterborn odds of supporting evolution dropped from 9.7 times to 4.6 times greater than firstborns. As the ideas gained scientific acceptance, firstborns were more comfortable advocating for them.

We assume that younger scientists will be more receptive to rebellious ideas than older scientists, who become conservative and entrenched in their beliefs with age. But remarkably, birth order was more consequential than age. "An 80-year-old laterborn was as open to evolutionary theory as a 25-year-old firstborn," Sulloway writes, arguing that evolutionary theory "only became a historical reality because laterborns outnumbered firstborns 2.6 to 1 in the general population."

Overall, laterborns were twice as likely as firstborns to champion major scientific upheavals. "The likelihood of this difference arising by chance is substantially less than one in a billion," Sulloway observes. "Laterborns have typically been half a century ahead of firstborns in their willingness to endorse radical innovations." Similar results emerged when he studied thirty-one political revolutions: laterborns were twice as likely as firstborns to support radical changes.

As a card-carrying firstborn, I was initially dismayed by these results. But as I learned about birth-order research, I realized that none of these patterns are set in stone. We don't need to cede originality to laterborn children. By adopting the parenting practices that are typically applied primarily to younger children, we can raise any child to become more original.

This chapter examines the family roots of originality. What's unique about being a younger child, how does family size figure in, and what are the implications for nurture? And how can we account for the cases that don't fit these patterns—the three only children on the base-stealing list, the firstborns who rebel, and the latterborn who conform? I'll use birth order as a launching pad for examining the impact of siblings, parents, and role models on our tendencies to take risks. To see why siblings aren't as alike as we expect them to be, I'll look at the upbringing of Jackie Robinson and the families of the most original comedians in America. You'll find out what determines whether children rebel in a constructive or destructive direction, why it's a mistake to tell children not to cheat, how we praise them ineffectively and read them the wrong books, and what we can learn from the parents of individuals who risked their lives to rescue Jews during the Holocaust.

Born to Rebel

In 1944, more than a decade before Rosa Parks made her heroic stand on a Montgomery bus, Jackie Robinson, then an army lieutenant, was court-martialed for refusing to sit at the back of a bus. The driver "shouted that if I didn't move to the rear of the bus he would cause me plenty of trouble," Robinson recounted. "I told him hotly that I couldn't care less about his causing me trouble." He gave a similar account for his mad dash toward home plate in the World Series opener. "I suddenly decided to shake things up," Robinson explained. "It was not the best baseball strategy to steal home with our team two runs behind, but I just took off and did it. I really didn't care whether I made it or not."

"I couldn't care less" and "I really didn't care" reveal something fundamental about how Jackie Robinson learned to approach risk.

According to eminent Stanford professor James March, when many of us make decisions, we follow a logic of consequence: Which course of action will produce the best result? If you're like Robinson, and you consistently challenge the status quo, you operate differently, using instead a logic of appropriateness: What does a person like me do in a situation like this? Rather than looking outward in an attempt to predict the outcome, you turn inward to your identity. You base the decision on who you are—or who you want to be.

When we use the logic of consequence, we can always find reasons not to take risks. The logic of appropriateness frees us up. We think less about what will guarantee the outcome we want, and act more on a visceral sense of what someone like us ought to do. And this tendency can be influenced by birth order.

For years, experts have touted the advantages of being firstborn. The eldest child in the family is typically set up for success, benefiting from the undivided attention, time, and energy of fawning parents. Evidence shows that firstborns are more likely to win the Nobel Prize in science, become U.S. congressmen, and win local and national elections in the Netherlands. It also appears that they're most likely to rise to the top of corporations: one analysis of more than 1,500 CEOs revealed that 43 percent were firstborn.

In a recent study, economists Marco Bertoni and Giorgio Brunello decided to take a closer look at the impact of birth order on career success. Tracking more than four thousand people over multiple decades in nearly a dozen European countries, they found that when entering the labor market, firstborns enjoy 14 percent higher starting salaries than laterborns. Firstborns benefit from greater education, which enables them to command these higher wages.

Yet this initial career advantage vanishes by age thirty. Laterborns have faster salary growth, because they are willing to switch to better-paying jobs sooner and more often. "Firstborns are more risk averse than laterborns," the economists write, noting that the laterborns were also more prone to bad drinking and smoking habits, and were less likely to buy retirement accounts and life insurance packages. Psychologist Dean Simonton explains: "It is not inferior ability that inclines later-borns to perform poorly on standardized tests, to achieve less in school, and to disfavor prestigious occupations. Rather, later-borns may find these first-born preoccupations to represent distasteful quests for authority and conformity."

Although it is beginning to gain some legitimacy, the science of birth order has a checkered past and remains controversial today. Birth order doesn't *determine* who you are; it only affects the *probability* that you'll develop in a particular way. There are many other contributing factors, both in your biology and your life experience. To isolate the impact of birth order, the research is inherently messy: you can't conduct randomized, controlled experiments, many studies stop at comparing siblings in different families when the more rigorous comparison would be within families, and there's little consensus about how to handle subjects like half siblings, stepsiblings, adopted siblings, deceased siblings, and cousins who share a household. Birth-order experts continue to fundamentally disagree on many of the conclusions. As a social scientist, I felt it was my responsibility to review the evidence and share my observations about what seems most likely to be true. When I examined the data, birth order was a better predictor of personality and behavior than I had expected.

In one study, people ranked their siblings and themselves on school achievement and rebellion. High academic achievers were 2.3 times as likely to be firstborn as lastborn. Rebels were twice as likely to be lastborn as firstborn. And when asked to write about the few most rebellious or unconventional things they had ever done in their lives, laterborns had longer responses and described more unconventional behaviors. Hundreds of studies point to the same conclusion: although firstborns tend to be more dominant, conscientious, and ambitious, laterborns are more open to taking risks and embracing original ideas.

Firstborns tend to defend the status quo; laterborns are inclined to challenge it.*

There are two dominant explanations for the laterborn tendency to take risks. One concerns how children themselves handle sibling rivalry; the other, how parents raise younger children differently. Although we can't control birth order, we can influence how it plays out.

Niche Picking: Competing by Not Competing

Look at lots of siblings, and you'll notice a baffling fact: the big differences in personality don't exist between families, but within them. When identical twins grow up in the same family, they're no more similar to each other than identical twins who are separated at birth and raised by different families. "The same is true of non-twin siblings—they are no more similar when reared together than when reared apart," Harvard psychologist Steven Pinker summarizes. "And adopted siblings are no more similar than two people plucked off the street at random." This holds for originality. In adulthood, adopted siblings don't resemble each other at all in tendencies toward non-conformity or risk taking, despite having been raised by the same parents.

Niche picking might help to make sense of this mystery. This concept has its roots in the work of the physician and psychotherapist Alfred Adler, who came to believe that Sigmund Freud's emphasis on parenting failed to account for the critical influence of siblings on personality development. Adler argued that because firstborn children

---

* There will always be counterexamples; my focus is on the average differences between firstborn and laterborn children in families. Middle children are less studied, because defining who counts as a middle child is more contested than identifying the firstborn or lastborn. Sulloway argues that, on average, middle children are the most inclined toward diplomacy. Facing a dominant firstborn, and prevented from dominating the youngest siblings by their parents and older siblings, they master the art of negotiation, persuasion, and coalition building. The irony of relegating middle children to a footnote is not lost on me.

start life as only children, they initially identify with their parents. When a younger sibling arrives, firstborns risk being "dethroned" and often respond by emulating their parents: they enforce rules and assert their authority over the younger sibling, which sets the stage for the younger child to rebel.

Faced with the intellectual and physical challenges of competing directly with an older sibling, the younger chooses a different way to stand out. "The niche of the responsible achiever is particularly likely to be open for an eldest child," Sulloway writes. "Once this niche is taken, it is difficult for a younger sibling to compete effectively for the same niche."* This depends, of course, on the age distance between siblings. If two children are only a year apart, the younger sibling may be smart enough or strong enough to hold her own; if they're seven years apart in age, the niche is open again for the younger sibling to participate without having to compete directly. In baseball, brothers who were two to five years apart in age were significantly more likely to play different positions than brothers who were less than two years apart or more than five years apart. Jackie Robinson ran track in college, but couldn't beat his older brother Mack, who was five years his senior and won an Olympic silver medal in the 200-meter dash. Robinson ended up differentiating himself by winning the NCAA broad jump championship—and lettering at UCLA in basketball and football, along with track and baseball.

Curious about whether niche picking could be observed in other families, I turned to the world of comedy. At its core, comedy is an act of rebellion. Evidence shows that compared to the norms in the population, comedians tend to be more original and rebellious—and the

---

* In one early study, psychologist Helen Koch asked teachers to rate more than three hundred children from two-child families, matched on birth order, sex, sibling sex, age, and social class. The firstborns scored significantly higher in assertiveness and dominance, regardless of whether they were male or female. As psychologist Frank Dumont notes, "First-born girls were actually *more masculine* on average than their second-born brothers. They tend to behave like alpha males."

higher they score on these dimensions, the more professional success they attain. After all, people laugh when a joke deviates from expectations or violates a sacred principle in a harmless way, making the unacceptable acceptable. To challenge expectations and question core values, comedians must take calculated risks; to do it without offending the audience to the point that they tune out, comedians need creativity. The very choice to become a comedian means abandoning the prospect of a stable, predictable career. Jim Carrey's father considered comedy, but chose accounting because it was a safer bet. As Jerry Seinfeld quipped, "I never had a job."

Based on what we know about niche picking, I suspected that laterborn children would be more likely to become great comedians. More conventional careers would already have been taken by older siblings, so instead of struggling to be smarter or stronger than them, the younger children could be funnier. Unlike other talents, the ability to make people laugh isn't dependent on age or maturity. The bigger your family is, the fewer options you have to distinguish yourself, and the more likely you'll be to choose humor as your niche.

Are great comedians more likely to be born last than first? To find out, I analyzed Comedy Central's 2004 list of the 100 greatest stand-up comics of all time. That tally is a who's who of original comedians known for rebellious material that challenges social norms and political ideologies, and includes figures ranging from George Carlin and Chris Rock to Joan Rivers and Jon Stewart.

Statistically, there should be an equal number of firstborns and lastborns. When I tracked the birth order of these hundred original comedians, though, forty-four of them were the lastborn, compared with only twenty firstborn. They came from families with an average of 3.5 children, yet nearly half of them were the baby of their families. On average, they were born 48 percent later in the sibling order than they should have been by chance. Comedians with siblings were 83 percent more likely to be born last than chance would predict. The odds of that many great comedians being lastborn by chance are two in a million.

When I turned to specific lastborn comedians, I found that their older siblings usually filled more conventional achievement niches. Stephen Colbert is the youngest of eleven; his older siblings include an intellectual property attorney, a congressional candidate, and a government lawyer. Chelsea Handler's five older siblings are a mechanical engineer, a chef, an accountant, a lawyer, and a nurse—all careers where it's possible to obtain education certifications and stable salaries. Louis C.K.'s three older sisters are a doctor, a teacher, and a software engineer. All five of Jim Gaffigan's older siblings are managers: three bank executives, a department store GM, and an operations manager. Mel Brooks's three older brothers were a chemist, a bookstore owner, and a government official.

Niche picking helps to solve the mystery of why siblings aren't terribly similar; laterborn children actively seek to be different. But there's more to this story than children's attempting to stand out. As hard as they may try to be consistent, parents treat children differently based on birth order, which wedges their personalities even further apart.*

The Slippery Slope of Strict Parenting

Psychologist Robert Zajonc observed that firstborns grow up in a world of adults, while the more older siblings you have, the more time

---

* Birth-order effects aren't purely environmental; there's reason to believe that biological factors can contribute as well. Evidence suggests that the more older brothers a man has, the more likely he is to be homosexual. Each older brother increases the probability that a man is homosexual by about 33 percent, possibly by causing maternal immune systems to produce more antibodies to testosterone, which influence the developing fetus. This birth-order effect holds only for men and is unique to the number of older brothers, not younger brothers or older or younger sisters. Researchers estimate that at least one in seven gay men can attribute their homosexuality to the effects of older brothers, and among gay men with at least three older brothers, the birth order effect is stronger than all other causes.

you spend learning from other children. Had Jackie Robinson been the first child, he would have been raised primarily by his mother. But with five children to feed, Mallie Robinson needed to work. As a result, Robinson's older sister, Willa Mae, reflected, "I was the little mother." She bathed him, dressed him, and fed him. When she went to kindergarten, she convinced her mother to let her bring her baby brother to school with her. A three-year-old Jackie Robinson played in the sandbox all day for a year, with Willa Mae poking her head out the window periodically to make sure he was okay. Meanwhile, Robinson's older brother Frank was ready to defend him in fights.

When older siblings serve as surrogate parents and role models, you don't face as many rules or punishments, and you enjoy the security of their protection. You also end up taking risks earlier: instead of emulating the measured, carefully considered choices of adults, you follow the lead of other children.

Even when the parenting role isn't delegated to children, parents tend to start out as strict disciplinarians with firstborns and become increasingly flexible with laterborns. Parents often relax as they gain experience, and there simply aren't as many chores for the lastborn children to do, because their older siblings handle them. When Robinson joined a neighborhood gang, he got caught stealing and shoplifting on a regular basis. On more than one occasion, instead of enforcing punishment, Robinson's mother marched to the police station and told the captain he was being too harsh on her son. "He could get away with these antics," writes biographer Mary Kay Linge, "because he had always . . . been coddled . . . after all, Jackie was the baby of the family, and he never had the same responsibilities that his siblings had."*

---

* The parental response to the youngest child can tilt in a darker direction. The poster victim of this path is Andre Agassi, the first man ever to win all four Grand Slams and an Olympic gold medal in singles tennis. His father dreamed of raising a tennis champion, and when the first three children fell short, the pressure was focused on the lastborn, Andre. His father was abusive, forcing him to practice for hours on end, dictating his schedule, and forbidding him from playing other sports. Andre grew up with the crushing awareness of being "the last best hope of the Agassi clan."

We can see this shift in parenting patterns in the experience of Lizz Winstead, who cocreated *The Daily Show*. It was the first news program to use comedy to challenge the established media's presentation of current events—looking like the news but parodying it at the same time. "We were going to make fun of them by *becoming* them," Winstead writes. "It simply had never been done before."

Growing up in Minnesota as the youngest of five children of extremely conservative parents, Winstead was given far more freedom than her siblings. "I walked all over my parents, because they were old. I had a lot of leeway. I stopped asking for permission to do things. I took public buses alone. I stayed out all night. They went on vacations and left me alone in high school. They were just more exhausted. They forgot to say 'You can't do that.'" When she was a child, despite the fact that she didn't know how to swim, her mother didn't warn her what would happen if she fell out of an inner tube in the middle of a lake. "I didn't know I was supposed to be scared. And in a nutshell, that is why I dove into everything headfirst," Winstead explains. "Then as now, I looked at life's challenges as dares rather than uphill battles, and consequently the results of this glaring parental oversight led to a lifetime of me torturing them with my chronic pluckiness."

From her earliest days, Winstead had to stand out to get noticed: as her brother Gene, now a mayor, recalls, "The whole family would pipe up all the time, so she being the runt would have to pipe up that much louder." At ten, Winstead questioned her Catholic teacher on why

---

Andre rebelled by flouting many of the game's unwritten rules: he donned a Mohawk, a mullet, and earrings; played in denim shorts and pink pants instead of traditional whites; and dated singer Barbra Streisand, twenty-eight years his senior. "Having no choice, having no say about what I do or who I am, makes me crazy," Agassi reflected. "Rebellion is the one thing I get to choose every day. . . . Bucking authority . . . sending a message to my father, thrashing against the lack of choice in my life." His story suggests that there are two opposing ways for parents to raise rebels: giving children the autonomy and protection to get away with it, or restricting their freedom to the point that they fight back.

dogs and Jews don't go to heaven. At twelve, when a priest told her she couldn't be an altar boy, she challenged him by proposing to become an altar girl—and wrote a letter championing the idea to the bishop, a notion her parents didn't discourage. Even when they did object to her values, her parents continued to support her. Years later, when she spoke out in favor of abortion, she overheard her father say, "At least my daughter says what she thinks and doesn't hide who she is."

The larger the family, the more laterborns face lax rules and get away with things that their elder siblings wouldn't have. "I'm from a very large family—nine parents," comedian Jim Gaffigan jokes. "When you're the youngest of a big family, by the time you're a teenager, your parents are insane."

While we can explain the risk taking of many originals by virtue of the unusual autonomy and protection that they received as the babies of their families, these parenting behaviors can nurture rebellion among children at any position in the birth order; they may just be most common with the youngest child. Interestingly, Sulloway finds that predicting personality is more challenging with only children than with children who have siblings. Like firstborns, only children grow up in a world of adults and identify with parents. Like lastborns, they are protected fiercely, which leaves them "freer to become radicals themselves."

The evidence on birth order highlights the importance of giving children freedom to be original. But one of the dangers of doing so is that they might use that freedom to rebel in ways that put themselves or others at risk. Once a child of any birth order is motivated to be original, what determines the direction in which she will channel that originality? I wanted to learn why Jackie Robinson abandoned gang life and became a civil rights activist—and what factors shape whether children use their freedom to become honorable or antisocial, proactive or passive, creative or destructive.

Answering this question has been the life's work of Samuel and Pearl Oliner, a sociologist and an education researcher. They conducted a pioneering study of non-Jews who risked their lives to save Jews during the Holocaust, comparing these heroic individuals with a group of neighbors who lived in the same towns but did not extend help to Jews. The rescuers had much in common with the bystanders: similar educational backgrounds, occupations, homes, neighborhoods, and political and religious beliefs. They were also equally rebellious in their childhoods—the rescuers were just as likely as the bystanders to be disciplined by their parents for disobeying, stealing, lying, cheating, aggressing, and failing to do what they were told. What differentiated the rescuers was how their parents disciplined bad behavior and praised good behavior.

Great Explanations

Years ago, researchers found that from ages two to ten, children are urged by their parents to change their behavior once every six to nine minutes. As developmental psychologist Martin Hoffman sums it up, this "translates roughly into 50 discipline encounters a day or over 15,000 a year!"

When the Holocaust rescuers recalled their childhoods, they had received a unique form of discipline from their parents. "*Explained* is the word most rescuers favored," the Oliners discovered:

It is in their reliance on reasoning, explanations, suggestions of ways to remedy the harm done, persuasion, and advice that the parents of rescuers differed most. . . . Reasoning communicates a message of respect. . . . It implies that had children but known better or understood more, they would not have acted in an inappropriate way. It is a mark of esteem for the listener; an indication of faith in his or her ability to comprehend, develop, and improve.

While reasoning accounted for only 6 percent of the disciplinary techniques that the bystanders' parents used, it accounted for a full 21 percent of how the rescuers' parents disciplined their children. One rescuer said her mother "told me when I did something wrong. She never did any punishing or scolding—she tried to make me understand with my mind what I'd done wrong."

This rational approach to discipline also characterizes the parents of teenagers who don't engage in criminal deviance and originals who challenge the orthodoxies of their professions. In one study, parents of ordinary children had an average of six rules, like specific schedules for homework and bedtime. Parents of highly creative children had an average of less than one rule and tended to "place emphasis on moral values, rather than on specific rules," psychologist Teresa Amabile reports.

If parents do believe in enforcing a lot of regulations, the way they explain them matters a great deal. New research shows that teenagers defy rules when they're enforced in a controlling manner, by yelling or threatening punishment. When mothers enforce many rules but offer a clear rationale for why they're important, teenagers are substantially less likely to break them, because they internalize them. In Donald MacKinnon's study comparing America's most creative architects with a group of highly skilled but unoriginal peers, a factor that distinguished the creative group was that their parents exercised discipline with explanations. They outlined their standards of conduct and explained their grounding in a set of principles about right and wrong, referencing values like morality, integrity, respect, curiosity, and perseverance. But "emphasis was placed upon the development of one's ethical code," MacKinnon wrote. Above all, the parents who raised highly creative architects granted their children the autonomy to choose their own values.

Reasoning does create a paradox: it leads both to more rule following and more rebelliousness. By explaining moral principles, parents encourage their children to comply voluntarily with rules that align with important values and to question rules that don't. Good explanations enable children to develop a code of ethics that often coincides with societal expectations; when they don't square up, children rely on the internal compass of values rather than the external compass of rules.

There's a particular kind of explanation that works especially well in enforcing discipline. When the Oliners examined the guidance of the Holocaust rescuers' parents, they found that they tended to give "explanations of why behaviors are inappropriate, often with reference to their consequences for others." While the bystanders' parents focused on enforcing compliance with rules for their own sake, the rescuers' parents encouraged their children to consider the impact of their actions on others.*

Highlighting consequences for others directs attention to the distress of the person who may be harmed by an individual's behavior, fueling empathy for her. It also helps children understand the role that their own actions played in causing the harm, resulting in guilt. As Erma Bombeck put it, "Guilt is the gift that keeps on giving." The dual moral emotions of empathy and guilt activate the desire to right wrongs of the past and behave better in the future.

---

* According to Martin Hoffman, explaining the impact of behavior on others should take shape differently depending on the child's age. When children are very young, parents can start by explaining how their behavior causes visible harm to a victim: "If you push him again, he'll fall down and cry" or "If you throw snow on their walk they will have to clean it up all over again." As children mature, parents can begin to explain the impact on basic feelings: "You really hurt Mary and made her feel sad when you took her doll" or "He feels bad when you don't share your toys with him, just like you would feel bad if he didn't share with you." Later, parents can direct attention to more subtle feelings: "She's upset because she was proud of her tower, and you knocked it down" or "Try to be quiet so he can sleep longer and feel better when he wakes up."

Emphasizing consequences for others can motivate adults, too. In hospitals, to encourage doctors and nurses to wash their hands more often, my colleague David Hofmann and I posted two different signs near soap and gel dispensers:

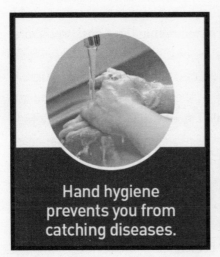
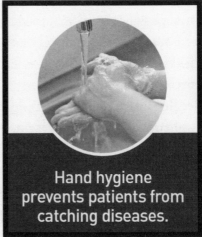

Over the next two weeks, a member of each hospital unit covertly counted the number of times that medical professionals washed their hands before and after each patient contact, while an independent team measured the amount of soap and gel used from each dispenser.

The sign on the left had no effect whatsoever. The sign on the right made a significant difference: merely mentioning *patients* instead of *you* led medical professionals to wash their hands 10 percent more often and use 45 percent more soap and gel.

Thinking about oneself invokes the logic of consequence: Will I get sick? Doctors and nurses can answer swiftly with a no: I spend a lot of time in a hospital, I don't always wash, and I rarely get sick, so this probably won't affect me. In general, we tend to be overconfident about our own invulnerability to harm. But thinking about patients prompts a logic of appropriateness: What should a person like me do in a situation like this? It changes the calculation from a cost-benefit equation to a contemplation of values, of right and wrong: I have a professional and moral obligation to care for patients.

An explanation of how his behavior affected others represented the first major turning point in Jackie Robinson's life. As a leader in the neighborhood gang, Robinson was hurling dirt at cars and rocks through windows, stealing golf balls and selling them back to players, and pilfering food and supplies from local stores. After one offense, the sheriff took him to jail at gunpoint. Seeing the gang in action, a mechanic named Carl Anderson took Robinson aside. "He made me see that if I continued with the gang it would hurt my mother," Robinson wrote. "He said it didn't take guts to follow the crowd, that courage and intelligence lay in being willing to be different. I was too ashamed to tell Carl how right he was, but what he said got to me." Once he considered how his behavior would affect his mother, Robinson didn't want to let her down, and he left the gang.*

Persona Noun Grata, or Why Nouns Are Better Than Verbs

Assuming that parents decide to give children the freedom to be original, what does it take to foster a sense of right and wrong? Values

---

* After I finished writing this section, our daughters were running around the family room, putting our crawling toddler son in jeopardy. I told them to stop running seven times, and it had no effect. Realizing I was failing to follow my own advice about explaining the impact on others, I changed my strategy. Turning to our six-year-old, I posed a question: "Why am I asking you not to run?" With a concerned look, she immediately responded, "Because we could hurt our brother." I asked, "Do you want to hurt him?" She shook her head, and our four-year-old piped up, "No!" I announced a new rule: no running in the family room, because we don't want to hurt anyone. I put the girls in charge of enforcing the rule, and they stopped running immediately. Their good behavior stuck. They spent the rest of the afternoon monitoring each other's nonrunning. But a few days later, they started running again. Only then did I learn that explanations of our impact on others are most likely to have a lasting effect if they're coupled with a statement of principles."She's crying because she wants to play with your toys" doesn't do much good alone; the more meaningful statement is: "She's crying because she wants to play with your toys, and in this family, we always share."

aren't formed only by how parents react when children misstep. In the study of Holocaust rescuers and bystanders, when the Oliners asked about the values they learned from their parents, the rescuers were three times more likely than the bystanders to reference moral values that applied to all people. The rescuers emphasized that their parents "taught me to respect all human beings." While bystanders also held moral values, they attached them to specific behaviors and in-group members—pay attention in school, don't get in fights with your peers, be polite to your neighbors, be honest with your friends and loyal to your families.

Moral standards are forged in part by what parents say after children do the *right* thing. The last time you saw a child engage in good behavior, how did you respond? My guess is that you praised the action, not the child. "That was really nice. That was so sweet." By complimenting the behavior you reinforce it, so the child will learn to repeat it.

Not so fast, says an experiment led by psychologist Joan Grusec. After children shared some marbles with their peers, a number of them were randomly assigned to have their *behavior* praised: "It was good that you gave some of your marbles to those poor children. Yes, that was a nice and helpful thing to do." Others received *character* praise: "I guess you're the kind of person who likes to help others whenever you can. Yes, you are a very nice and helpful person."

Children who received character praise were subsequently more generous. Of the children who were complimented for being helpful people, 45 percent gave craft materials to cheer up kids at a hospital two weeks later, compared with only 10 percent of the children who were commended for engaging in helpful behavior. When our character is praised, we internalize it as part of our identities. Instead of seeing ourselves as engaging in isolated moral acts, we start to develop a more unified self-concept as a moral person.

Affirming character appears to have the strongest effect in the critical periods when children are beginning to formulate strong identities. In one study, for example, praising character boosted the moral actions of eight-year-olds but not five-year-olds or ten-year-olds. The ten-year-olds may already have crystallized self-concepts to the degree that a single comment didn't affect them, and the five-year-olds may have been too young for an isolated compliment to have a real impact. Character praise leaves a lasting imprint when identities are forming.*

But even among very young children, an appeal to character can have an influence in the moment. In an ingenious series of experiments led by psychologist Christopher Bryan, children between ages three and six were 22 percent to 29 percent more likely to clean up blocks, toys, and crayons when they were asked *to be helpers* instead of *to help.* Even though their character was far from gelled, they wanted to earn the identity.

Bryan finds that appeals to character are effective for adults as well. His team was able to cut cheating in half with the same turn of phrase: instead of "Please don't cheat," they changed the appeal to "Please don't be a cheater." When you're urged not to cheat, you can do it and still see an ethical person in the mirror. But when you're told not to be a cheater, the act casts a shadow; immorality is tied to your identity, making the behavior much less attractive. Cheating is an isolated action that gets

---

* There's an interesting tension between this research on the benefits of praising character and a famous body of research on the value of praising effort. In *Mindset*, the Stanford psychologist Carol Dweck describes her groundbreaking studies demonstrating that when we praise children for their intelligence, they develop a fixed view of ability, which leads them to give up in the face of failure. Instead of telling them how smart they are, it's wise to praise their effort, which encourages them to see their abilities as malleable and persist to overcome obstacles. How can we reconcile these competing ideas about praising the person in the moral domain but the behavior in the skill domain? Praising character can lead children to think, "I'm a good person, so I can do a bad thing"—or, more frighteningly, "I'm a good person, so how could this be a bad thing?" This is why it's so important to exercise discipline as described above: it motivates children to develop clear moral standards and emotions that discourage bad behaviors. My bet is that character praise coupled with discipline leads to the most moral choices.

evaluated with the logic of consequence: Can I get away with it? Being a cheater evokes a sense of self, triggering the logic of appropriateness: What kind of person am I, and who do I want to be?

In light of this evidence, Bryan suggests that we should embrace nouns more thoughtfully. "Don't Drink and Drive" could be rephrased as: "Don't Be a Drunk Driver." The same thinking can be applied to originality. When a child draws a picture, instead of calling the artwork creative, we can say "You are creative." After a teenager resists the temptation to follow the crowd, we can commend her for being a non-conformist.

When we shift our emphasis from behavior to character, people evaluate choices differently. Instead of asking whether this behavior will achieve the results they want, they take action because it is the right thing to do. In the poignant words of one Holocaust rescuer, "It's like saving somebody who is drowning. You don't ask them what God they pray to. You just go and save them."

Why Parents Aren't the Best Role Models

We can afford to give children a great deal of freedom if we explain the consequences of their actions on others and emphasize how the right moral choices demonstrate good character. This increases the odds that they will develop the instinct to express their original impulses in the form of moral or creative actions, as opposed to deviant ones. But as they grow up, they often don't aim high enough.

When psychologists Penelope Lockwood and Ziva Kunda asked college students to list what they hoped to achieve over the following decade, they came up with perfectly ordinary objectives. Another group of students was instructed to read a newspaper article about an outstanding peer and then list their goals; they aimed much higher. Having a role model elevated their aspirations.

Role models have a foundational impact on how children grow up to express their originality. When hundreds of women who graduated from Radcliffe College were asked in their early thirties to name the people who had the greatest influence on their lives, the vast majority mentioned parents and mentors. Seventeen years later, psychologists Bill Peterson and Abigail Stewart measured the women's commitments to changing things for the better for future generations. Naming a parent as a major influence accounted for less than one percent of the women's motivations to drive meaningful change. The women who were pursuing originality had been influenced a decade and a half earlier not by their parents, but by their mentors: Mentioning a mentor accounted for 14 percent of differences in women's desires to improve the world.

The paradox of encouraging children to develop strong values is that parents effectively limit their own influence. Parents can nurture the impulse to be original, but at some point, people need to find their own role models for originality in their chosen fields. In comedy, Lizz Winstead drew inspiration from comedian Roseanne Barr—both for her talents on stage and her support of women off it. When Winstead went public with her rebellious political views, her father quipped, "I screwed up. I raised you to have an opinion, and I forgot to tell you it was supposed to be mine."

If we want to encourage originality, the best step we can take is to raise our children's aspirations by introducing them to different kinds of role models. "I might have become a full-fledged juvenile delinquent," Jackie Robinson acknowledged, "if it had not been for the influence of two men." One was the mechanic who explained how his gang behavior was hurting his mother. The other was a young minister, Karl Downs. Noticing that adolescents were being forced by their parents to attend church and many were dropping out, Downs instituted some unconventional changes, holding dances at the church and building a badminton court. Many of the members protested, clinging to the traditions of the past, but Downs persisted. Inspired by a man who was willing to challenge orthodoxy in order to engage children, Robinson volunteered to become a Sunday school teacher, and became determined to open doors for others as Downs had done for him.

In baseball, Robinson found another original mentor in Branch Rickey, the Dodgers owner who recruited him to break the color barrier. Robinson was already twenty-six when Rickey summoned him to his office. Rickey had been scouting black players who could run, throw, and hit, and once he had a group of candidates with similarly extraordinary ability, he started evaluating their character, inviting them to meet in the guise of starting a new Negro League. Once he chose Robinson, Rickey encouraged him to take some risks on the base path—"run wild, to steal the pants off them"—but urged him to be more cautious outside the lines. "I want a ballplayer with guts enough not to fight back."

Finding the right mentor is not always easy. But we can locate role models in a more accessible place: the stories of great originals throughout history. Human rights advocate Malala Yousafzai was moved by reading biographies of Meena, an activist for equality in Afghanistan, and of Martin Luther King, Jr. King was inspired by Gandhi, as was Nelson Mandela.

In some cases, fictional characters may be even better role models. Growing up, many originals find their first heroes in their most beloved novels, where protagonists exercise their creativity in pursuit of unique accomplishments. When asked to name their favorite books, Elon Musk and Peter Thiel each chose *Lord of the Rings,* the epic tale of a hobbit's adventures to destroy a dangerous ring of power. Sheryl Sandberg and Jeff Bezos both pointed to *A Wrinkle in Time,* in which a young girl learns to bend the laws of physics and travel through time. Mark Zuckerberg was partial to *Ender's Game,* where it's up to a group of kids to save the planet from an alien attack. Jack Ma named his favorite childhood book as *Ali Baba and the Forty Thieves*, about a woodcutter who takes the initiative to change his own fate.

It's likely that they were all highly original children, which accounts for why they were drawn to these tales in the first place. But it's also possible that these stories helped elevate their aspirations. Remarkably, there are studies showing that when children's stories emphasize original achievements, the next generation innovates more. In one study, psychologists tracked unique accomplishments in American children's stories from 1800 to 1950. After original achievement themes in American children's books rose by 66 percent from 1810 to 1850, the patent rate shot up sevenfold from 1850 to 1890. Children's books reflected the values popular at the time, but also helped to nurture those values: When stories emphasized original achievement, patent rates typically soared twenty to forty years later. As Dean Simonton summarizes, "It took time for the children exposed to the achievement imagery in school to grow up and contribute to the creation of new inventions."

Unlike biographies, in fictional stories characters can perform actions that have never been accomplished before, making the impossible seem possible. The inventors of the modern submarine and helicopter were transfixed by Jules Verne's visions in *Twenty Thousand Leagues Under the Sea* and *The Clipper of the Clouds*. One of the earliest rockets was built by a scientist who drew his motivation from an H. G. Wells novel. Some of the earliest mobile phones, tablets, GPS navigators, portable digital storage disks, and multimedia players were designed by people who watched *Star Trek* characters using similar devices. As we encounter these images of originality in history and fiction, the logic of consequence fades away. We no longer worry as much about what will happen if we fail.

Undoubtedly, the next generation of originals will draw inspiration from the *Harry Potter* series, which is brimming with references to original accomplishment: Harry Potter is the only wizard who can defeat Voldemort. With his friends Hermione and Ron, he learns unique spells and invents new ways of defending against the dark arts. We see the children's spirits rise when they succeed, and they are crestfallen when they fail. Along with giving a generation of children role models for originality, J. K. Rowling embedded a moral message in her novels. Recent experiments show that reading *Harry Potter* can improve children's attitudes toward marginalized groups. As they see Harry and Hermione face discrimination for not having pure wizard blood, they empathize and become less prejudiced toward minority groups in their own lives.

When children identify strongly enough with heroes who exemplify originality, it might even change the way that niche picking unfolds. Among siblings, laterborns often become original after their siblings fill conventional niches. But wherever we fall in the birth order, when we have compelling role models for originality, they expand our awareness of niches that we had never considered. Instead of causing us to rebel because traditional avenues are closed, the protagonists in our favorite stories may inspire originality by opening our minds to unconventional paths.

7

Rethinking Groupthink

The Myths of Strong Cultures, Cults, and Devil's Advocates

"In fact, the only sin which we never forgive
in each other is difference of opinion."

Ralph Waldo Emerson

Standing on stage in front of a captive audience, a technology icon pulled a new device out of his pocket. It was so much smaller than competing products that no one in the room could believe his eyes. The founder's flair for theatrical product launches wasn't the only source of his fame. He was known for his singular creative vision, a passion for blending science and art, an obsession with design and quality, and a deep disdain for market research. "We give people products they do not even know they want," he remarked after introducing a revolutionary gadget that helped to popularize the selfie.

The man urged people to think different. He led his company to greatness and redefined multiple industries, only to be unceremoniously forced out by his own board of directors, and then watch the empire he created start to crumble before his eyes.

As much as this story seems to describe Steve Jobs, the visionary was actually one of Jobs's heroes: Edwin Land, the founder of Polaroid. Today, Land is best remembered for inventing the instant camera, which gave rise to an entire generation of amateur photographers—and enabled Ansel Adams to take his famous landscape photographs,

Andy Warhol to make his celebrity portraits, and NASA astronauts to capture the sun. But Land was responsible for something bigger: the polarizing light filter that's still used in billions of products, from sunglasses and digital watches to pocket calculators and 3-D movie glasses. He also played a vital role in conceiving and designing the U-2 spy plane for President Dwight Eisenhower, which changed the course of the Cold War. In total, Land amassed 535 patents, more than any American before him other than Thomas Edison. In 1985, just a few months before getting kicked out of Apple, Steve Jobs shared his admiration for Land, "one of the great inventors of our time. . . . The man is a national treasure."

Land may have been a great original, but he failed to instill those attributes in his company's culture. In an ironic twist, Polaroid was one of the companies that pioneered the digital camera, yet ultimately went bankrupt because of it. As early as 1981, the company was making major strides in electronic imaging. By the end of the decade, Polaroid's digital sensors could capture quadruple the resolution of competitors' products. A high-quality prototype of a digital camera was ready in 1992, but the electronic-imaging team could not convince their colleagues to launch it until 1996. Despite earning awards for technical excellence, Polaroid's product floundered, as by then more than forty competitors had released their own digital cameras.

Polaroid fell due to a faulty assumption. Within the company, there was widespread agreement that customers would always want hard copies of pictures, and key decision makers failed to question this assumption. It was a classic case of groupthink—the tendency to seek consensus instead of fostering dissent. Groupthink is the enemy of originality; people feel pressured to conform to the dominant, default views instead of championing diversity of thought.

In a famous analysis, Yale psychologist Irving Janis identified groupthink as the culprit behind numerous American foreign-policy disasters, including the Bay of Pigs invasion and the Vietnam War. According to

Janis, groupthink occurs when people "are deeply involved in a cohesive in-group," and their "strivings for unanimity override their motivation to realistically appraise alternative courses of action."

Before the Bay of Pigs fiasco, Undersecretary of State Chester Bowles wrote a memo opposing the idea of sending Cuban exiles to overthrow Fidel Castro, but was dismissed for being fatalistic. A number of President John F. Kennedy's advisers, in fact, had reservations about the invasion: Some were silenced by group members, and others chose not to speak up. In the meeting on the final decision, only a lone rebel voiced opposition. The president called for a straw poll, a majority voted in favor of the proposal, and the conversation quickly shifted to tactical decisions about its execution.

Janis argued that members of the Kennedy administration were concerned about "being too harsh" and destroying the "cozy, 'we-feeling' atmosphere." Insiders who were present at the discussions shared the view that it was this sort of cohesion that promoted groupthink. As Bill Moyers, who handled correspondence between Kennedy and Lyndon Johnson, recalls:

> *Men who handled national security affairs became too close, too personally fond of each other. They tended to conduct the affairs of state as if they were a gentlemen's club. . . . If you are very close . . . you are less inclined, in a debating sense, to drive your opponent to the wall and you very often permit a viewpoint to be expressed and to go unchallenged except in a peripheral way.*

When a group becomes that cohesive, it develops a strong culture—people share the same values and norms, and believe in them intensely. And there's a fine line between having a strong culture and operating like a cult.

For nearly half a century, leaders, policymakers, and journalists have accepted the Janis theory of groupthink: Cohesion is dangerous, and strong cultures are deadly. To solve problems and make wise decisions, groups need original ideas and dissenting views, so we need to make sure that their members don't get too chummy. Had Kennedy's advisers not been so tight-knit, they could have welcomed minority opinions, prevented groupthink, and avoided the Bay of Pigs disaster altogether.

There's just one tiny problem with the cohesion theory: It isn't true.

When Janis completed his analysis in 1973, it was too early for him to have access to classified documents and memoirs concerning the Bay of Pigs incident. These critical sources of information reveal that the key decision was not made by one small, cohesive group. Richard Neustadt, a political scientist and presidential adviser, explained that Kennedy held "a series of *ad hoc* meetings with a small but shifting set of top advisers." Subsequent studies have also demonstrated that cohesion takes time to develop: A group without stable membership has no opportunity to form a sense of closeness and camaraderie. University of Toronto researcher Glen Whyte points out that in the year after the Bay of Pigs, Kennedy led a cohesive group of mostly the same advisers to an effective resolution of the Cuban missile crisis. We now know that the consensus to launch the Cuban invasion "was not the result of a desire to maintain the group's cohesiveness or esprit de corps," explains Stanford psychologist Roderick Kramer.

Cohesion doesn't cause groupthink anywhere else, either. There was another fatal flaw in Janis's analysis: He studied mostly cohesive groups making bad choices. How do we know that it was actually cohesion—and not the fact that they all ate cereal for breakfast or wore shoes with laces—that drove dysfunctional decisions? To draw an accurate conclusion about cohesion, he needed to compare bad *and* good decisions, and then determine whether cohesive groups were more likely to fall victim to groupthink.

When researchers examined successful and failed strategic decisions in top management teams at seven Fortune 500 companies, they discovered that cohesive groups weren't more likely to seek agreement and dismiss divergent opinions. In fact, in many cases, cohesive groups tended to make better business decisions. The same was true in politics. In a comprehensive review, researchers Sally Riggs Fuller and Ray Aldag write, "There is no empirical support. . . . Cohesiveness, supposedly the critical trigger in the groupthink phenomenon, has simply not been found to play a consistent role." They observe that "the benefits of group cohesion" include "enhanced communication," and members of cohesive groups "are likely to be secure enough in their roles to challenge one another." After carefully combing through the data, Whyte concludes that "cohesiveness should be deleted from the groupthink model."

In this chapter, I want to examine what really causes groupthink and what we can do to prevent it. Why are some cohesive groups vulnerable to bad decisions while others do just fine? What does it take to maintain a strong culture without spawning a cult? To figure out how to fight groupthink and promote the expression of original opinions, I'll analyze Polaroid's errors and take a deep dive into an organization whose billionaire founder has a radical approach to preventing conformity pressures. You'll learn why dissenting opinions often fall on deaf ears, why most groups use devil's advocates ineffectively, why it's sometimes better to encourage people to complain about problems than to solve them, and why having people share their preferences can reduce the odds that minority opinions prevail. Ultimately, you'll see what ordinary people and organizations can do to foster a climate that breeds originality early on—and embraces it over time.

A Bolt from the Blueprint

In the mid-1990s, a group of experts became curious about how founders shape the destinies of their companies. Led by sociologist James Baron, they interviewed the founders of nearly two hundred high-tech startups in Silicon Valley, spanning computer hardware and software to telecommunications and networking, medical devices and biotech to research, and manufacturing to semiconductors. Baron and his colleagues asked the founders about their original blueprints: What organizational models did they have in mind when they started their companies?

Across industries, there were three dominant templates: professional, star, and commitment. The professional blueprint emphasized hiring candidates with specific skills: Founders looked for engineers who could code in JavaScript or C++, or scientists who had deep knowledge about synthesizing proteins. In the star blueprint, the focus shifted from current skills to future potential, placing a premium on choosing or poaching the brightest hires. The individuals in question might have less current expertise in a particular area, but they had the raw brainpower to acquire it.

Founders with a commitment blueprint went about hiring differently. Skills and potential were fine, but cultural fit was a must. The top priority was to employ people who matched the company's values and norms. The commitment blueprint involved a unique approach to motivation, too. Whereas founders with professional and star blueprints gave employees autonomy and challenging tasks, those with commitment blueprints worked to build strong emotional bonds among employees and to the organization. They often used words like *family* and *love* to describe the companionship in the organization, and employees tended to be intensely passionate about the mission.

Baron's team wanted to see which founder blueprint predicted the greatest success. When they tracked the firms through the internet boom of the late 1990s and after the bubble burst in 2000, one blueprint was far superior to the others: commitment.

When founders had a commitment blueprint, the failure rate of their firms was zero—not a single one of them went out of business.

The future wasn't nearly as bright when founders used other models: Failure rates were substantial for the star blueprint and more than three times worse for the professional blueprint. The commitment blueprint also meant a better chance of making it to the stock market, with odds of an initial public offering more than triple those of the star model and more than quadruple those of the professional model.*

Since many of the startups replaced their founder with a new CEO, Baron and colleagues interviewed the CEOs about their own blueprints as well. The founders' blueprints mattered even after controlling for the CEOs' blueprints—and they were at least as consequential, if not more so. Founders cast a long shadow. Skills and stars are fleeting; commitment lasts.

We can see the benefits of a commitment blueprint in the early days of Polaroid's culture, which revolved around the core values of intensity, originality, and quality. When Edwin Land was developing the instant camera, he once worked for eighteen days in a row without even bothering to change his clothes. "Every concept in it is new," he said of the final product, "the kind of photography, the kind of image making, the kind of photographic system, the way of developing, the way of taking it."

While Kodak hired men with advanced science degrees, Land sought a more diverse workforce, employing women with artistic backgrounds and men straight out of the navy. Just like the Silicon

---

* Baron and his collaborators, Michael Hannan and Diane Burton, also tracked how common each blueprint was. The professional blueprint was the most common, adopted by 31 percent of founders. The commitment and star blueprints were the next most common, characterizing 14 percent and 9 percent of founders. There were two other blueprints—autocracy and bureaucracy—with 6.6 percent each. Both models meant hiring based on skills, but autocracies relied primarily on money and direct oversight to make sure that employees performed, whereas bureaucracies focused more on challenging tasks coupled with detailed rules and procedures. Not surprisingly, the autocratic and bureaucratic blueprints were the most likely to fail. The remaining third of the founders used a combination of these blueprints. The autocratic blueprint was the most likely to fail, eight times higher than star; hybrid and bureaucratic blueprints had survival rates between the professional and star blueprints.

Valley founders with commitment blueprints, he didn't worry about the specific skills or star qualities of the people he took on; his focus was rather on whether they would value generating novel ideas and dedicate themselves to the mission. Surrounded by others who shared the same passions and goals, his employees felt a strong sense of belonging and cohesiveness. When you're bonded that strongly with your colleagues and your organization, it's hard to imagine working anywhere else.

After the instant camera itself, two of the key inventions that contributed to Polaroid's early success were advances in film technology. The first was Polaroid's debut with sepia film, as black-and-white instant photos were prone to fading. The lab leader who proved indispensable in solving the problem was a woman named Meroë Morse, an art history major who had taken no physics or chemistry courses in college, and who later paved the way for a groundbreaking insight on color vision. She was so dedicated that her lab ran twenty-four hours a day, with technicians working in three different shifts. The second breakthrough was instant color photography—Howard Rogers, an automobile mechanic with no formal education in the field, toiled for fifteen years to crack the color code.

Growing Pains: The Dark Side of Commitment Cultures

As fruitful as commitment cultures are in the early stages of an organization's life, over time, they tend to falter. In the Silicon Valley study, although founders' commitment blueprints gave startups a better chance of surviving and going public, once they did so, they suffered from slower growth rates in stock-market value. Firms with commitment blueprints grew their stock values 140 percent slower than star blueprints and 25 percent slower than professional blueprints; even the bureaucratic blueprint performed better. It seems, as executive coach Marshall Goldsmith says, that what got you here won't get you there. When organizations mature, what goes wrong in commitment cultures?

"Commitment firms have greater difficulty attracting, retaining, or integrating a diverse workforce," Baron and his colleagues suggest. There's data to back it up: Psychologist Benjamin Schneider finds that organizations tend to become more homogeneous over time. As they attract, select, socialize, and retain similar people, they effectively weed out diversity in thoughts and values. This is especially likely in established firms with strong commitment cultures, where similarity is the basis for hiring, and employees face intense pressure to fit in or get out.

Stanford sociologist Jesper Sørensen finds that in stable industries, large companies with strong cultures of this type have more reliable financial performance than their peers. When employees are committed to a shared set of goals and values, they can execute effectively in predictable environments. But in volatile settings like the computer, aerospace, and airline industries, the benefits of strong cultures disappear. Once a market becomes dynamic, big companies with strong cultures are too insular: They have a harder time recognizing the need for change, and they're more likely to resist the insights of those who think differently. As a result, they don't learn and adapt, and don't have better or more reliable financial results than their competitors.

These findings map directly onto the rise and fall of Polaroid. After Land invented the instant camera in 1948, the company took off, its revenues jumping from under $7 million in 1950 to nearly $100 million in 1960 and $950 million by 1976. Throughout that period, the photography industry remained stable: Customers loved high-quality cameras that printed instant pictures. But as the digital revolution began, the market became volatile, and Polaroid's once-dominant culture was left in the dust.

In 1980, Land was approached by Sony founder Akio Morita, who confided that the chemical processing of film might not be the wave of the future, and expressed interest in collaborating on an electronic camera. Land saw the world in terms of chemistry and physics, not zeros and ones. He dismissed the idea, insisting that customers would always want prints, and that the quality of digital photos would never approach that of chemically processed ones.

As the company began to struggle in the face of disruption, Land became even less receptive to outside input. "He surrounded himself with devoted followers who would do his bidding," one longtime colleague observed. Land's pet project now was Polavision, an instant movie camera. When Polaroid president William McCune questioned the concept, Land complained to the board of directors and gained complete control over the project, working on a separate floor where naysayers were denied access. "He has to be able to override all kinds of objections and obvious reasons why things are not going to work," McCune said. "When he is doing something wild and risky, he is careful to insulate himself from anyone who's critical."

Land's response was all too typical: In a study by strategy researchers Michael McDonald and James Westphal, the worse companies performed, the more CEOs sought advice from friends and colleagues who shared their perspectives. They favored the comfort of consensus over the discomfort of dissent, which was precisely the opposite of what they should have done. Company performance only improved when CEOs actively gathered advice from people who weren't their friends and brought different insights to the table, which challenged them to fix mistakes and pursue innovations.*

---

* There's a common belief that creativity flourishes when criticism is withheld, but this turns out to be false. It became pronounced in the advertising age of the 1950s, when Alex Osborn introduced the notion of brainstorming, with the second rule being "withhold criticism." The assumption was that criticism would discourage people from trying wild ideas, yet original breakthroughs come after more criticism, not less. In one experiment in the United States and France, people were instructed to brainstorm, and randomly assigned either "not to criticize" or "feel free to debate, even criticize." The groups that debated and criticized weren't afraid to share ideas, and they generated 16 percent more ideas than those that didn't. In high-stakes creative settings, debate and criticism improve the quality of ideas, too. Research suggests that in the most

"Minority viewpoints are important, not because they tend to prevail but because they stimulate divergent attention and thought," finds Berkeley psychologist Charlan Nemeth, one of the world's leading experts on group decisions. "As a result, even when they are wrong they contribute to the detection of novel solutions and decisions that, on balance, are qualitatively better."

Dissenting opinions are useful *even when they're wrong.*

Nemeth first demonstrated this in the 1980s, and her results have been replicated many times. In one experiment, people were asked to choose between three candidates for a job. John was objectively superior, but they didn't realize it, and they all started the experiment with a preference for the wrong candidate, Ringo. When someone made an argument for a different wrong candidate, George, it quadrupled their chances of hiring the right one. Disrupting consensus by including George in the running encouraged the group members to engage in divergent thinking. They reexamined the hiring criteria and the qualifications of every candidate, which led them to reconsider John.

Without dissenting opinions, Land's instant movie camera was a complete bust. Although it was technologically clever, it carried only a few minutes of video, compared to the several hours that successful video camcorders already on the market were capable of capturing. The effort burned about $600 million, and the board dethroned him. Although Land cut ties with Polaroid, his beliefs remained firmly embedded in the company's DNA, and employees were hired and socialized to share them. He built the company to last, but his blueprint unwittingly doomed it to perish. Land knew how to "think different," yet he created a company that didn't.

The evidence suggests that social bonds don't drive groupthink;

---

successful microbiology labs, when scientists present new evidence, their skeptical colleagues don't applaud; they challenge the interpretations and propose alternatives. The same is true in hospitals: the teams with the most dissent make the best decisions, as long as members feel that their colleagues are looking out for one another's best interests.

the culprits are overconfidence and reputational concerns. At Polaroid, in keeping with Land's blueprint, leaders were overconfident that customers would always want their pictures printed, and continued manufacturing cheap cameras to earn profits on film—like selling cheap razors to make money on blades. When confronted with the idea of a digital camera, leaders repeatedly asked, "Where's the film? There's no film?" When presented with projections of 38 percent profit margins, decision makers scoffed, noting that they earned 70 percent on film. It was a "constant fight," recalls a member of the electronic imaging team. "We constantly challenged the notion of the current business model, the core business, as being old, antiquated and unable to go forward."

Those who disagreed were quickly marginalized. In the minds of leaders, dissenters didn't appreciate the value of an instant, permanent record. When an engineer named Carl Yankowski was hired as the vice president in charge of business imaging for Polaroid, he proposed to acquire a startup with electronic imaging technology. But the CEO, Mac Booth, dismissed the idea and shut down the discussion by announcing that "Polaroid doesn't sell what it didn't invent," reflecting overconfidence in the company's ability to predict the future and create the best products. "I think instant film is going to be the dominant factor in electronic photography, and we know more about that than anyone in the world," Booth said in 1987. "Anyone who says instant photography is dying has his head in the sand."

Yankowski recalls that when he recommended finding an external electronics expert to guide the company into the digital age, Booth retorted, "I don't know if I should punch you in the nose or fire you!" There's the reputational risk. Finally, Yankowski gave up and left for Sony, where he launched the PlayStation and nearly doubled revenue within four years. He went on to lead the turnaround of Reebok and become the CEO of Palm, but despite his success in driving innovation and saving failing companies, "I could never conquer the culture paradigms prevalent in Polaroid," Yankowski lamented, decrying the "closed-minded thinking" and "inbred" mentality of key decision makers. "Many of us certainly drank the 'Kool-Aid' along with the executives," notes Milton Dentch, who spent twenty-seven years at Polaroid. "The culture ingrained in several generations of Polaroid management always came back to the strategy that the engine that will drive Polaroid has to be hard-copy media. . . . The real cause was Polaroid's unique culture."*

Polaroid came close to being a pioneer in digital photography, and could have easily been a fast settler. Instead, leaders fiddled while the company burned. Had they embraced original ideas instead of adhering rigidly to Land's beliefs in hard-copy chemical imaging, the company might have survived. How can you build a strong culture that welcomes dissent?

"Think Different" Culture

When I polled executives and students about the strongest culture they had ever encountered in an organization, the landslide winner was Bridgewater Associates. Headquartered in a Connecticut town,

---

* You might be thinking that the safe strategy is to start with a commitment culture and then shift to another blueprint. Although this seems like a natural solution, it's not effective. Changing a blueprint is both difficult and dangerous. In the Silicon Valley study, half of the startups altered their blueprints—and those that did more than doubled their chances of failing. Firms that deviated from the founder's original blueprint had 2.3 times higher odds of failure compared to similar firms that stayed with the founder's original model. Even a small adjustment was enough to cause big problems. More than half of the firms that shifted their blueprints only made one change, like hiring on potential instead of skills, but they suffered anyway. A new blueprint boosted turnover by more than 25 percent. Many employees who used to feel part of the team decided it was time to leave for greener pastures. And if companies shifted blueprints and still became successful enough to go public, over the next three years their value on the stock market grew almost three times slower than those that stayed with the original blueprint. Overall, changing the blueprint had a more negative impact than replacing the founder. Here's the kicker: the negative effects of change were most pronounced for firms with commitment blueprints.

Bridgewater handles over $170 billion in investments for governments, pension funds, universities, and charities. Its philosophy is outlined in a set of over two hundred principles written by the founder. Although the company manages money, the principles don't contain a word about investing. They are maxims about how to think and act in any situation you might encounter at work or in life if you want to do meaningful work and build meaningful relationships.

The principles have been downloaded more than two million times, and they range from the philosophical ("Realize you have nothing to fear from truth") to the practical ("Recognize that behavior modification typically takes about 18 months of constant reinforcement"). New employees are hired based on an assessment of how well they fit with the way of operating that's outlined in the principles. They are trained in an intensive boot camp modeled after the military, where they are asked to reflect on and discuss the principles, placed in emotionally intense situations to practice them, and evaluated on how well they integrate them into their behaviors. Although there's always a lot of debate, Bridgewater is a highly cohesive, close-knit community, to the point that its staff frequently call it a family, and it's common for employees to stay for decades.

Bridgewater has a strong commitment culture in the volatile financial industry, but its performance hasn't waned over time. The company has two major funds, both of which have delivered consistently excellent returns through two decades. They've been recognized for making more money for clients than any hedge fund in the history of the industry. In 2010, Bridgewater's returns exceeded the combined profits of Google, eBay, Yahoo, and Amazon.

Bridgewater's secret is promoting the expression of original ideas. The company has been consistently praised for its innovative investment strategies, one of which has involved reducing risk by embracing a much greater degree of diversification than typical investment funds. And in the spring of 2007, Bridgewater started warning clients about the impending financial crisis. According to *Barron's,* "Nobody was better prepared for the global market crash."

In the investment world, you can only make money if you think different from everyone else. Bridgewater has prevented groupthink by inviting dissenting opinions from every employee in the company. When employees share independent viewpoints instead of conforming to the majority, there's a much higher chance that Bridgewater will make investment decisions no one else has considered and recognize financial trends no one else has discerned. That makes it possible to be right when the rest of the market is wrong.

My goal isn't to analyze Bridgewater's brilliant financial decisions, but to take a deeper look at the culture that underlies those decisions. It starts with Bridgewater's billionaire founder, Ray Dalio. Although he has been called the Steve Jobs of investing, employees don't communicate with him as if he's anyone special. Here's an email that Jim, a client adviser, sent to Dalio after a meeting with an important potential client:

> *Ray— you deserve a "D-" for your performance today . . . you rambled for 50 minutes . . . It was obvious to all of us that you did not prepare at all because there is no way you could have and been that disorganized at the outset if you had prepared. We told you this prospect has been identified as a "must-win" . . . today was really bad . . . we can't let this happen again.*

At a typical company, sending an email this critical of a boss would be career suicide. But instead of reacting defensively, Dalio responded by asking others who attended the meeting to give him honest feedback and grade him on a scale from A to F. Then, instead of hiding Dalio's shortcomings or attacking the author of the note, Bridgewater's co-CEO copied the email trail to the entire company so that everyone could learn from the exchange.

In many organizations, people give negative feedback only behind closed doors. As Jack Handey advised in one of his "Deep Thoughts" on *Saturday Night Live*, before you criticize people, you should walk a mile in their shoes. That way, when you criticize them, you're a mile away and you have their shoes.

At Bridgewater, employees are expected to voice concerns and critiques directly to each other. "Don't let 'loyalty' stand in the way of truth and openness," Dalio writes in the principles. "No one has the right to hold a critical opinion without speaking up about it." In a typical organization, people are punished for raising dissent. At Bridgewater, they're evaluated on whether they speak up—and they can be fired for failing to challenge the status quo.

Strong cultures exist when employees are intensely committed to a shared set of values and norms, but the effects depend on what those values and norms are. If you're going to build a strong culture, it's paramount to make diversity one of your core values. This is what separates Bridgewater's strong culture from a cult: The commitment is to promoting dissent. In hiring, instead of using similarity to gauge cultural fit, Bridgewater assesses cultural contribution.* Dalio wants people who will think independently and enrich the culture. By holding them accountable for dissenting, Dalio has fundamentally altered the way people make decisions.

In a cult, core values are dogma. At Bridgewater, employees are expected to challenge the principles themselves. During training, when employees learn the principles, they're constantly asked: Do you agree? "We have these standards that are stress tested over time, and you have to either operate by them or disagree with them and fight for

---

* If you hire people who fit your culture, you'll end up with people who reinforce rather than challenge one another's perspectives. "Cultural fit has become a new form of discrimination," Northwestern University sociologist Lauren Rivera finds. Too often, it is a "catchall used to justify hiring people who are similar to decision makers and rejecting people who are not." At IDEO, the design consulting firm that created the mouse for Apple, managers throw cultural fit out the window, focusing instead on how potential candidates can improve the culture.

better ones," explains Zack Wieder, who works with Dalio on codifying the principles.

Rather than deferring to the people with the greatest seniority or status, as was the case at Polaroid, decisions at Bridgewater are based on quality. The goal is to create an idea meritocracy, where the best ideas win. To get the best ideas on the table in the first place, you need radical transparency.

Later, I'm going to challenge some of Dalio's principles, but first I want to explain the weapons he has used to wage a war on groupthink.

The Devil You Know

After the Bay of Pigs debacle, President Kennedy asked his brother Robert to argue against majority opinions and consider every idea. When Irving Janis analyzed the disease of groupthink, one of his main cures was to appoint a devil's advocate. The practice dates back to 1587, when Pope Sixtus V instituted a new process for vetting candidates for sainthood in the Roman Catholic Church. He assigned a *promotor fidei*, or promoter of the faith, to oppose canonization by critically evaluating the character of candidates and challenging claims of miracles they had performed. The promoter of the faith argued against the *advocatus Dei*, God's advocate, and became known as the devil's advocate. Half a millennium later, this is effectively what most leaders do to foster dissent: bring in someone to oppose the majority. But Charlan Nemeth shows that we're doing it wrong.

In an experiment inspired by Nemeth's work, over two hundred business and government managers in Germany were assigned to represent a company transferring its production abroad. They were given a choice between two countries—say, Peru and Kenya—and, after reading some initial information, were asked to select one or the other. The ones that favored Peru joined a group with two other people who shared their preference, and before making a decision, they had access to a dozen articles that offered more detailed information about each country. Half of the articles recommended Peru and half favored Kenya, and they didn't have time to read them all.

The managers chose to read 26 percent more articles that favored Peru. This is what psychologists call confirmation bias: When you have a preference, you seek out information supporting it, while overlooking information that challenges it.

But would that bias change if one of the teammates had been randomly assigned to be a devil's advocate? His role was to challenge the majority preference for Peru, identifying its disadvantages and questioning the group's assumptions.

With a devil's advocate present, the managers became more balanced: they read only 2 percent more pro-Peru articles than pro-Kenya articles. Yet the advocate's input ultimately wasn't sufficient to change their minds. The managers paid lip service to the advocate by selecting an evenhanded mix of articles, but their confidence in their original preference dropped by only 4 percent. Because of confirmation bias, they were persuaded by the arguments that affirmed their preference, and discounted those that didn't. To overcome a majority preference, groups would need to consider more articles against it than in support of it.

If assigning a devil's advocate doesn't work, what does?

The researchers formed another set of groups with two managers who favored Peru. For the third member, instead of assigning a devil's advocate to argue for Kenya, they picked someone who actually preferred Kenya. Those groups selected 14 percent more articles *against* the majority preference than for it. And now, they were 15 percent less confident in their original preference.

While it can be appealing to *assign* a devil's advocate, it's much more powerful to *unearth* one. When people are designated to dissent, they're just playing a role. This causes two problems: They don't argue forcefully or consistently enough for the minority viewpoint, and group members are less likely to take them seriously. "Dissenting for the sake of dissenting is not useful. It is also not useful if it is 'pretend dissent'—for example, if role-played," Nemeth explains. "It is not useful if motivated by considerations other than searching for the truth or the best solutions. But when it is authentic, it stimulates thought; it clarifies and it emboldens."

The secret to success is sincerity, the old saying goes: Once you can fake that, you've got it made. In fact, it's not easy to fake sincerity. For devil's advocates to be maximally effective, they need to really believe in the position they're representing—and the group needs to believe that they believe it, too. In one experiment led by Nemeth, groups with an authentic dissenter generated 48 percent more solutions to problems than those with an assigned devil's advocate, and their solutions tended to be higher in quality. This was true regardless of whether the group knew the devil's advocate held the majority opinion or was unsure of the person's actual opinion. And even if a devil's advocate did believe in the minority perspective, informing the other members that the role had been assigned was enough to undermine the advocate's persuasiveness.* Whereas people doubt assigned dissenters, genuine dissenters challenge people to doubt themselves.

Even though the assigned position is less effective, it's an attractive option because it seems to provide cover. It's precarious to genuinely challenge the status quo when you're in the minority; if you can claim that you're just playing devil's advocate, you feel protected against

---

* In light of this evidence that authentic dissent works best, I asked Nemeth what she thought of Robert Kennedy's assigned devil's advocate role in the Cuban missile crisis. "I think Bobby Kennedy's role there was to ensure a process of questioning each possibility," she replied. "What he did was at least make them go through the motions of reconsidering positions—at least defending them. I still don't think this has the same effect as authentic dissent but it was certainly an improvement over a rush to judgment." It seems that Robert Kennedy was less of a pure devil's advocate, and more of what Harvard political scientist Roger Porter calls an honest broker: someone who guided the group through an effective decision process that brought different arguments to the table and evaluated their quality.

criticism or hostility from the group. But this isn't what Nemeth found. Compared to assigned dissenters, authentic dissenters don't make group members substantially angrier, and they're actually liked slightly more (at least they have principles).

Instead of appointing devil's advocates, Bridgewater unearths them. In 2012, Ray Dalio drew out authentic dissenters by sending a poll asking everyone in the company to hold others accountable for speaking their minds:

Of the people you work with on a regular basis, what percentage of those people would you rely on to speak up and to fight to make sense of things even when it's difficult?

Are you such a person?

Let's test your forthrightness. Of the people you work with, who is not doing their part to fight for right? (add exactly three answers)

Have you told them? If not, why not?

Dalio included an open-ended prompt for employees to provide feedback. As the feedback poured in, the exercise turned out to be unusually polarizing for a company with strong consensus around principles. Some employees objected to the idea of naming names; others balked at the format. One person said it was "very much Nazi Germany as opposed to idea meritocracy." Another commented that "today's poll is outrageous. . . . It is asking me to choose three people for a piece of feedback that is extremely specific, and highly charged, and do it in a format that is highly impersonal and gives a mean-spirited edge to it."

But other employees had the opposite reaction: They felt that Bridgewater was enacting the principles it espoused. If there were people who weren't speaking their minds, they were jeopardizing the nucleus of the culture. One wrote that it "caused me to reflect" and "generated conversation—someone emailed me that she put my name down for not fighting for right—and we got in sync." Another admitted that "this is probably the toughest and most valuable bit of homework I've done in over two years."

Dalio loved the cacophony, which provided an opportunity for both sides to learn. Instead of assigning a devil's advocate, Dalio was uncovering actual areas of disagreement. "The greatest tragedy of mankind," Dalio says, "comes from the inability of people to have thoughtful disagreement to find out what's true." Through the process of open-minded debate, Dalio expects employees to reconcile their differences. Instead of reaching consensus because some people are overconfident or others are afraid to speak up, the staff get on the same page by duking it out. In the language of futurist Paul Saffo, the norm is to have "strong opinions, weakly held."

To get people in sync about their conflicting views of the poll, Dalio hosted a discussion. In an effort to foster a balanced dialogue, he selected three people with strong negative opinions and three who were extremely enthusiastic. Dalio turned to one of the critical employees and asked for his point of view. The employee expressed concerns about "creating an indictment culture, something where it felt McCarthyist." Another employee agreed, arguing that "the naming names feels pretty tone-deaf."

A leader pushed back: "I think it's tone-deaf *not* to share that info." The poll data revealed that 40 percent of people who had critical thoughts about others hadn't shared them—while every single employee wanted to know others' critical thoughts. With a few dozen people in the room, the debate raged for more than an hour.

As founder of a firm that manages investments, why would Dalio spend so much time on a conversation about naming names? If employees can get in sync about making sure that everyone speaks up, they don't need to worry as much about groupthink. Dalio can be confident that members of his staff won't feel pressured to nod and smile whenever he presents an opinion; his whole team will be radically transparent in challenging his assumptions about markets, and they'll be the same with one another.* Decisions will be made based on an idea meritocracy, not a status hierarchy or democracy.

When all was said and done, 97 percent of Bridgewater employees were more worried about too little accountability than too much. By devoting more than an hour to the debate on that matter, employees reached consensus that they needed to push one another to share original ideas. That transparency would shield them against groupthink, enabling them to avoid countless bad decisions over time. By building a culture in which people are constantly encouraging one another to disagree, Dalio has created a powerful way to combat conformity. Yet the kind of disagreement he seeks is the opposite of what most leaders invite.

Finding the Canary in the Coal Mine

If you're a leader talking to your employees, how would you fill in the blanks in this sentence?

> *Don't bring me* _____;
> *bring me* _____.

I learned about this question from organizational psychologist David Hofmann, who posed it while serving as a member of the

---

* Valuing transparency doesn't mean employees should speak up about everything. "It has to be goal relevant," one employee explains. "You can tell people you don't like their jeans, but then you'll get criticized. How is that relevant?!" To hold employees accountable for being transparent, virtually all meetings and calls at Bridgewater are videotaped. If you're slamming people, they deserve the opportunity to learn from your perspective. When everything you say is being recorded, you might as well be open about it—and if you're not, they'll find out anyway. As a Bridgewater employee, if you talk behind someone's back, they'll call you a slimy weasel to your face. If you do it more than once, you might be sent packing.

committee investigating British Petroleum's Deepwater Horizon explosion and oil spill. Since then, I've presented the question to thousands of leaders in groups, asking them to shout out the full sentence. Without fail, multiple people chime in unison, as if they've rehearsed the chorus many times before: "Don't bring me problems; bring me solutions."

This seems like a wise philosophy for leaders. We don't want people to stop at complaining; when they see something wrong, they ought to take the initiative to fix it. As management researcher Jeff Edwards advises, if you're going to tell the emperor he has no clothes, you'd better be a good tailor. And extensive research shows that leaders do react much more positively when employees bring solutions rather than problems to the table.

But when it comes to groupthink, there's a dark side to encouraging solutions. Hofmann is one of the world's preeminent authorities on creating organizational cultures that detect, correct, and prevent errors. After the space shuttle *Columbia* exploded upon reentry into the atmosphere in 2003, Hofmann's research was instrumental in assessing and documenting improvements in NASA's safety culture. The culture survey he helped create was completed by every NASA employee and has since reached over two hundred thousand employees across more than a thousand companies. Hofmann found that a culture that focuses too heavily on solutions becomes a culture of advocacy, dampening inquiry. If you're always expected to have an answer ready, you'll arrive at meetings with your diagnosis complete, missing out on the chance to learn from a broad range of perspectives. A day after the *Columbia* shuttle took off, a "mystery object" was seen floating away in orbit. If an inquiry had been launched, the team might have discovered that the mystery object had caused a hole in the left wing, and been able to repair it before hot gas eventually entered the ship.

Advocacy is fine if you're on the jury at a courtroom trial. Since all twelve members get to hear the entire case, when it's time to deliberate, they can start debating about whether the defendant is innocent or guilty. But organizational life doesn't work like a courtroom, Hofmann admonishes. It's more like sitting through a twelve-hour trial where each juror hears only one hour of testimony, and no two jurors listen to the same hour. When every member of a group has different information, inquiry needs to precede advocacy—which means you have to raise the problems before pursuing solutions. To make sure that problems get raised, leaders need mechanisms for unearthing dissenters.

In 2007, Google's head of people operations, Laszlo Bock, decided to move annual performance reviews from December to March to avoid the holiday crunch. His team ran the idea by dozens of people and decided to announce the change to the company on a Friday. On late Thursday afternoon, Bock emailed managers with a heads-up, only to face an avalanche of strong objections. After fielding hundreds of emails and forty phone conversations between 6 P.M. and midnight, Bock was persuaded to move the reviews up to October. Before that input, his team had fallen victim to groupthink, having obtained only supportive opinions from like-minded people. "The experience underscored not just the importance of listening to our people, but also the need to have a reliable channel for opinions well before decisions are made," Bock writes in *Work Rules!*

To ensure that authentic dissenters voiced their viewpoints earlier, Bock's team created the "Canaries"—a group of trusted engineers across the company who represent diverse viewpoints, and have a reputation both for being sensitive to adverse conditions and for speaking their minds. They took their name from the nineteenth-century practice of using canaries to detect deadly gases in coal mines. Before Google's people operations team introduces a major change in policy, they often run it by the Canaries for critical feedback. They're part advisory board, part focus group, and they've become an invaluable safeguard to make sure Googlers' voices are heard. By reaching out to them in advance, one member of Bock's team explains, "Our biggest complainers become our strongest advocates."

Polaroid never systematically engaged canaries to call out problems. In contrast, Bridgewater is designed to be a whole company of canaries. In my first conversation about the company, a former junior employee told me she was known there informally as the canary in the coal mine. I expected that status to stall her career, but it was highlighted as a major strength in her performance reviews and gave her credibility with senior management as a champion of the culture.

Ray Dalio doesn't want employees to bring him solutions; he expects them to bring him problems. One of his first inventions was the issue log, an open-access database for employees to flag any problem they identify and to rate its severity. Getting problems noted is half the battle against groupthink; the other is listening to the right opinions about how to solve them. The Bridgewater procedure for the latter is to gather a group of credible people to diagnose the problems, share their reasoning, and explore the causes and possible solutions.

Although everyone's opinions are welcome, they're not all valued equally. Bridgewater is not a democracy. Voting privileges the majority, when the minority might have a better opinion. "Democratic decision making—one person, one vote—is dumb," Dalio explains, "because not everybody has the same believability."*

---

* The futility of democratic voting as a decision-making process has been clear since the Bay of Pigs debacle, when President Kennedy's straw poll silenced the opposition. Having learned from that experience, in the Cuban missile crisis, Kennedy sought to bring more dissenting opinions to the table. To prevent the committee from favoring for political reasons the option that pleased him, he started by limiting his own role in the decision-making process, which forced the group to make a more balanced assessment of a broader range of possibilities. As psychologists Andreas Mojzisch and Stefan Schulz-Hardt find, "knowing others' preferences degrades the quality of group decisions." Next, instead of discussing alternatives one at a time, they compared and contrasted each of the alternatives. Evidence shows that when groups consider options one at a time, a majority preference can emerge too early. It's better to rank order the options, because comparing your third and fourth choice might surface information that shifts the entire decision. Psychologist Andrea Hollingshead finds that when groups are instructed to rank order the

At Bridgewater, every employee has a believability score on a range of dimensions. In sports, statistics for every player's performance history are public. In baseball, before you sign a player, you can look up his batting average, home runs, and steals; assess his strengths and weaknesses; and adjust accordingly. Dalio wanted Bridgewater to work the same way, so he created baseball cards that display statistics on every employee's performance, which can be accessed by anyone at the company. If you're about to interact with a few Bridgewater colleagues for the first time, you can see their track records on seventy-seven different dimensions of values, skills, and abilities in the areas of higher-level thinking, practical thinking, maintaining high standards, determination, open-mindedness yet assertiveness, and organization and reliability.

During regular review cycles, employees rate one another on different qualities like integrity, courage, living in truth, taking the bull by its horns, not tolerating problems, being willing to touch a nerve, fighting to get in sync, and holding people accountable. Between cycles, employees can give real-time, open feedback to anyone in the company. At any time, employees can submit dots, or observations— they assess peers, leaders, or subordinates on the metrics and give short explanations of what they've observed. The baseball cards create a "pointillist picture" of staff members, aggregating across review cycles and dots, and incorporate various assessments that employees take. The cards' display changes over time, revealing who's best suited to play each position, and flagging areas to "rely on" and "watch out for" with green and red lights.

When you express an opinion, it's weighted by whether you've established yourself as believable on that dimension. Your believability is a probability of being right in the present, and is based on your

---

alternatives, instead of choosing the best alternative, they're more likely to consider each option, share information about the unpopular ones, and make a good decision.

judgment, reasoning, and behavior in the past. In presenting your views, you're expected to consider your own believability by telling your audience how confident you are. If you have doubts, and you're not known as believable in the domain, you shouldn't have an opinion in the first place; you're supposed to ask questions so you can learn. If you're expressing a fierce conviction, you should be forthright about it—but know that your colleagues will probe the quality of your reasoning. Even then, you're supposed to be assertive and open-minded at the same time. As management scholar Karl Weick advises, "Argue like you're right and listen like you're wrong."

When Principles Collide

What happens, though, when believable people don't agree? In the summer of 2014, Bridgewater conducted an anonymous survey to find out about dissent that hadn't been voiced. When co-CEO Greg Jensen led an all-hands meeting to discuss the results, an employee, "Ashley," commented that some people were misinterpreting Bridgewater's principles. Greg asked if she was correcting them when that occurred, and Ashley mentioned that she had recently called someone out for a misinterpretation.

By speaking up, Ashley was exemplifying one of Bridgewater's principles. But rather than responding to the substance of her comment, Greg called her out for violating another Bridgewater principle, which emphasizes the importance of understanding the difference between the forest and the trees, and navigating between the two. He wanted a synthesis of how she handled such situations in general, not her account of a specific case.

A senior manager, Trina Soske, felt that Greg made a bad leadership decision. Although he was attempting to adhere to one Bridgewater principle, Trina was concerned that Ashley—and others—might be discouraged from speaking up in the future. In most organizations, since Greg had higher status than her, a manager in Trina's position would remain silent and go home thinking he was a jerk. But Trina wrote honest feedback for the whole company to read. She praised Ashley for having the courage and integrity to speak up, and cautioned Greg that his response "signaled the exact opposite of what you, as a CEO, should model."

In a typical organization, as the senior leader Greg's opinion would prevail over Trina's, and her career might be in jeopardy for criticizing him. But at Bridgewater, Trina wasn't punished, and the resolution wasn't based on authority, seniority, majority, or who spoke the most loudly or forcefully. It started with a debate via email: Greg disagreed with Trina's views, as he felt he was being open and direct; after all, principle three stated that no one has the right to hold a critical opinion without speaking up. But Trina had heard two different people criticize Greg's behavior in informal conversations. "The dampening impact is going to be more about what you don't see and don't hear," she wrote to him. She worried that Greg's behavior would instigate groupthink, causing people to stay silent rather than to challenge leaders. Greg stood his ground: By allowing people to talk behind his back, Trina was failing to hold people accountable for confronting him with their critical opinions. She was allowing them to violate one of Bridgewater's principles by acting like "slimy weasels."

It's extremely rare to see a senior leader open to this kind of thoughtful disagreement, but even more unusual was what Greg did next. "I doubt we'll be able to resolve this ourselves," he wrote to Trina, copying the entire management committee—a group of people who had established their believability as leaders. "It's like agreeing on a judge or a mediator," Dalio explains. By escalating the disagreement to them, Greg was allowing the idea meritocracy to sort out who was right.

Instead of leaving it to the management committee to resolve, though, Dalio asked Greg and Trina to collaborate on turning their conflict into a case to share with all of Bridgewater. Along with making their debate transparent, it forced them to inquire about each other's perspectives instead of just advocating for their own viewpoints. When the case was finished, to continue the inquiry process Greg and Trina each generated questions to ask the entire company.

Several months after the issue first occurred, it was still being discussed, and the analytics team was preparing to share the data on employees' reactions. But "resolving the issue itself is in some ways less important than understanding the path to resolving such things in the future, and agreeing on that," Zack Wieder explains. "No one (including our CEO) has any monopoly on the truth."

I can't help but wonder: If Polaroid leaders had called people slimy weasels for talking behind Edwin Land's back about the problems with his instant movie camera, would the company still be thriving today? Had NASA's culture allowed for this kind of open disagreement, would the seven *Columbia* astronauts still be alive?

Even if your organization doesn't currently embrace critical upward feedback, holding an open season on leaders might be an effective way to begin changing the culture. At the software company Index Group, CEO Tom Gerrity asked a consultant to tell him everything he did wrong in front of his entire staff of roughly a hundred employees. By role modeling receptivity to feedback, employees across the company became more willing to challenge him—and one another. I've learned to do something similar in the classroom. I collect anonymous feedback from students after the first month, focusing on constructive criticism and suggestions for improvement, and then email the full set of verbatim comments to the entire class. In the next class session, I summarize what I thought were the key suggestions, seek feedback on my interpretations, and propose changes to address these issues. Students often report that this dialogue makes them feel more comfortable in becoming active contributors to improving the class.

It's not just Dalio's openness that makes people comfortable challenging senior leaders. It's the fact that early in the training, employees
are encouraged to question the principles. Rather than waiting for
employees to become experienced, Bridgewater reveals that we can
start encouraging originality on day one. In most organizations, the
socialization period is passive: We're busy learning the ropes and
familiarizing ourselves with the culture. By the time we're up to speed,
we're already swamped with work and beginning to see the world in
the company way. The early period is the perfect time for employees to
pay attention to opportunities to improve the culture.

A few years ago, I was hired by Goldman Sachs to identify steps for
attracting and retaining talented investment banking analysts and
associates by allowing them to improve the work environment. One of
the initiatives that we introduced was an entry interview. Instead of
waiting to ask employees for ideas on their way out, managers hold
meetings to learn about new hires' ideas when they first join the organization. It's easier to start a relationship with the door open than to
pry open a door that's already been slammed shut.

The Moment of Truth

I was eager to find out for myself if Ray Dalio was anything like Edwin
Land. Was he too attached to his own blueprint? How did he handle
challenges to his principles? I had done enough inquiry at Bridgewater
to develop some critical opinions of my own. By virtue of unearthing
devil's advocates and conducting a thorough inquiry process before
moving into advocacy, the company was unusually good at preventing
groupthink. But that didn't mean they were perfect.

Soon enough, I found myself sitting with Dalio at the kitchen table
in his apartment. In the past, I would have hesitated to speak my mind.
I've never enjoyed conflict, but my time studying Bridgewater had

begun to change me; I'd become more direct in giving critical feedback, and who better to challenge than the forefather of radical transparency? I'd come to believe that no one had the right to hold a critical opinion without speaking up about it, I explained to Dalio, and since that's what their culture prizes, I wouldn't pull any punches. "I'm unoffendable," he replied, giving me the green light to go ahead.

If I were running the show, I began, Bridgewater's principles would be rank ordered in a hierarchy, from most to least important. The disagreement between Greg and Trina centered on two different principles: being open with critical opinions and encouraging others to be open with theirs. Both of these principles appeared in a list, without any information about which one mattered more. After studying values for more than forty years, psychologist Shalom Schwartz has found that their main purpose is to help people choose between conflicting options. "The relative importance of multiple values guides action," Schwartz explains.

I pointed out to Dalio that when organizations fail to prioritize principles, their performance suffers. In a study of over one hundred professional theaters by researchers Zannie Voss, Dan Cable, and Glenn Voss, leaders rated the importance of five values: artistic expression (innovative plays), entertainment (audience satisfaction), giving to the community (providing access, outreach, and education), achievement (being recognized for excellence), and financial performance (fiscal viability). The more strongly leaders disagreed about the importance of these values, the lower their ticket revenues and net income. It didn't matter what their principles were, as long as leaders established consensus about their significance.

I added that establishing relative importance is especially essential when organizations have a large number of principles. In a study of over 150 hospitals led by Wharton professor Drew Carton, a compelling vision was necessary but not sufficient for strong health and financial performance. The more core principles a hospital emphasized, the less a vivid vision helped. When hospitals had more than four core values, a clear mission no longer offered any benefits for reducing heart attack readmission rates or increasing return on assets. The more principles you have, the greater the odds that employees focus on different values or interpret the same values differently. If that proved to be an issue with five to ten principles, wouldn't it be an even greater problem with two hundred or more?

"I agree with you," Dalio said. "I can see that I might not have been clear enough that there's a hierarchy, because these 200 are not all the same. A principle is just some type of event happening over and over again, and how to deal with that event. Life consists of billions of these events, and if you can go from those billions to 250, you can make the connection, 'Ah, this is one of those.'"

A lightbulb went off for me: We have lots of categories to describe people's personalities, but few frameworks for describing the personalities of situations. Now I saw the value of having a large number of these principles, but I still wanted to know which ones mattered most.

A few years earlier, Dalio had been asked whether it was his personal dream to have everyone live by the principles. "No. No, no, no, no, no, no, no. Nooo. Nooo. Absolutely not. No. Just please. No," he replied emphatically. "That's not my dream. . . . The number one principle is that you must think for yourself."

The independent search for truth stood at the very top of the principle hierarchy, but I wanted to see Dalio go further in ranking the rest of the principles. Was it more important for leaders to share their critical opinions openly or self-censor when there was a risk of discouraging more junior employees from speaking up? "I need to be clearer about that," Dalio acknowledged. I worried that I'd offended him, but he broke out into a grin. "Is that all you've got?" he asked. "Is that the best you can do?"

My other piece of feedback was tougher to deliver, because it got to the very heart of the idea meritocracy, which holds that people should fight for right and seek the truth. But Bridgewater's methods of adjudicating which idea wins fall short of my own standards of rigor. Dalio's default approach to resolving problems like the disagreement between Greg and Trina is to unearth three believable people with strong opinions from each side, and have them discuss and debate until they're in sync. Yet this leaves decisions up to subjective opinions, which are notoriously flawed as a form of evidence. Believability takes into account test results, performance reviews, and other assessments, but a major component is the judgments of others. As one Bridgewater employee described it to me, "You gain believability by other believable people saying you're believable."

In the centuries since the Roman Catholic Church assigned the *promotor fidei* to argue against the *advocatus Dei*, humanity has developed a tool more powerful than debate for resolving disagreement. It's called science. In the field of medicine, I told Dalio, there's widespread consensus among experts that the quality of evidence can be classified on a scale of strength from one to six. The gold standard is a series of randomized, controlled experiments with objective outcomes. The least rigorous evidence: "the opinion of respected authorities or expert committees." The same standards are part of the growing field of evidence-based management and people analytics, in which leaders are encouraged to design experiments and gather data instead of relying solely on logic, experience, intuition, and conversation.

If I were running Bridgewater, I would have resolved Greg and Trina's debate by running some small experiments. In various meetings, people would be randomly assigned to speak up. In some cases, leaders would criticize the speaker's delivery, as Greg had with Ashley; in other cases, they would affirm the speaker's courage, as Trina wanted Greg to do; and the rest of the time, they would do both or neither. I would then track how frequently and boldly the attendees voiced their concerns in subsequent meetings. This might be tough to execute, but at minimum, I would measure whether the people who saw Greg criticize Ashley—or reacted negatively to it—were speaking up less.

This time, Dalio disagreed. "I might be wrong," he qualified, but he explained that he favored the debate format between believable people, because it was the fastest way to reach the right answer and it enabled them to learn from each other's reasoning. He had been testing out different cultural practices at Bridgewater for years, and although they're not controlled experiments, he felt he'd seen enough to have a good sense of what works. He believes that thoughtful disagreement between experts creates an efficient marketplace of ideas, where the best ones emerge over time. Here, we agreed to disagree. Dalio places more faith than I do in the triangulated opinions of experts. For me, a critical test would be assigning some units to rely on believability-weighted debate and others to run experiments, and see which units make better decisions. Then, every unit would try the opposite method and analyze the results again. As a social scientist, my bet is that, on average, groups that make decisions based on experiments will outperform those guided by debate between experts. But only the data will tell.

Movers and Shapers

To his credit, Dalio has been running an investigation of his own. Fascinated with understanding people who shape the world and eager to discern what they have in common, he's been interviewing many of the most influential originals of our time, and studying historical figures from Benjamin Franklin to Albert Einstein to Steve Jobs. Of course, all of them were driven and imaginative, but I was intrigued by three other qualities on Dalio's list. "Shapers" are independent thinkers: curious, non-conforming, and rebellious. They practice brutal, nonhierarchical honesty. And they act in the face of risk, because their fear of not succeeding exceeds their fear of failing.

Dalio himself fits this description, and the hurdle facing him now is to find another shaper to fill his shoes. If he doesn't, Bridgewater may vanish like Polaroid's instant pictures. But Dalio knows that preventing groupthink is about more than the vision of a single leader. The greatest shapers don't stop at introducing originality into the world. They create cultures that unleash originality in others.

8

Rocking the Boat and
Keeping It Steady

Managing Anxiety, Apathy, Ambivalence, and Anger

"I learned that courage was not the absence of fear,
but the triumph over it. . . . The brave man is not he who does not feel
afraid, but he who conquers that fear."

Nelson Mandela

In 2007, a lawyer named Lewis Pugh plunged into the Arctic Sea wearing only a Speedo, a swim cap, and goggles. The ice had melted to the point that it was no longer frozen solid, and his plan was to become the first person ever to survive a long-distance swim across the North Pole. Hailing from England and South Africa, Pugh had served in the British Special Air Service and worked as a maritime lawyer before becoming the best cold-water swimmer on the planet. Two years earlier, he had broken a world record for the northernmost long-distance swim in frigid seas. Later that same year, he broke the southernmost record by leaping off an iceberg to swim a full kilometer in Antarctica.

Pugh, who has been called a human polar bear, is capable of a feat that has never been documented in another human: Before a swim, his core body temperature elevates from 98.6°F to 101°F. His sports scientist coined a term for it, "anticipatory thermogenesis," and it appears to be the fruit of decades of Pavlovian conditioning: When it's time to plunge into frosty waters, his body automatically prepares.

Pugh calls it the art of self-heating. But unlike many world-class athletes, he does not consider it his mission simply to be the best in the world or to prove what's possible. He is an ocean advocate, an environmentalist who swims to raise awareness about climate change.

The passengers on the *Titanic* perished in 41°F water. In Pugh's Antarctic swim, the water temperature was at the freshwater freezing point of 32°F. At the North Pole he was facing something even more lethal: less than 29°F. After falling into that water, a British explorer had lost fingers due to frostbite in only three minutes; Pugh's team estimated that his swim would require almost twenty. Two days before the big effort, Pugh took a dip for a five-minute practice swim, and afterward he couldn't feel his entire left hand or any of the fingers on his right—and he wouldn't again for four more months. The cells in his fingers burst, and he was hyperventilating.

Instead of visualizing success, Pugh began to imagine failure. *Great depths don't normally hold any fear for me, but this is different,* he thought. If he failed, he would die, and his body would sink more than two and a half miles to the bottom of the Arctic. Paralyzed by fear, he began to question whether he could survive. Would he have been better off envisioning the best-case scenario?

This chapter examines the emotional drama involved in going against the grain. In my own research at a health-care company, I tested how much employees knew about effective strategies for managing emotions, comparing their responses to expert ratings on how best to handle emotionally challenging situations like being demoted from a job, being nervous before a major presentation, getting blamed for a mistake, and having teammates turn in shoddy work. Those who aced the emotion regulation test spoke up more often with ideas and suggestions to challenge the status quo—and their managers rated them as more effective in doing so. They marshaled the courage to rock the boat and mastered the techniques for keeping it steady.

To understand these skills, I'll consider how Pugh heated up to brave icy waters and Martin Luther King, Jr., prepared civil rights activists to keep their cool. I'll also explore how a group of activists overthrew a dictator and a technology leader convinced engineers to make a radical change to their product. By studying effective strategies for managing emotions, you'll discover when it's better to plan like an optimist or a pessimist, whether calming yourself down can fight fear and venting can quench anger, and what it takes to maintain your resolve when the odds are against you.

The Positive Power of Negative Thinking

Although many originals come across as beacons of conviction and confidence on the outside, their inner experiences are peppered with ambivalence and self-doubt. When outstanding U.S. government leaders described their most difficult decisions, they reported struggling not with complex problems, but with choices that required courage. And new research led by Rice professor Scott Sonenshein indicates that even the most dedicated environmentalists wrestle with constant uncertainty about whether they can succeed in their mission. Choosing to challenge the status quo is an uphill battle, and there are bound to be failures, barriers, and setbacks along the way.

Psychologist Julie Norem studies two different strategies for handling these challenges: strategic optimism and defensive pessimism. Strategic optimists anticipate the best, staying calm and setting high expectations. Defensive pessimists expect the worst, feeling anxious and imagining all the things that can go wrong. If you're a defensive pessimist, about a week before a big speech you convince yourself that you're doomed to fail. And it won't be just ordinary failure: You'll trip on stage and then forget all your lines.

Most people assume it's better to be a strategic optimist than a

defensive pessimist. Yet Norem finds that although defensive pessimists are more anxious and less confident in analytical, verbal, and
creative tasks, they perform just as well as strategic optimists. "At first,
I asked how these people were able to do so well *despite* their pessimism," Norem writes. "Before long, I began to realize that they were
doing so well *because* of their pessimism."

In one experiment, Norem and a colleague asked people to throw
darts after being randomly assigned to picture a perfect performance,
envision a bad performance, or relax. Defensive pessimists were about 30
percent more accurate in their dart throws when they thought about
negative outcomes rather than imagining positive outcomes or relaxing.
In another experiment, on a tracing task that demanded focus and accuracy, defensive pessimists were 29 percent more accurate when they
were not encouraged than when they were told they would probably do
very well. (Those same words of encouragement boosted the performance of strategic optimists by 14 percent.) And in preparing a mental
math test that required adding and subtracting in their heads (calcula-
tions like $23 - 68 + 51$), defensive pessimists scored about 25 percent
higher when they made a list of the worst things that could happen in the
test and how they would feel than when they distracted themselves.

"Defensive pessimism is a strategy used in specific situations to
manage anxiety, fear, and worry," Norem explains. When self-doubts
creep in, defensive pessimists don't allow themselves to be crippled by
fear. They deliberately imagine a disaster scenario to intensify their
anxiety and convert it into motivation. Once they've considered the
worst, they're driven to avoid it, considering every relevant detail to
make sure they don't crash and burn, which enables them to feel a
sense of control. Their anxiety reaches its zenith before the event, so
that when it arrives, they're ready to succeed. Their confidence springs
not from ignorance or delusions about the difficulties ahead, but from
a realistic appraisal and an exhaustive plan. When they don't feel

anxious, they become complacent; when encouraged, they become discouraged from planning. If you want to sabotage the performance of chronic defensive pessimists, just make them happy.

Lewis Pugh was usually an optimist; he saw possibilities where others wouldn't and persevered when others would give up. But in the weeks before major swims, he often operated like a defensive pessimist. Much of his inspiration came not from the high expectations of his own team, but from the discouragement of doubters. Two years earlier, when gearing up for his record-breaking northern swim, he had been fueled by an outdoorsman telling him it was impossible and he would die. Before another big swim, he reminded himself of skeptics and imagined them gloating to their friends that he couldn't achieve it. "Being the first to undertake a swim is exponentially harder than going second. You don't know what will happen. The fear can be crippling," he writes.

As Pugh stood shaking at the North Pole, his instincts warned him of "the calamity that was about to unfold." But instead of trying to cheer up, he found that his negative thinking "shows where things can go wrong, and it gets rid of complacency." Considering the worst-case scenario impelled him to prepare thoroughly and mitigate against every single possible risk.* He started formulating plans to spend less time on the ice before the swim and return to the boat immediately afterward. "The trick is to make fear your friend," he notes. "Fear forces you to prepare more rigorously and see potential problems more quickly." That was an important step, but it wasn't enough to keep him going. As you'll see, defensive pessimism is a valuable resource when commitment to the task is steadfast. But when commitment flutters, anxiety and doubt can backfire.

---

* Research shows that when American presidents' inaugural addresses feature positive thoughts about the future, employment rates and gross domestic product decline during their terms in office. When presidents are too optimistic, the economy gets worse. Negative thoughts can direct our attention to potential problems, and the absence of those thoughts predicts a failure to take preventative and corrective actions.

Don't Stop Believin'

When ordinary people list their fears, one tends to be more common than death: public speaking. As Jerry Seinfeld jokes, "If you have to go to a funeral, you're better off in the casket than doing the eulogy."

If we want to understand how to manage fear, we don't have to threaten people's lives; we need only threaten to put them on stage. Alison Wood Brooks, a professor at Harvard Business School, asked college students to deliver a persuasive speech on why they would make good collaborators at work. A critical experimenter sat in the audience, and all the speeches were videotaped. A committee of peers would be enlisted later to evaluate each speaker's persuasiveness and confidence. With only two minutes to prepare, many of the students were visibly shaking.

If you were in this situation, how would you manage your fear? When Brooks asked three hundred working Americans to offer advice on this matter, the most popular recommendation was "Try to relax and calm down." This is the most obvious suggestion, favored by more than 90 percent of professionals. Yet it isn't the best one.

Before the college students gave their speeches, Brooks asked them to speak three words out loud. She randomly assigned them to say either "I am calm" or "I am excited."

That one word—*calm* versus *excited*—was sufficient to significantly alter the quality of their speeches. When students labeled their emotions as excitement, their speeches were rated as 17 percent more persuasive and 15 percent more confident than those of students who branded themselves calm. Reframing fear as excitement also motivated the speakers, boosting the average length of their speeches by 29 percent; they had the courage to spend an extra thirty-seven seconds on stage. In another experiment, when students were nervous before taking a tough math test, they scored 22 percent better if they were told "Try to get excited" instead of "Try to remain calm."

But is reframing fear as excitement the best way to cope with nerves? To find out whether it's better to just acknowledge anxiety, Brooks gave students another frightening task: She asked them to sing eighties rock music in public.

Standing in front of a group of peers, students belted out the Journey song "Don't Stop Believin'" into a microphone. A voice recognition program on the Nintendo Wii automatically scored their performance on an accuracy scale from 0 to 100 percent, assessing volume, pitch, and note duration. They would earn a bonus for high scores. Before they started singing, she randomly assigned the students to say "I am anxious" or "I am excited."

A control group who said nothing prior to performing averaged an accuracy score of 69 percent. Labeling the emotion as anxiety reduced accuracy to 53 percent. Instead of helping them accept fear, it reinforced that they were afraid. Calling it excitement was enough to spike accuracy to 80 percent.

To overcome fear, why does getting excited work better than trying to calm yourself down? Fear is an intense emotion: You can feel your heart pumping and your blood coursing. In that state, trying to relax is like slamming on the brakes when a car is going 80 miles per hour. The vehicle still has momentum. Rather than trying to suppress a strong emotion, it's easier to convert it into a different emotion—one that's equally intense, but propels us to step on the gas.

Physiologically, we have a stop system and a go system. "Your stop system slows you down and makes you cautious and vigilant," explains *Quiet* author Susan Cain. "Your go system revs you up and makes you excited." Instead of hitting the stop switch, we can motivate ourselves to act in the face of fear by pressing the go switch. Fear is marked by uncertainty about the future: We're worried that something bad will happen. But because the event hasn't occurred yet, there's also a possibility, however slim, that the outcome will be positive. We can step on the gas by focusing on the reasons to move forward—the sliver of excitement that we feel about breaking loose and singing our song.

When we're not yet committed to a particular action, thinking like a defensive pessimist can be hazardous. Since we don't have our hearts set on charging ahead, envisioning a dismal failure will only activate anxiety, triggering the stop system and slamming our brakes. By looking on the bright side, we'll activate enthusiasm and turn on the go system.

But once we've settled on a course of action, when anxieties creep in, it's better to think like a defensive pessimist and confront them directly. In this case, instead of attempting to turn worries and doubts into positive emotions, we can shift the go system into higher gear by embracing our fear. Since we've set our minds to press forward, envisioning the worst-case scenario enables us to harness anxiety as a source of motivation to prepare and succeed. Neuroscience research suggests that when we're anxious, the unknown is more terrifying than the negative. As Julie Norem describes it, once people have imagined the worst, "they feel more in control. In some sense, they've peaked in anxiety before their actual performance. By the time they get to the event itself they've taken care of almost everything."

In every previous cold-water swim, Lewis Pugh had the unshakable conviction that he could succeed, so the defensive pessimist strategy was effective: analyzing the potential hazards left him as prepared as possible. At the North Pole, that approach worked initially, but after the disastrous test swim, "[m]y belief system was splintered. . . . If five minutes in this water had caused so much pain and damage to my hands, what would twenty minutes do?" He couldn't shake the fear that the swim could be deadly: "What I felt on that stupid test swim wasn't like anything I'd felt before. I don't believe I can do this."

With his commitment wavering, it was time to shift away from defensive pessimism and activate the go system by focusing on the reasons to do the swim. A friend gave him three ideas to get excited: First, they would plant national flags at key markers along the way to remind Pugh of the twenty-nine people from ten countries who helped make the swim possible. In earlier swims, Pugh had been "motivated by those who doubted you," but now, his friend said, he should "focus on those people who believe in you, who have inspired you." Second, he should look back and remember how his parents inspired him to care about protecting the environment. And third, he should look ahead and think of the legacy he could establish to fight climate change. "After listening to him, the idea of abandoning the swim disappeared," Pugh reflects. He dove into the frigid water and started swimming against the current. Eighteen minutes and fifty seconds later, he successfully finished—and sustained no physical damage. Three years after that, he swam across the highest lake on Mount Everest.

Whereas Pugh's biggest hurdle was regulating his own fear, many originals have to manage other people's emotions. When others are afraid to act, how can we activate their go systems?

In the summer of 2009, fifteen young tourists made a pilgrimage to Belgrade, the capital of Serbia. After walking them around the city's square, the tour guide, a lanky Serbian in his midthirties, regaled them with stories about the country's recent history of inflated potato prices, free rock concerts, and wars with neighboring countries. But as the guide sprinkled his comments about Serbia with references to Monty Python humor and Tolkien fantasies, the tourists grew impatient. They weren't just an ordinary group of travelers. They had come to Belgrade to learn how to overthrow their own country's dictator.

Searching for a way to fight back against a tyrant, they asked the tour guide about how his countrymen had defeated the Serbian dictator Slobodan Milosevic. You don't need to take big risks, the guide told them. You can demonstrate your resistance in small ways—drive slower than usual, throw Ping-Pong balls onto the streets, or put food coloring in fountains to make the water look different. The foreigners scoffed at his advice: such trivial actions wouldn't make a dent in an iron curtain. It can never happen in our country, a man insisted. If we stand up to him, a woman challenged, our dictator will simply make us vanish. How can we even plan a revolution, when he has made it illegal to gather in groups of more than three?

They didn't know it, but the tour guide had heard all these objections before. He heard them in 2003 from Georgian activists, in 2004 from Ukrainian activists, in 2005 from Lebanese activists, and in 2008 from Maldivian activists. In each case, they overcame fear and apathy and took down their respective dictators.

The tour guide, Srdja Popovic, had trained them all.

Popovic was one of the masterminds behind Otpor!, the grassroots youth nonviolence movement that overthrew Milosevic. A decade earlier, he had suffered through ethnic cleansing and martial law, and gaped in horror as his mother's building was bombed. He was arrested, jailed, and beaten; his life flashed before his eyes when an officer of the law jammed a pistol into his mouth.

When psychologist Dan McAdams and his colleagues asked adults to tell their life stories and plotted their emotional trajectories over time, they discovered two different desirable patterns. Some people had consistently pleasant experiences: they were content throughout the major periods of their lives. The people who had been recognized for making original contributions to their communities shared many more stories that started negatively but surged upward: they struggled early and triumphed only later. Despite being confronted with more negative events, they reported greater satisfaction with their lives and a stronger sense of purpose. Instead of merely enjoying good fortune all along, they endured the battle of turning bad things good—and judged it as a more rewarding route to a life well lived. Originality brings more bumps in the road, yet it leaves us with more happiness and a greater sense of meaning. "Proper revolutions are not cataclysmic explosions," Popovic observes. "They are long, controlled burns."

After working with friends to lead the movement that toppled Milosevic and brought democracy to Serbia, Popovic dedicated his life to preparing activists to lead nonviolent revolutions. In 2010, the fifteen foreigners he trained a year earlier used his methods to overthrow the Egyptian dictator. Not every group has succeeded, but we can learn a lot from Popovic's approaches to conquering fear, overcoming apathy, and channeling anger. His first step mirrors how a technology leader dealt with fear among his employees.

Outsourcing Inspiration

When Josh Silverman took the reins of Skype in February 2008, the company was facing significant challenges. Employee morale was plummeting as the company was failing to maintain the explosive growth that Skype had experienced after pioneering free computer-to-computer calls and cheap long-distance calls between phones and computers. Silverman decided to make a big bet on an original feature: full-screen video calls. In April, he announced a moon-shot goal to release Skype 4.0 with the video feature by the end of the year. "The emotion among many employees was passionately negative. A lot of people thought it was too big a change, and we were going to kill the company," Silverman recalls. They worried that the timeline was too short, video quality would be poor, and users would hate a full-screen format.

Instead of trying to calm them down, Silverman decided to psych them up by developing a Skype vision that would get them inspired about video. At a series of all-hands meetings, he emphasized the impact of the product on people's lives, articulating a vision that he later formalized during a conversation with actor and technology investor Ashton Kutcher. "It's not about making cheap phone calls. It's about being together when you're not in the same room."

When originals come up with a vision for transforming anxiety into excitement, they usually take it upon themselves to communicate it. But just because it's your idea doesn't mean you're the best person to activate the go system. In a series of experiments, Dave Hofmann and I found that the most inspiring way to convey a vision is to outsource it to the people who are actually affected by it. Consider university fund-raisers, who are often extremely nervous about calling alumni, interrupting their dinners, and asking them to donate money. When two leaders spoke passionately to them about how the money they were being asked to solicit would make a difference, the callers didn't become any more effective.

The amount of money the average caller raised more than tripled, however, when leaders outsourced inspiration to a scholarship student, who described how the callers' efforts had enabled him to afford university tuition and study abroad in China. On average, callers went from raising under $2,500 in the two weeks before the student spoke to over $9,700 in the two weeks after.* They were suspicious of the leaders, who clearly had the ulterior motive of convincing them to work harder. When the same message came from a scholarship student, they found

---

* We wanted to prove that even when the message was held constant, it would be more effective when it was delivered by a beneficiary than by a leader. So in our next experiment, we asked people to edit a paper by an international graduate student that contained many minor grammatical errors. We explained that it was for a program that existed to help these students improve their papers so that they could obtain jobs. To provide an example of how the editing could make a difference, we randomly assigned participants to watch one of two versions of a video clip of the same woman speaking about a student who had received three job offers as a direct result of the program's editing help. She introduced herself as Priya Patel, either the director in charge of the program or the student who benefited from the program. Seeing the leader speak about the impact of the program didn't make a difference: on average, that group spotted fewer than twenty-five errors, the same as a control group who didn't see the video at all. But when she described herself as a student who benefited from the program, they caught an average of thirty-three errors—a boost of 34 percent. We also gave them a chance to write open-ended comments to the student, and had independent coders rate how constructive and helpful they were. The comments were 21 percent better when they saw the beneficiary video than the leader video.

it more authentic, honest, and truthful. They empathized with the student, and instead of being anxious about asking for money, they were excited to solicit donations to help more students like him.

This doesn't mean, though, that leaders need to step out of the picture altogether. In later studies, I found that people are inspired to achieve the highest performance when leaders describe a vision and then invite a customer to bring it to life with a personal story. The leader's message provides an overarching vision to start the car, and the user's story offers an emotional appeal that steps on the accelerator.

At Skype, Josh Silverman knew the best way to activate the go system wasn't through his words alone. After talking about how Skype enabled his own children to have a deep personal relationship with their grandparents despite living eight time zones apart, he breathed life into the vision by giving the floor to Skype users as a regular feature of his all-hands meetings. A married couple shared how they survived a yearlong separation during their engagement "only thanks to daily talks on Skype." A serviceman spoke about how Skype had allowed him to maintain a close relationship with his children while serving in Iraq; they even opened Christmas presents together. "Bringing the customer into the room connected them to the mission, and reached their hearts and minds," Silverman says. "It helped employees see what a difference we could make in the world."

As they grasped that Skype was about connecting people, the team's anxiety gave way to excitement. Inspired to build a video feature that would enable more meaningful conversations, they shipped Skype 4.0 on schedule with high-quality, full-screen video calls. Soon, Skype was adding about 380,000 users per day; by the end of the last quarter of the year, more than a third of the 36.1 billion computer-to-computer minutes spent on Skype were video calls. Less than three years after Silverman shared his vision and brought in users to inspire the team, Microsoft bought Skype for $8.5 billion, a 300 percent climb in value.

In Serbia, Srdja Popovic and his friends launched the Otpor! revolution by outsourcing inspiration. They knew that the words of a charismatic leader wouldn't suffice to overcome the terror inflicted by a violent dictator. Many qualified candidates were too afraid to put their lives on the line, and even if one could be found, Milosevic could squash the resistance by making that brave soul disappear. So, instead of appointing a leader to activate the go system, Popovic outsourced inspiration to a symbol: a black clenched fist.

The effort began in the fall of 1998, when Popovic and his friends were college students. They spray painted three hundred clenched fists around the town square and plastered stickers of the image throughout buildings in Belgrade. Without that fist, he says, the revolution would never have happened.

In the spring of 2010, a year after training the Egyptian activists, Popovic stopped cold in front of a newspaper stand. The clenched fist of Otpor! was featured on a front page, pictured on a poster held by a woman under the headline "The Fist Shakes Cairo!" The Egyptian activists had chosen to galvanize their own go systems by outsourcing inspiration to the same symbol. What made the fist so energizing?

Strength in Small Numbers

In a classic experiment, psychologist Solomon Asch asked people to judge the lengths of different lines. Imagine that you're brought into a room with seven other people and are shown the following images:

Your task is to look at the line on the left and decide whether line A, B, or C is the same length. The correct answer is obviously B, and everyone in the group provides it. You all agree in the next round, too. Then comes the third trial:

The right answer in this case is clearly C. But strangely, the first person in your group insists it's B. You're stunned when the second person picks B as well. The third and fourth group members call out B, too. What would you do?

The other people in your group are confederates in cahoots with the research team. There are eighteen trials in total, and the others have been instructed to intentionally give the wrong answer on twelve of them, to determine if you'll go against your better judgment and follow the majority. Over a third of the time, participants conformed: They chose the line they knew didn't match just because the rest of the group did. Three quarters of participants conformed at least once with a wrong answer.

When they were tested alone, people virtually never erred. When they went along with the group, they knew they were giving an incorrect answer, but they were afraid of being ridiculed. It doesn't take a violent dictator to silence us through fear. Just flying solo with an opinion can make even a committed original fearful enough to conform to the majority.

The easiest way to encourage non-conformity is to introduce a single dissenter. As entrepreneur Derek Sivers put it, "The first follower is what transforms a lone nut into a leader." If you were sitting with seven other people and six group members picked the wrong answer, but the remaining one chose the correct answer, conformity dropped dramatically. Errors fell from 37 percent to just 5.5 percent. "The presence of a supporting partner depleted the majority of much of its pressure," Asch wrote.

Merely knowing that you're not the only resister makes it substantially easier to reject the crowd. Emotional strength can be found even in small numbers. In the words of Margaret Mead, "Never doubt that a small group of thoughtful citizens can change the world; indeed, it's the only thing that ever has." To feel that you're not alone, you don't need a whole crowd to join you. Research by Sigal Barsade and Hakan Ozcelik shows that in business and government organizations, just having one friend is enough to significantly decrease loneliness.

If you want people to go out on a limb, you need to show them that they're not alone. That was the first key to the success of Otpor! and a number of other revolutions. When Popovic and his friends displayed the fist around Belgrade, they included slogans like "Resistance, because I love Serbia," "Bite the system," and "Resistance until victory!" Prior to that, Serbians who privately opposed Milosevic's dictatorship feared expressing their disapproval in public. But when they saw the Otpor! fist, they realized that others were willing to step forward. Later, when members of the movement were arrested, police officers asked them who was in charge. Popovic and his friends trained them to introduce themselves as "one of 20,000 leaders of Otpor!"

Around the world, resistance movements have helped people overcome fear by turning on the go system with small actions that signal the support of a larger group. When Popovic trained the Egyptian activists, he shared a story from 1983 of how Chilean miners had mounted a protest against the country's dictator, Pinochet. Instead of taking the risk of going on strike, they issued a nationwide call for citizens to demonstrate their resistance by turning their lights on and off. People weren't afraid to do that, and soon they saw that their neighbors weren't, either. The miners also invited people to start driving slowly. Taxi drivers slowed down; so did bus drivers. Soon, pedestrians were walking in slow motion down the streets and driving their cars and trucks at a glacial pace. In his inspiring book *Blueprint for Revolution*, Popovic explains that prior to these activities:

> *People were afraid to talk openly about despising Pinochet, so if you hated the dictator, you might have imagined that you were the only one. Tactics like these, Chileans used to say, made people realize that "we are the many and they are the few." And the beauty was that there was no risk involved: Not even in North Korea was it illegal for cars to drive slowly.*

In Poland, when activists objected to government lies dominating the news, they knew that simply turning off their televisions wouldn't show their fellow citizens that they were ready to stand in protest. Instead, they put their TV sets in wheelbarrows and pushed them around the streets. Soon, it was happening in towns throughout Poland—and the opposition eventually won power. In Syria, activists poured red food-coloring in fountains around the squares of Damascus, symbolizing that citizens would not accept the bloody rule of their dictator, Assad. Instead of facing the terror of standing out as lone resisters, people were able to see themselves as members of a group. It's easier to rebel when it feels like an act of conformity. Other people are involved, so we can join, too.

In Serbia, Otpor! found an ingenious way to activate the go system. The country was in such dire straits that excitement wasn't an easy emotion to cultivate. Popovic and his friends were able to transform fear into another strong positive emotion: hilarity. Flouting the solemn, resolute demeanor of great moral leaders like Gandhi, Otpor! used humor to attract allies and subvert enemies. They sent birthday presents to Milosevic: a one-way ticket to the Hague to be tried for his war crimes, handcuffs, and a prison uniform. To celebrate the lunar eclipse, they invited downtown shoppers to gaze into a telescope, which showed an eclipse of Milosevic's face. Later, Otpor! produced a commercial with Milosevic's image on a T-shirt. "I've been trying to clean this stain for ten years," a woman said, standing next to a washing machine. "Believe me, I've tried everything. But now there is a new machine. It has a great program which . . . permanently cleans this and similar stains." In another case, as a crowd gathered, an Otpor! activist grabbed a microphone and announced:

We are here reporting from in front of the Niš police station. And here is an example of a terrorist, on the border between Serbia and Montenegro. The terrorist is about six feet tall, and he is wearing a T-shirt of the terrorist organization Otpor! He is wearing eyeglasses, which means he reads a lot. It's dangerous to read a lot in this country, so beware.

In his workshops, Popovic trains revolutionaries to use humor as a weapon against fear. Not long after he spent some time with the Egyptian activists, an image began to spread around Egypt—a parody of a Microsoft Windows program installation:

It was accompanied by an error message:

As the image gained popularity, fear slowly faded. It's hard to be afraid of speaking up when you're laughing at the target of your rebellion.

Effective displays of humor are what Popovic calls dilemma actions: choices that put oppressors in a lose-lose situation. In Syria, activists emblazoned slogans like "Freedom" and "Enough" on thousands of Ping-Pong balls and dumped them onto the streets of Damascus. When they heard the sound of the bouncing balls, Popovic observes, the people of Syria knew "the nonviolent opposition was sticking its finger into the eye of Assad's regime." Soon enough the police showed up. "Huffing and puffing, these guys scoured the capital, scooping up Ping-Pong balls one by one. What the police didn't seem to realize," Popovic explains, "was that in this slapstick comedy, the Ping-Pong balls were just the props. It was they themselves, the regime's enforcers, who had been cast to star as the clowns."

It's easy to see how this kind of humor thrives against dictators, who don't take kindly to jokes. But it can work in ordinary environments, too. Stanford professor Robert Sutton describes a group of young surgeons who regularly endured verbal abuse from attending surgeons. They were treated so poorly that they began to elect an "Attending *sshole of the Week," who became known as the AAOTW. Every Friday at a happy hour, they would nominate candidates and vote for a winner. They so despised one particular surgeon that they set a rule: in the event of a tie, he would win—even if he wasn't a finalist that week. They recorded the names of the biggest offenders in a leather-bound journal and wrote a summary of the behaviors that qualified the contestants for the top spot among the losers. The humor made surgeons' behavior less demoralizing and eventually dampened the young doctors' fear; they worked up the courage to pass the journal along to the entering chief resident each year. Twenty years later, the journal is still in use by residents at the hospital. The surgeons who created it have themselves climbed to positions of power at hospitals around the country, vowing not to perpetrate or tolerate the kind of treatment to which they had been subjected.

Popovic sees a role for amusement wherever fear runs rampant. Instead of trying to decelerate the stop system, he uses laughter to rev up the go system. When you have no power, it's a powerful way to convert strong negative emotions into positive ones. In one of his workshops, students were up in arms over the exorbitant price of tuition at their university. After hearing Popovic's stories, they proposed to approach the university president, show him pictures of their ramen-only diet, and invite themselves to weekly dinners at his house. Popovic smiled and nodded in approval: whether they went ahead with the campaign or not, he had taught them how to fight fear with humor. If the president didn't welcome them for dinner, Popovic suggested, they ought to at least ask for his leftovers.*

But then he had a more somber message to deliver: The struggle for freedom is not all roses and unicorns. On the surface, Srdja Popovic is the picture of an optimist. When others were living in apathy, he envisioned a better future for Serbia. When others were crippled by fear, he brought laughter, and was hopeful enough to believe that a group of students could defeat a formidable dictator. But when I asked whether his confidence was ever shaken, he immediately said yes. "Did I feel self-doubt? Always, for ten years." Even today, having led a successful revolution and trained so many activists to unseat dictators, he thinks about the lives lost in those movements and feels responsible for not having taught them enough.

It's one thing to motivate people to push a TV in the streets. Giving

---

* When we're dealing with anxiety, excitement and amusement aren't the only positive emotions that can activate the go system. When Elvis Presley had his personnel file created by the U.S. military, government clerks completed the forms using manual typewriters. By the 1980s, the IBM Selectric had replaced the antiquated manual typewriters, but little else had changed. When it came time to automate the process with desktop computers, the government employees responsible for completing these forms were already anxious that computers would eventually replace their jobs. Instead of trying to calm them down or reassure them, leaders activated the go system by evoking curiosity. They plunked the computers down on their desks right next to their trusted typewriters and simply announced that a test program would take place later; they didn't even plug them in. After about a week they installed a few simple games and encouraged the clerks to try them out in their free time. The clerks were so intrigued that a few months later, when they started their official training, they had already taught themselves some of the key operations. As Brian Goshen, one of the leaders involved at the time, recalls: "By the time we were ready to start, they weren't afraid of it anymore; they were comfortable with the newer technology."

them the courage to take more meaningful action is a much greater challenge. When I asked Popovic how originals can activate the go system to mobilize a more substantial effort, he replied that we usually do it wrong.

The Burning Platform

On New Year's Eve in 2000, Popovic and his friends organized a celebration in Republic Square. They lined up the hottest Serbian rock bands and spread the word that midnight would feature a live concert by the Red Hot Chili Peppers—an international sensation and a huge hit in Serbia. Thousands of people packed the square in Belgrade, dancing to the local bands and buzzing with anticipation about the main event. One minute before midnight, the square went dark and people began counting down. But when the clock struck twelve, no famous rock band appeared.

The only audible sound was depressing music. As the audience listened in shock, a psychologist named Boris Tadic delivered a clear message from behind the stage. "We have nothing to celebrate," he said, asking them to go home and think about what action they would take. "This year has been a year of war and oppression. But it doesn't have to be that way. Let's make the coming year count. Because 2000 is *the* year."

Research by management professors Lynne Andersson and Thomas Bateman sheds light on the impact of that gesture. In a study of hundreds of managers and employees who championed environmental issues at their companies, the successful campaigns didn't differ from the failures in the amount of emotion they expressed, their use of metaphors or logical arguments, their efforts to consult key stakeholders, or their framing of a green movement as an opportunity or threat. The distinguishing factor was a sense of urgency. To convince leaders to sponsor the issue, create a task force, and spend time and money on it, the environmental champions had to articulate why the original cause needed to be adopted *now*.

When Harvard professor John Kotter studied more than one hundred companies trying to institute major changes, he found that the first error they made was failing to establish a sense of urgency. Over 50 percent of leaders fell short of convincing their employees that change needed to happen, and it needed to happen now. "Executives underestimate how hard it can be to drive people out of their comfort zones," Kotter writes. "Without a sense of urgency, people ... won't make needed sacrifices. Instead they cling to the status quo and resist." Otpor! conveyed urgency with slogans like "It's time" and "He's finished." When they announced, "This is *the* year," it was clear to the Serbians that there was a pressing need to act immediately.

To further illuminate the effectiveness of an act like sending everyone home on New Year's Eve, let's take a look at a piece of research that transformed one field, spawned another, and ultimately won a Nobel Prize. Imagine that you're an executive at a car manufacturer, and due to economic challenges, you need to close three plants and lay off six thousand employees. You can choose between two different plans:

Plan A will save one of the three plants and two thousand jobs.

Plan B has a one-third chance of saving all three plants and all six thousand jobs, but a two-thirds chance of saving no plants and no jobs.

Most people prefer Plan A. In the original study, 80 percent chose to play it safe rather than take a chance. But suppose we gave you a different set of options:

Plan A will lose two of the three plants and four thousand jobs.

Plan B has a two-thirds chance of losing all three plants and all six thousand jobs, but a one-third chance of losing no plants and no jobs.

Logically, these are the same options as the first set of choices. But psychologically, they don't feel the same. In the latter option, 82 percent of people prefer Plan B. Their preferences reverse.

In the first case, the options are framed as gains. We prefer Plan A because we tend to be risk averse in the domain of benefits. When we have a certain gain, we like to hold on to it and protect it. We play it safe to guarantee saving two thousand jobs instead of taking a risk that might leave us saving no jobs. After all, a bird in the hand is worth two in the bush.

But in the second case, we're presented with a guaranteed loss. Now, we're willing to do whatever it takes to avoid that loss, even if it means risking an even bigger one. We're going to lose thousands of jobs anyway, so we throw caution to the wind and make the big gamble, hoping that we'll lose nothing.

This line of research was conducted by psychologists Amos Tversky and Daniel Kahneman; it helped give rise to the field of behavioral economics and win Kahneman a Nobel Prize. It revealed that we can dramatically shift risk preferences just by changing a few words to emphasize losses rather than gains. This knowledge has major implications for understanding how to motivate people to take risks.

If you want people to modify their behavior, is it better to highlight the benefits of changing or the costs of not changing? According to Peter Salovey, one of the originators of the concept of emotional intelligence and now the president of Yale, it depends on whether they perceive the new behavior as safe or risky. If they think the behavior is safe, we should emphasize all the good things that will happen if they do it—they'll want to act immediately to obtain those certain gains. But when people believe a behavior is risky, that approach doesn't work. They're already comfortable with the status quo, so the benefits of change aren't attractive, and the stop system kicks in. Instead, we need to destabilize the status quo and accentuate the bad things that will happen if they don't change. Taking a risk is more appealing when they're faced with a guaranteed loss if they don't. The prospect of a certain loss brings the go system online.

At the pharmaceutical giant Merck, CEO Kenneth Frazier decided to motivate his executives to take a more active role in leading innovation and change. He asked them to do something radical: generate ideas that would put Merck out of business.

For the next two hours, the executives worked in groups, pretending to be one of Merck's top competitors. Energy soared as they developed ideas for drugs that would crush theirs and key markets they had missed. Then, their challenge was to reverse their roles and figure out how to defend against these threats.*

This "kill the company" exercise is powerful because it reframes a gain-framed activity in terms of losses. When deliberating about innovation opportunities, the leaders weren't inclined to take risks. When they considered how their competitors could put them out of business, they realized that it was a risk *not* to innovate. The urgency of innovation was apparent.

To counter apathy, most change agents focus on presenting an inspiring vision of the future. This is an important message to convey, but it's not the type of communication that should come first. If you want people to take risks, you need first to show what's wrong with the present. To drive people out of their comfort zones, you have to cultivate dissatisfaction, frustration, or anger at the current state of affairs, making it a guaranteed loss. "The greatest communicators of all time," says communication expert Nancy Duarte—who has spent her career studying the shape of superb presentations—start by establishing "what is: here's the status quo." Then, they "compare that to what could be," making "that gap as big as possible."

We can see this sequence in two of the most revered speeches in American history. In his famous inaugural address, President Franklin D.

---

* The exercise capitalizes on a psychological difference between playing defense and playing offense. In studying counterterrorism teams in the intelligence community, Carnegie Mellon professor Anita Woolley finds that when teams are on defense, they tend to play it safe, attempting to protect against all competitive threats. They search for a lot of information, but can end up overwhelmed, with confidence waning. When teams are on offense, they consider many creative possibilities, but then drill down into one or two plans of attack.

Roosevelt opened by acknowledging the current state of affairs. Promising to "speak the whole truth, frankly and boldly," he described the dire straits of the Great Depression, only then turning to what could be, unveiling his hope of creating new jobs and forecasting, "This great nation . . . will revive and will prosper. . . . The only thing we have to fear is fear itself."

When we recall Martin Luther King, Jr.'s, epic speech, what stands out is a shining image of a brighter future. Yet in his 16-minute oration, it wasn't until the eleventh minute that he first mentioned his dream. Before delivering hope for change, King stressed the unacceptable conditions of the status quo. In his introduction, he pronounced that, despite the promise of the Emancipation Proclamation, "one hundred years later, the life of the Negro is still sadly crippled by the manacles of segregation and the chains of discrimination."

Having established urgency through depicting the suffering that was, King turned to what could be: "But we refuse to believe that the bank of justice is bankrupt." He devoted more than two thirds of the speech to these one-two punches, alternating between what was and what could be by expressing indignation at the present and hope about the future. According to sociologist Patricia Wasielewski, "King articulates the crowd's feelings of anger at existing inequities," strengthening their "resolve that the situation must be changed." The audience was only prepared to be moved by his dream of tomorrow after he had exposed the nightmare of today.

Psychologists Minjung Koo and Ayelet Fishbach find that when we're experiencing doubts on the way toward achieving a goal, whether we ought to look backward or forward depends on our commitment. When our commitment is wavering, the best way to stay on track is to consider the progress we've already made. As we recognize what we've invested and attained, it seems like a waste to give up, and our confidence and commitment surge. In the early days of Otpor!, Srdja Popovic and his friends dealt with doubt and fear by helping people laugh and accumulate small wins. That way, they could look back and gain a sense of progress, which turned anxiety into enthusiasm and secured their dedication.

Once commitment is fortified, instead of glancing in the rearview mirror, it's better to look forward by highlighting the work left to be done. When we're determined to reach an objective, it's the gap between where we are and where we aspire to be that lights a fire under us. In Serbia, as the Otpor! movement drew a loyal following that was no longer frozen in fear, it was time to show them how much distance they had yet to travel.

That's why Popovic and his friends halted the concert and sent the citizens of Belgrade home on New Year's Eve. In the span of less than two years, Otpor! had accumulated more than 70,000 members in 130 different branches. But to actually overthrow Milosevic, they would need millions of votes. A few years earlier, Milosevic had agreed to a relatively democratic election—and won. His minions controlled the ballot boxes. Even if Serbians could vote him out of office, would he concede? Popovic and his allies understood that they needed intense emotions to propel action across the country. It was time to destabilize the status quo and turn on the go system by reminding them that there was nothing to celebrate because the present was intolerable. "Instead of courage," management guru Tom Peters recommends fostering "a level of fury with the status quo such that one cannot not act."

The Show Must Go On

Anger counteracts apathy: We feel that we've been wronged, and we're compelled to fight. But it can also go too far. Anger doesn't just activate the go system; it drops a heavy brick on the gas pedal. It's a force that motivates people to speak up and act, but it can also make them less effective in doing so. After studying activists, Debra Meyerson and Maureen Scully suggest that the key is to be "simultaneously hot- and cool-headed. The heat fuels action and change; the coolness shapes the action and change into legitimate and viable forms." But once the heat is on, how do we keep our cool?

According to Berkeley sociologist Arlie Hochschild, if you're feeling an intense emotion like anxiety or anger, there are two ways to manage it: surface acting and deep acting. Surface acting involves putting on a mask—modifying your speech, gestures, and expressions to present yourself as unfazed. If you're a flight attendant, and an angry passenger begins yelling at you, you might smile to feign warmth. You're adjusting your outward appearance, but your internal state is unchanged. You're furious with the passenger, and the passenger probably knows it. Russian theater director Constantin Stanislavski observed that in surface acting, actors were never fully immersed in the role. They were always aware of the audience, and their performances never came across as authentic. Stanislavski wrote that surface acting "will neither warm your soul nor penetrate deeply into it . . . delicate and deep human feelings are not subject to such technique."

In deep acting, known as method acting in the theater world, you actually become the character you wish to portray. Deep acting involves changing your inner feelings, not just your outer expressions of them. If you're the flight attendant in the above example, you might imagine that the passenger is stressed, afraid of flying, or going through a messy divorce. You feel empathy for the passenger, and the smile comes naturally to you, creating a more genuine expression of warmth. Deep acting dissolves the distinction between your true self and the role you are playing. You are no longer acting, because you are actually experiencing the genuine feelings of the character.

Before Lewis Pugh embarks on a freezing swim, he engages in deep acting. While listening to songs by Eminem and P. Diddy, he calls up vivid memories of leaping out of an airplane from his days in the

British special forces. He is reliving the intense excitement he wants to experience again. The Oscar-winning actor Daniel Day-Lewis goes a step further. To prepare himself for a role in Arthur Miller's *The Crucible*, he built a house using seventeenth-century tools and lived with no running water or electricity. When he played a writer with cerebral palsy in *My Left Foot*, he spent the entire production process in a wheelchair, speaking in broken dialect and allowing crew members to feed him with a spoon. As an actor, he's ultimately still playing a character, but the purpose of deep acting is to feel the emotions he wants to display.

Deep acting turns out to be a more sustainable strategy for managing emotions than surface acting. Research shows that surface acting burns us out: Faking emotions that we don't really feel is both stressful and exhausting. If we want to express a set of emotions, we need to actually experience them.

When Srdja Popovic and his colleagues train activists, they teach deep acting through role-playing exercises. In the Maldives, for example, they had people play the parts of business leaders, hotel owners, island elders, expatriates in India, and police and security guards. This gave them the chance to anticipate how others would react and practice their own responses.

Fanning the Flame

Less than a year after Rosa Parks was arrested for refusing to sit in the back of a Montgomery bus, the Supreme Court outlawed segregation. To prepare citizens for the racial conflicts that might ensue on integrated buses, Martin Luther King, Jr., designed and delivered workshops for thousands of black Alabamans, working in concert with nonviolence experts like James Lawson, Bayard Rustin, and Glenn

Smiley. The team simulated a bus by setting up rows of chairs, and assigned about a dozen different audience members to play the driver and passengers. The "white passengers" called the black ones names. They spat on them, smashed gum and flicked cigarette ashes in their hair, dumped milk on their heads, and squirted ketchup and mustard in their faces.

In this deep-acting exercise, King wanted to make black citizens angry enough to stand in protest, but not so angry that they would resort to violence. What would be the best way to handle their anger? The most popular strategy for doing so is venting. Therapists advise us to blow off steam by hitting a pillow or screaming. By expressing our pent-up rage, Freud argued, we can relieve the pressure and find catharsis. In the movie *Analyze This*, Billy Crystal plays a psychiatrist tasked with helping mobster Robert De Niro manage his anger. Crystal recommends hitting a pillow, and De Niro grabs a gun, aims at a couch, and starts shooting at a pillow. Crystal, shaken, asks, "Feel better?" "Yeah," De Niro replies. "I do."

To test whether venting helps with managing anger, psychologist Brad Bushman designed a shrewd experiment to make people angry. The participants were asked to write an essay about whether they were against abortion or pro-choice. They then received some harsh written feedback from a peer with the opposite view, who rated their essays as disorganized, unoriginal, poorly written, unclear, unpersuasive, and low in quality, adding, "This is one of the worst essays I have read!"

The angry recipients were then randomly assigned to one of three responses: venting, distraction, or control. The members of the venting group were allowed to hit a punching bag as hard as they wanted for as long as they liked, while thinking about the jerk who criticized their essays and looking at his picture. The distraction group hit the punching bag but was instructed to think about becoming physically fit, and was shown a photo of someone exercising. In the control group, there was no punching bag; participants sat quietly for two minutes while the computer was being fixed. Which group would become the most aggressive toward the peer who insulted them?

To find out, Bushman gave each of the groups the chance to blast their essay's critic with noise, letting them determine the volume and duration of the sonic blasts.

The venting group was the most aggressive. They slammed the critic with more intense noise, and held the button down longer, than the distraction and control groups. One participant got so angry after thinking about the insulting feedback that hitting the punching bag wasn't enough: he punched a hole in the wall of the lab.

Venting doesn't extinguish the flame of anger; it feeds it. When we vent our anger, we put a lead foot on the gas pedal of the go system, attacking the target who enraged us. Hitting the punching bag without thinking of the target, though, keeps the go system on but enables us to consider alternative ways of responding. Sitting quietly begins to activate the stop system.*

In other studies, Bushman has demonstrated that venting doesn't work even if you think it does—and even if it makes you feel good. The better you feel after venting, the more aggressive you get: not only toward your critic, but also toward innocent bystanders.

Avoiding venting was a central theme in the training of activists

---

* Catharsis seems to work best once a certain period of time has passed. After the terrorist attacks of September 11, legions of more than nine thousand counselors descended upon New York, hoping to prevent post-traumatic stress and relieve symptoms of anxiety, depression, and grief. Psychologist Timothy Wilson describes how many of the counselors conducted critical incident stress debriefing, encouraging trauma victims and observers to spend several hours expressing their thoughts and feelings as soon as possible. Unfortunately, this didn't do much good for local citizens, firefighters, and other people close to the tragedy. In one study of people who suffered severe burns in a fire, those who went through critical incident stress debriefing had *higher* rates of post-traumatic stress disorder, depression, and anxiety more than a year later. Psychologist James Pennebaker has demonstrated that expressing our thoughts and feelings about a stressful or traumatic event is most salutary after we've had some time to process the event, when we're not blinded by anger or consumed by distress.

in the civil rights movement. Since nonviolent resistance depends on controlling anger, King and his colleagues made a concerted effort in their workshops to stop venting in its tracks. "Sometimes the person playing a white man put so much zeal into his performance that he had to be gently reproved from the sidelines," King reflected. In response, a citizen playing a black man often "forgot his nonviolent role and struck back with vigor; whenever this happened we worked to rechannel his words and deeds in a nonviolent direction." After every performance, the group provided feedback and suggestions for responding more constructively.

One of the fundamental problems with venting is that it focuses attention on the perpetrator of injustice. The more you think about the person who wronged you, the more violently you want to lash out in retaliation. "Anger is a powerful mobilizing tool," Srdja Popovic explains, "but if you make people angry, they might start breaking things." On New Year's Eve at midnight in 2000, when Otpor! shut down the concert, turned off the lights, and played sad music, only one sight was visible: a gigantic screen, on which a slide show of pictures was being played, none of which featured the despised Milosevic.

The images instead were of Serbian soldiers and police officers who had been killed under Milosevic's rule.

To channel anger productively, instead of venting about the harm that a perpetrator has done, we need to reflect on the victims who have suffered from it. Management researchers Andrew Brodsky, Joshua Margolis, and Joel Brockner find that focusing on the victims of injustice spurs us to speak truth to power. In one experiment, adults witnessed a CEO overpaying himself and underpaying a star employee. When they were prompted to focus on the employee who was treated unfairly, they were 46 percent more likely to challenge the CEO's payment decision.

In the civil rights movement, Martin Luther King, Jr., frequently called attention to victims of violence and injustice. "We are not out to defeat or humiliate the white man," he pronounced in a 1956 speech defending the Montgomery bus boycott, but to "free our children from a life of permanent psychological death." Focusing on the victim activates what psychologists call empathetic anger—the desire to right wrongs done unto another. It turns on the go system, but it makes us thoughtful about how to best respect the victim's dignity. Research demonstrates that when we're angry *at* others, we aim for retaliation or revenge. But when we're angry *for* others, we seek out justice and a better system. We don't just want to punish; we want to help.

When Otpor! displayed the images of dead soldiers, Serbians were pumped with empathetic adrenaline and broke out into a chant: "Let's make the coming year count." They weren't going to get excited about actually taking down their dictator, but they could feel enough righteous indignation that they were determined to do so. In Popovic's words, "There was an energy in the air that no rock band could ever re-create. Everybody felt that they had something important to do."

That autumn, Otpor! mobilized one of the largest voter turnouts in Serbia's history, defeating Milosevic and shepherding in a new era of democracy. Boris Tadic, the psychologist who had sent everyone home because there was nothing to celebrate, was elected president of Serbia four years later.

———

"I arise in the morning torn between a desire to improve the world and a desire to enjoy the world," E. B. White once wrote. "This makes it difficult to plan the day."

The Declaration of Independence promises Americans the unalienable rights to life, liberty, and the pursuit of happiness. In the quest for happiness, many of us choose to enjoy the world as it is. Originals embrace the uphill battle, striving to make the world what it could be. By struggling to improve life and liberty, they may temporarily give up some pleasure, putting their own happiness on the back burner. In the long run, though, they have the chance to create a better world. And that—to borrow a turn of phrase from psychologist Brian Little—brings a different kind of satisfaction. Becoming original is not the easiest path in the pursuit of happiness, but it leaves us perfectly poised for the happiness of pursuit.

Actions for Impact

If you're seeking to unleash originality, here are some practical actions that you can take. The first steps are for individuals to generate, recognize, voice, and champion new ideas. The next set is for leaders to stimulate novel ideas and build cultures that welcome dissent. The final recommendations are for parents and teachers to help children become comfortable taking a creative or moral stand against the status quo.

To gauge your originality with a free assessment, visit www.adamgrant.net.

Individual Actions:

A. Generating and Recognizing Original Ideas

1. ***Question the default.*** Instead of taking the status quo for granted, ask why it exists in the first place. When you remember that rules and systems were created by people, it becomes clear that they're not set in stone—and you begin to consider how they can be improved.

2. ***Triple the number of ideas you generate.*** Just as great baseball players only average a hit for every three at bats, every innovator swings and misses. The best way to boost your originality is to produce more ideas.

3. ***Immerse yourself in a new domain.*** Originality increases when you broaden your frame of reference. One approach is to learn a new craft, like the Nobel Prize–winning scientists who expanded their creative repertoires by taking up painting, piano, dance, or poetry. Another strategy is to try a job rotation: get trained to do a position that requires a new base of knowledge and skills. A third option is to learn about a different culture, like the fashion designers who became more innovative when they lived in foreign countries that were very different from their own. You don't need to go abroad to diversify your experience; you can immerse yourself in the culture and customs of a new environment simply by reading about it.

4. ***Procrastinate strategically.*** When you're generating new ideas, deliberately stop when your progress is incomplete. By taking a break in the middle of your brainstorming or writing process, you're more likely to engage in divergent thinking and give ideas time to incubate.

5. ***Seek more feedback from peers.*** It's hard to judge your own ideas, because you tend to be too enthusiastic, and you can't trust your gut if you're not an expert in the domain. It's also tough to rely on managers, who are typically too critical when they evaluate ideas. To get the most accurate reviews, run your pitches by peers—they're poised to spot the potential and the possibilities.

B. Voicing and Championing Original Ideas

6. ***Balance your risk portfolio.*** When you're going to take a risk in one domain, offset it by being unusually cautious in another realm of your life. Like the entrepreneurs who kept their day jobs

while testing their ideas, or Carmen Medina taking a job to protect against security leaks when she was pushing the CIA to embrace the internet, this can help you avoid unnecessary gambles.

7. ***Highlight the reasons not to support your idea.*** Remember Rufus Griscom, the entrepreneur in chapter 3 who told investors why they shouldn't invest in his company? You can do this, too. Start by describing the three biggest weaknesses of your idea and then ask them to list several more reasons not to support it. Assuming that the idea has some merit, when people have to work hard to generate their own objections, they will be more aware of its virtues.

8. ***Make your ideas more familiar.*** Repeat yourself—it makes people more comfortable with an unconventional idea. Reactions typically become more positive after ten to twenty exposures to an idea, particularly if they're short, spaced apart by a few days, and mixed in with other ideas. You can also make your original concept more appealing by connecting it with other ideas that are already understood by the audience—like when the *Lion King* script was reframed as *Hamlet* with lions.

9. ***Speak to a different audience.*** Instead of seeking out friendly people who share your values, try approaching disagreeable people who share your methods. In the U.S. Navy, a young aviator named Ben Kohlmann created a highly effective rapid-innovation cell by assembling a band of junior officers who had disciplinary actions brought against them for challenging authority. They had a history of principled dissent, and although they held different objectives, their habits of loyal opposition meshed well. Your best allies are the people who have a track record of being tough and solving problems with approaches similar to yours.

10. **Be a tempered radical.** If your idea is extreme, couch it in a more conventional goal. That way, instead of changing people's minds, you can appeal to values or beliefs that they already hold. You can use a Trojan horse, as Meredith Perry did when she masked her vision for wireless power behind a request to design a transducer. You can also position your proposal as a means to an end that matters to others, like Frances Willard reframing the right to vote as a way for conservative women to protect their homes from alcohol abuse. And if you're already known as too extreme, you can shift from leader to lightning rod, allowing more moderate people to take the reins.

C. Managing Emotions

11. **Motivate yourself differently when you're committed vs. uncertain.** When you're determined to act, focus on the progress left to go—you'll be energized to close the gap. When your conviction falters, think of the progress you've already made. Having come this far, how could you give up now?

12. **Don't try to calm down.** If you're nervous, it's hard to relax. It's easier to turn anxiety into intense positive emotions like interest and enthusiasm. Think about the reasons you're eager to challenge the status quo, and the positive outcomes that might result.

13. **Focus on the victim, not the perpetrator.** In the face of injustice, thinking about the perpetrator fuels anger and aggression. Shifting your attention to the victim makes you more empathetic, increasing the chances that you'll channel your anger in a constructive direction. Instead of trying to punish the people

who caused harm, you'll be more likely to help the people who were harmed.

14. ***Realize you're not alone.*** Even having a single ally is enough to dramatically increase your will to act. Find one person who believes in your vision and begin tackling the problem together.

15. ***Remember that if you don't take initiative, the status quo will persist.*** Consider the four responses to dissatisfaction: exit, voice, persistence, and neglect. Only exit and voice improve your circumstances. Speaking up may be the best route if you have some control over the situation; if not, it may be time to explore options for expanding your influence or leaving.

Leader Actions:

A. Sparking Original Ideas

1. ***Run an innovation tournament.*** Welcoming suggestions on any topic at any time doesn't capture the attention of busy people. Innovation tournaments are highly efficient for collecting a large number of novel ideas and identifying the best ones. Instead of a suggestion box, send a focused call for ideas to solve a particular problem or meet an untapped need. Give employees three weeks to develop proposals, and then have them evaluate one another's ideas, advancing the most original submissions to the next round. The winners receive a budget, a team, and the relevant mentoring and sponsorship to make their ideas a reality.

2. ***Picture yourself as the enemy.*** People often fail to generate new ideas due to a lack of urgency. You can create urgency by

implementing the "kill the company" exercise from Lisa Bodell, CEO of futurethink. Gather a group together and invite them to spend an hour brainstorming about how to put the organization out of business—or decimate its most popular product, service, or technology. Then, hold a discussion about the most serious threats and how to convert them into opportunities to transition from defense to offense.

3. ***Invite employees from different functions and levels to pitch ideas.*** At DreamWorks Animation, even accountants and lawyers are encouraged and trained to present movie ideas. This kind of creative engagement can add skill variety to work, making it more interesting for employees while increasing the organization's access to new ideas. And involving employees in pitching has another benefit: When they participate in generating ideas, they adopt a creative mindset that leaves them less prone to false negatives, making them better judges of their colleagues' ideas.

4. ***Hold an opposite day.*** Since it's often hard to find the time for people to consider original viewpoints, one of my favorite practices is to have "opposite day" in the classroom and at conferences. Executives and students divide into groups, and each chooses an assumption, belief, or area of knowledge that is widely taken for granted. Each group asks, "When is the opposite true?" and then delivers a presentation on their ideas.

5. ***Ban the words*** **like, love, *and* hate.** At the nonprofit DoSomething.org, CEO Nancy Lublin forbade employees from using the words *like, love,* and *hate,* because they make it too easy to give a visceral response without analyzing it. Employees aren't allowed to say they prefer one Web page over another; they have to explain their reasoning with statements like "This page

is stronger because the title is more readable than the other options." This motivates people to contribute new ideas rather than just rejecting existing ones.

B. Building Cultures of Originality

6. ***Hire not on cultural fit, but on cultural contribution.*** When leaders prize cultural fit, they end up hiring people who think in similar ways. Originality comes not from people who match the culture, but from those who enrich it. Before interviews, identify the diverse backgrounds, skill sets, and personality traits that are currently missing from your culture. Then place a premium on those attributes in the hiring process.

7. ***Shift from exit interviews to entry interviews.*** Instead of waiting to ask for ideas until employees are on their way out the door, start seeking their insights when they first arrive. By sitting down with new hires during onboarding, you can help them feel valued and gather novel suggestions along the way. Ask what brought them in the door and what would keep them at the firm, and challenge them to think like culture detectives. They can use their insider-outsider perspectives to investigate which practices belong in a museum and which should be kept, as well as potential inconsistencies between espoused and enacted values.

8. ***Ask for problems, not solutions.*** If people rush to answers, you end up with more advocacy than inquiry, and miss out on the breadth of knowledge in the room. Following Bridgewater's issue log, you can create an open document for teams to flag problems that they see. On a monthly basis, bring people together to review them and figure out which ones are worth solving.

9. ***Stop assigning devil's advocates and start unearthing them.***
Dissenting opinions are useful even when they're wrong, but
they're only effective if they're authentic and consistent. Instead
of assigning people to play the devil's advocate, find people
who genuinely hold minority opinions, and invite them to present their views. To identify these people, try appointing an
information manager—make someone responsible for seeking
out team members individually before meetings to find out what
they know.

10. ***Welcome criticism.*** It's hard to encourage dissent if you don't
practice what you preach. When Ray Dalio received an email
criticizing his performance in an important meeting, copying it
to the entire company sent a clear message that he welcomed
negative feedback. By inviting employees to criticize you publicly, you can set the tone for people to communicate more
openly even when their ideas are unpopular.

Parent and Teacher Actions:

1. ***Ask children what their role models would do.*** Children feel
free to take initiative when they look at problems through the
eyes of originals. Ask children what they would like to improve
in their family or school. Then have them identify a real person
or fictional character they admire for being unusually creative
and inventive. What would that person do in this situation?

2. ***Link good behaviors to moral character.*** Many parents and
teachers praise helpful actions, but children are more generous
when they're commended for being helpful people—it becomes

part of their identity. If you see a child do something good, try saying, "You're a good person because you ___." Children are also more ethical when they're asked to be moral people—they want to earn the identity. If you want a child to share a toy, instead of asking, "Will you share?" ask, "Will you be a sharer?"

3. ***Explain how bad behaviors have consequences for others.*** When children misbehave, help them see how their actions hurt other people. "How do you think this made her feel?" As they consider the negative impact on others, children begin to feel empathy and guilt, which strengthens their motivation to right the wrong—and to avoid the action in the future.

4. ***Emphasize values over rules.*** Rules set limits that teach children to adopt a fixed view of the world. Values encourage children to internalize principles for themselves. When you talk about standards, like the parents of the Holocaust rescuers, describe why certain ideals matter to you and ask children why they're important.

5. ***Create novel niches for children to pursue.*** Just as laterborns sought out more original niches when conventional ones were closed to them, there are ways to help children carve out niches. One of my favorite techniques is the Jigsaw Classroom: bring students together for a group project, and assign each of them a unique part. For example, when writing a book report on Eleanor Roosevelt's life, one student worked on her childhood, another on her teenage years, and a third on her role in the women's movement. Research shows that this reduces prejudice—children learn to value each other's distinctive strengths. It can also give them the space to consider original ideas instead of

falling victim to groupthink. To further enhance the opportunity for novel thinking, ask children to consider a different frame of reference. How would Roosevelt's childhood have been different if she grew up in China? What battles would she have chosen to fight there?

Acknowledgments

Writing a book was different the second time around. This time, I didn't throw away 103,000 words and start over from scratch—yet I was also more acutely aware that someone might actually read what I wrote, which left me second-guessing my taste. Thankfully, my wife, Allison, has an uncanny ability to recognize originality and quality (and also happens to possess the nose of a jungle cat). She instantly knew when a direction was worthwhile and when one stunk somethin' awful, Sookie. My writing would be significantly less fun without her. She patiently talked with me about every idea, lovingly read the first iteration of each chapter, and deftly reworded and reorganized multiple sections. Her standards are as high as can be, and when she was happy I knew I would be, too. This book would not exist without her passion as a writer and reader and her compassion as a wife and mother.

My agent Richard Pine, a true original, was indispensable in helping to develop the idea for this book and in providing sage advice at every step along the way. It was a treat to work with Rick Kot, who is more than an editor. Along with bringing rare levels of grace to enrich the content and thoughtfulness to refine the structure, he went to bat for this book as if it were his own child.

Sheryl Sandberg read every word with remarkable care and made the book dramatically better by sharpening the logic, style, and practical advice. She contributed more than I could have possibly imagined. Justin Berg endured countless chapter drafts and conversations, and provided just as many creative sparks to improve the substance and the narrative. Reb Rebele read the first full draft, giving his signature blend of deep questions and expert guidance on concepts and writing. Dan Pink racked up multiple assists for suggesting a chapter on timing, reminding me of the narcissism of small differences, and introducing me to one of the most fascinating people profiled.

I was fortunate to work with Alexis Hurley, Eliza Rothstein, and the rest of the InkWell team, and the dedicated group at Viking—particularly Carolyn Coleburn, Kristin Matzen, and Lindsay Prevette for publicity; Jane Cavolina, Diego Nunez, and Jeannette Williams for editing; and Pete Garceau, Jakub Gojda, Roseanne Serra, and Alissa Theodor for the cover and interior design. Jon Cohen and Sarah Cho at SurveyMonkey were swift, effective, and generous in designing and deploying a survey that allowed us to test different subtitles, as well as collect input about the cover design and concept.

The community of colleagues at Wharton—most notably Sigal Barsade, Drew Carton, Samir Nurmohamed, and Nancy Rothbard—has been invaluable. Special thanks to the Impact Lab and Lindsay Miller for their staunch enthusiasm. This project also benefited considerably from the support of Geoff Garrett, Mike Gibbons, Amy Gutmann, Dan Levinthal, and Nicolaj Siggelkow. For insights and introductions to people profiled or quoted in the book, I thank Jennifer Aaker, Teresa Amabile, Niko Canner, Rosanne Cash, Christine Choi, Kate Drane, Lisa Gevelber, David Hornik, Tom Hulme, Jimmy Kaltreider, Daphne Koller, John Michel, Andrew Ng, Bobby Turner, and Lauren Zalaznick.

I appreciate help with finding stories and examples from Josh Berman, Jesse Beyroutey, Wendy De La Rosa, Priti Joshi, Stacey Kalish, Victoria Sakal, and Jenny Wang, and for consistently generative feedback on chapter drafts from James An, Sarah Beckoff, Kelsey Gliva, Nicole Granet, Shlomo Klapper, Nick LoBuglio, Casey Moore, Nicole Pollack, Julianna Pillemer, Sreyas Raghavan, Anna Reighart, Eric Shapiro, Jacob Tupler, Danielle Tussing, and Kimberly Yao. For stimulating conversations about originals, I am grateful to Sue Ashford, Caroline Barlerin, Kipp Bradford, Danielle Celermajer, Annicken Day, Kathryn Dekas, Lisa Donchak, Angela Duckworth, Jane Dutton, Mike Feinberg, Anna Fraser, Malcolm Gladwell, Marc Grossman, Saar Gur, Julie Hanna, Emily Hunt, Karin Klein, Josh Kopelman, Stephanie Landry, Ellen Langer, Ryan Leirvik, Dave Levin, Tamar Lisbona, Brian Little, Nancy Lublin, Joshua Marcuse, Cade Massey, Deb Mills-Scofield, Sean Parker, Meredith Petrin, Phebe Port, Rick Price, Ben Rattray, Fred Rosen, Spencer Scharff, Nell Scovell, Scott Sherman, Phil Tetlock, Colleen Tucker, Jeanine Wright, and Amy Wrzesniewski. (Oh, and Stacy and Kevin Brand for requesting this acknowledgment.)

At one point or another, many family members have modeled or encouraged originality—my parents, Susan and Mark; my sister, Traci; my grandparents, Marion and Jay Grant and the late Florence and Paul Borock; and my in-laws, Adrienne and Neal Sweet.

Our children, Joanna, Elena, and Henry, mean the world to me, and they led me to think differently about this book. They taught me that to become original, adults need to spend less time learning and more time unlearning. And they inspired me to conform less in the hopes of creating a better world for them.

References

1: Creative Destruction

1 **"The reasonable man adapts himself":** George Bernard Shaw, *Man and Superman* (New York: Penguin Classics, 1903/1963).

2 **They called the company Warby Parker:** Personal interviews with Neil Blumenthal and Dave Gilboa, June 25, 2014, and March 23 and 24, 2015; David Zax, "Fast Talk: How Warby Parker's Cofounders Disrupted the Eyewear Industry and Stayed Friends," *Fast Company,* February 22, 2012, www.fastcompany.com/1818215/fast-talk-how-warby-parkers-cofounders-disrupted-eyewear-industry-and-stayed-friends; "A Chat with the Founders of Warby Parker," *The Standard Culture,* September 5, 2012, www.standardculture.com/posts/6884-A-Chat-with-the-Founders-of-Warby-Parker; Blumenthal, "Don't Underinvest in Branding," *Wall Street Journal, Accelerators,* July 18, 2013, http://blogs.wsj.com/accelerators/2013/07/18/neil-blumenthal-branding-is-a-point-of-view; Curan Mehra and Anya Schultz, "Interview: Dave Gilboa, Founder and CEO of Warby Parker," *Daily Californian,* September 5, 2014, www.dailycal.org/2014/09/05/interview-dave-gilboa-founder-ceo-warby-parker/; "The World's 50 Most Innovative Companies," *Fast Company,* February 9, 2015, www.fastcompany.com/section/most-innovative-companies-2015.

3 **"a person who is different . . . inventive capacity":** *Merriam-Webster Dictionary,* accessed on August 24, 2014, at www.merriam-webster.com/dictionary/original.

3 **conformity and originality:** Harrison Gough, *California Psychological Inventory Administrator's Guide* (Palo Alto, CA: Consulting Psychologists Press, Inc., 1987); see also Thomas S. Bateman and J. Michael Crant, "The Proactive Component of Organizational Behavior: A Measure and Correlates," *Journal of Organizational Behavior* 14 (1993): 103–18; Gregory J. Feist and Frank X. Barron, "Predicting Creativity from Early to Late Adulthood: Intellect, Potential, and Personality," *Journal of Personality* 37 (2003): 62–88; Adam M. Grant and Susan J. Ashford, "The Dynamics of Proactivity at Work," *Research in Organizational Behavior* 28 (2008): 3–34; Mark A. Griffin, Andrew Neal, and Sharon K. Parker, "A New Model

of Work Role Performance: Positive Behavior in Uncertain and Interdependent Contexts," *Academy of Management Journal* 50 (2007): 327–47.

3 **vulnerable to "kleptomnesia":** "Kleptomnesia" coined by Dan Gilbert; see C. Neil Macrae, Galen V. Bodenhausen, and Guglielmo Calvini, "Contexts of Cryptomnesia: May the Source Be with You," *Social Cognition* 17 (1999): 273–97.

5 **Internet Explorer is built into :** Personal correspondence with Michael Housman, January 30, February 25 and 27, March 9 and 27, and April 6, 2015; Housman presentation at the Wharton People Analytics Conference, March 28, 2015; "How Might Your Choice of Browser Affect Your Job Prospects?" *Economist*, April 10, 2013, www.economist.com/blogs/economist-explains/2013/04/economist-explains-how-browser-affects-job-prospects.

6 **Jost's team developed a theory:** John T. Jost, Brett W. Pelham, Oliver Sheldon, and Bilian Ni Sullivan, "Social Inequality and the Reduction of Ideological Dissonance on Behalf of the System: Evidence of Enhanced System Justification Among the Disadvantaged," *European Journal of Social Psychology* 33 (2003): 13–36; John T. Jost, Vagelis Chaikalis-Petritsis, Dominic Abrams, Jim Sidanius, Jojanneke van der Toorn, and Christopher Bratt, "Why Men (and Women) Do and Don't Rebel: Effects of System Justification on Willingness to Protest," *Personality and Social Psychology Bulletin* 38 (2012): 197–208; Cheryl J. Wakslak, John T. Jost, Tom R. Tyler, and Emmeline S. Chen, "Moral Outrage Mediates the Dampening Effect of System Justification on Support for Redistributive Social Policies," *Psychological Science* 18 (2007): 267–74; John T. Jost, Mahzarin R. Banaji, and Brian A. Nosek, "A Decade of System Justification Theory: Accumulated Evidence of Conscious and Unconscious Bolstering of the Status Quo," *Political Psychology* 25 (2004): 881–919.

7 **we experience *vuja de*:** Karl E. Weick, "The Collapse of Sensemaking in Organizations: The Mann Gulch Disaster," *Administrative Science Quarterly* 38 (1993): 628–52; see also Robert I. Sutton, *Weird Ideas That Work: 11½ Practices for Promoting, Managing, and Sustaining Innovation* (New York: Simon & Schuster, 2001).

8 **"man-made and therefore reversible":** Jean H. Baker, *Sisters: The Lives of America's Suffragists* (New York: Hill and Wang, 2006).

9 **Child prodigies:** Ellen Winner, "Child Prodigies and Adult Genius: A Weak Link," in *The Wiley Handbook of Genius*, ed. Dean Keith Simonton (Hoboken, NJ: Wiley-Blackwell, 2014).

10 **The least favorite students:** Erik L. Westby and V. L. Dawson, "Creativity: Asset or Burden in the Classroom," *Creativity Research Journal* 8 (1995): 1–10.

10 **the world's most excellent sheep:** William Deresiewicz, *Excellent Sheep: The Miseducation of the American Elite and the Way to a Meaningful Life* (New York: Free Press, 2014).

10 **"only a fraction of gifted children":** Ellen Winner, "Child Prodigies and Adult Genius: A Weak Link," in *The Wiley Handbook of Genius*, ed. Dean Keith Simonton (Hoboken, NJ: Wiley-Blackwell, 2014).

10 **But as cultures rack up:** Dean Keith Simonton, "Creative Cultures, Nations, and Civilizations: Strategies and Results," *Group Creativity: Innovation Through Collaboration*, eds. Paul B. Paulus and Bernard A. Nijstad (New York: Oxford University Press, 2013).

10 **The more you value achievement:** Robert J. Sternberg and Todd I. Lubart, *Defying the Crowd: Simple Solutions to the Most Common Relationship Problems* (New York: Simon & Schuster, 2002); see also John W. Atkinson, "Motivational Determinants of Risk-Taking Behavior," *Psychological Review* 64 (1997): 359–72.

11 **lifted up by followers and peers:** Jane M. Howell and Boas Shamir, "The Role of Followers in the Charismatic Leadership Process: Relationships and Their Consequences," *Academy of Management Review* 30 (2005): 96–112; J. Mark Weber and Celia Moore, "Squires: Key Followers and the Social Facilitation of Charismatic Leadership," *Organizational Psychology Review* 4 (2014): 199–227.

11 **From our perspective today, the Declaration:** Jack Rakove, *Revolutionaries: A New History of the Invention of America* (New York: Houghton Mifflin, 2010); Ron Chernow, *Washington: A Life* (New York: Penguin, 2011).

11 **his dream was:** Martin Luther King, Jr., *The Autobiography of Martin Luther King, Jr.* (New York: Warner Books, 1998); see also Howell Raines, *My Soul Is Rested: Movement Days in the Deep South Remembered* (New York: Penguin, 1983).

12 **at the pope's insistence:** Giorgio Vasari, *Lives of the Most Excellent Painters, Sculptors, and Architects, from Cimabue to Our Times* (New York: Modern Library Classics, 1568/2006).

12 **astronomy stagnated for decades:** Frank J. Sulloway, *Born to Rebel: Birth Order, Family Dynamics, and Creative Lives* (New York: Vintage, 1997).

13 **"I still intended to be at that company forever":** Livingston, *Founders at Work*, 42, 45.

13 **act of creative destruction** Joseph A. Schumpeter, *Capitalism, Socialism & Democracy* (New York: Harper Perennial Modern Classics, 1942/2008).

13 **fear of rocking the boat:** Jennifer J. Kish-Gephart, James R. Detert, Linda Klebe Treviño, and Amy C. Edmondson, "Silenced by Fear: The Nature, Sources, and Consequences of Fear at Work," *Research in Organizational Behavior* 29 (2009): 163–93; "Politics Threaten Science at FDA," *National Coalition Against Censorship*, July 22, 2006, http://ncac.org/update/politics-threaten-science-at-fda; Frances J. Milliken, Elizabeth W. Morrison, and Patricia F. Hewlin, "An Exploratory Study of Employee Silence: Issues That Employees Don't Communicate Upward and Why," *Journal of Management Studies* 40 (2003): 1453–76.

14 **"There are so few originals":** Personal interview with Mellody Hobson, May 12, 2015, and Hobson USC commencement speech, May 19, 2015, http://time .com/3889937/mellody-hobson-graduation-speech-usc/.

14 **The word *entrepreneur*:** Richard Cantillon, *An Essay on Economic Theory* (Auburn, AL: Ludwig von Mises Institute, 1755/2010); see also James Surowiecki, "Epic Fails of the Startup World," *New Yorker*, May 19, 2014, www.newyorker.com /magazine/2014/05/19/epic-fails-of-the-startup-world.

17 **Entrepreneurs who kept their day jobs:** Joseph Raffiee and Jie Feng, "Should I Quit My Day Job? A Hybrid Path to Entrepreneurship," *Academy of Management Journal* 57 (2014): 936–63.

17 **Phil Knight:** Bill Katovsky and Peter Larson, *Tread Lightly: Form, Footwear, and the Quest for Injury-Free Running* (New York: Skyhorse Publishing, 2012); David C. Thomas, *Readings and Cases in International Management: A Cross-Cultural Perspective* (Thousand Oaks, CA: Sage Publications, 2003).

17 **Steve Wozniak:** Jessica Livingston, *Founders at Work: Stories of Startups' Early Days* (Berkeley, CA: Apress, 2007).

18 **"We almost didn't start Google":** Personal conversations with Larry Page on September 15 and 16, 2014, and "Larry Page's University of Michigan Commencement Address," May 2, 2009, http://googlepress.blogspot.com /2009/05/larry-pages-university-of-michigan.html; Google Investor Relations, https://investor.google.com/financial/tables.html.

18 **Ava DuVernay:** "With Her MLK Drama *Selma,* Ava DuVernay Is Directing History," *Slate,* December 5, 2014, www.slate.com/blogs/browbeat/2014/12/05 /ava_duvernay_profile_the_selma_director_on_her_mlk_drama_and_being_a _black.html.

18 **"We Will Rock You":** Laura Jackson, *Brian May: The Definitive Biography* (New York: Little, Brown, 2011).

18 **Grammy winner John Legend:** Tiffany McGee, "5 Reasons Why John Legend Is No Ordinary Pop Star," *People,* November 6, 2006, www.people.com/people /archive/article/0,20060910,00.html; "Singer/Songwriter John Legend Got Early Start," *USA Today,* July 28, 2005, http://usatoday30.usatoday.com/life/music /news/2005-07-28-legend-early-start_x.htm; John Legend, "All in on Love," *Huffington Post,* May 20, 2014, www.huffingtonpost.com/john-legend/penn -commencement-speech-2014_b_5358334.html.

18 **Stephen King:** Lucas Reilly, "How Stephen King's Wife Saved 'Carrie' and Launched His Career," *Mental Floss,* October 17, 2013, http://mentalfloss.com/article/53235/how-stephen-kings-wife-saved -carrie-and-launched-his-career.

18 ***Dilbert* author Scott Adams:** Scott Adams, *Dilbert 2.0: 20 Years of Dilbert* (Kansas City, MO: Andrews McMeel Publishing, 2008).

19 **Risk portfolios:** Clyde H. Coombs and Lily Huang, "Tests of a Portfolio Theory of Risk Preference," *Journal of Experimental Psychology* 85 (1970): 23–29; Clyde H. Coombs and James Bowen, "Additivity of Risk in Portfolios," *Perception & Psychophysics* 10 (1971): 43–46, and "Test of the Between Property of Expected Utility," *Journal of Mathematical Psychology* 13 (323–37).

19 **Baseball owner Branch Rickey:** Lee Lowenfish, *Branch Rickey: Baseball's Ferocious Gentleman* (Lincoln: University of Nebraska Press, 2009).

19 **T. S. Eliot's landmark work:** Paul Collins, "Ezra Pound's Kickstarter Plan for
T. S. Eliot," *Mental Floss,* December 8, 2013, http://mentalfloss.com/article/54098
/ezra-pounds-kickstarter-plan-ts-eliot.

19 **Polaroid founder Edwin Land:** Victor K. McElheny, *Insisting on the Impossible:
The Life of Edwin Land* (New York: Basic Books, 1999).

19 **Pierre Omidyar:** Adam Cohen, *The Perfect Store: Inside eBay* (New York: Little,
Brown, 2008).

20 **"take the risk out of risk-taking":** Jane Bianchi, "The Power of Zigging: Why
Everyone Needs to Channel Their Inner Entrepreneur," LearnVest, October 22,
2014, http://www.learnvest.com/2014/10/crazy-is-a-compliment-the-power-of
-zigging-when-everyone-else-zags/; Marco della Cava, "Linda Rottenberg's Tips
for 'Crazy' Entrepreneurs," *USA Today*, October 15, 2014, www.usatoday.com
/story/tech/2014/10/02/linda-rottenberg-crazy-is-a-compliment-book/16551377;
"Myths About Entrepreneurship," *Harvard Business Review, IdeaCast*, October
2010, https://hbr.org/2014/10/myths-about-entrepreneurship; Linda Rottenberg,
Crazy Is a Compliment: The Power of Zigging When Everyone Else Zags
(New York: Portfolio, 2014).

20 **Sara Blakely:** Clare O'Connor, "Top Five Startup Tips from Spanx
Billionaire Sara Blakely," *Forbes,* April 2, 2012, www.forbes.com/sites/
clareoconnor/2012/04/02/top-five-startup-tips-from-spanx-billionaire-sara
-blakely/.

20 **Henry Ford:** "Henry Ford Leaves Edison to Start Automobile Company," History
.com, www.history.com/this-day-in-history/henry-ford-leaves-edison-to-start
-automobile-company.

20 **"Bill Gates might more accurately":** Rick Smith, *The Leap: How 3 Simple
Changes Can Propel Your Career from Good to Great* (New York: Penguin, 2009).

20 **having co-CEOs:** Matteo P. Arena, Stephen P. Ferris, and Emre Unlu, "It Takes
Two: The Incidence and Effectiveness of Co-CEOs," *The Financial Review* 46
(2011): 385–412; see also Ryan Krause, Richard Priem, and Leonard Love, "Who's
in Charge Here? Co-CEOs, Power Gaps, and Firm Performance," *Strategic
Management Journal* (2015)

22 **"entrepreneurs are significantly more risk-averse":** Hongwei Xu and Martin Ruef, "The Myth of the Risk-Tolerant Entrepreneur," *Strategic Organization* 2 (2004): 331–55.

23 **successful entrepreneurs . . . stealing valuables:** Ross Levine and Yona Rubinstein, "Smart and Illicit: Who Becomes an Entrepreneur and Does It Pay?," National Bureau of Economic Research working paper no. 19276 (August 2013); Zhen Zhang and Richard D. Arvey, "Rule Breaking in Adolescence and Entrepreneurial Status: An Empirical Investigation," *Journal of Business Venturing* 24 (2009): 436–47; Martin Obschonka, Hakan Andersson, Rainer K. Silbereisen, and Magnus Sverke, "Rule-Breaking, Crime, and Entrepreneurship: A Replication and Extension Study with 37-Year Longitudinal Data," *Journal of Vocational Behavior* 83 (2013): 386–96; Marco Caliendo, Frank Fossen, and Alexander Kritikos, "The Impact of Risk Attitudes on Entrepreneurial Survival," *Journal of Economic Behavior & Organization* 76 (2010): 45–63.

23 **"Many entrepreneurs take":** Malcolm Gladwell, "The Sure Thing," *New Yorker*, January 18, 2010, www.newyorker.com/magazine/2010/01/18/the-sure-thing.

23 **In a comprehensive analysis:** Hao Zhao, Scott E. Seibert, and G. T. Lumpkin, "The Relationship of Personality to Entrepreneurial Intentions and Performance: A Meta-Analytic Review," *Journal of Management* 36 (2010): 381–404; Scott Shane, *The Illusions of Entrepreneurship: The Costly Myths That Entrepreneurs, Investors, and Policy Makers Live By* (New Haven, CT: Yale University Press, 2008).

23 **When hundreds of historians:** Ronald J. Deluga, "American Presidential Proactivity, Charismatic Leadership, and Rated Performance," *Leadership Quarterly* 9 (1998): 265–91; Steven J. Rubenzer and Thomas R. Faschingbauer, *Personality, Character, and Leadership in the White House: Psychologists Assess the Presidents* (Dulles, VA: Brassey's, 2004).

24 **Before signing the Emancipation Proclamation:** Todd Brewster, *Lincoln's Gamble: The Tumultuous Six Months That Gave America the Emancipation Proclamation and Changed the Course of the Civil War* (New York: Simon & Schuster, 2014), 60.

24 **To unlock their mindsets:** Amy Wrzesniewski, Justin M. Berg, Adam M. Grant, Jennifer Kurkoski, and Brian Welle, "Dual Mindsets at Work: Achieving Long-Term Gains in Happiness," under revision, *Academy of Management Journal* (2015).

2: Blind Inventors and One-Eyed Investors

29 **"Creativity is allowing yourself":** Scott Adams, *The Dilbert Principle* (New York: HarperBusiness, 1996).

30 **"Segway as an investment":** PandoMonthly, "John Doerr on What Went Wrong with Segway," accessed on February 12, 2015, at www.youtube.com/watch?v=oOQzjpBkUTY.

30 **Why did such savvy:** Personal interviews with Aileen Lee, February 6, 2015, Randy Komisar, February 13, 2015, and Bill Sahlman, March 11, 2015; Steve Kemper, *Reinventing the Wheel: A Story of Genius, Innovation, and Grand Ambition* (New York: HarperCollins, 2005); Hayagreeva Rao, *Market Rebels: How Activists Make or Break Radical Innovations* (Princeton, NJ: Princeton University Press, 2008); Mathew Hayward, *Ego Check: Why Executive Hubris Is Wrecking Companies and Careers and How to Avoid the Trap* (New York: Kaplan Business, 2007); Jordan Golson, "Well, That Didn't Work: The Segway Is a Technological Marvel. Too Bad It Doesn't Make Any Sense," *Wired*, January 16, 2015, www.wired.com/2015/01/well-didnt-work-segway-technological-marvel-bad-doesnt-make-sense; Paul Graham, "The Trouble with the Segway," July 2009, www.paulgraham.com/segway.html; Mike Masnick, "Why Segway Failed to Reshape the World: Focused on Invention, Rather Than Innovation," *Techdirt*, July 31, 2009, www.techdirt.com/articles/20090730/1958335722.shtml; Gary Rivlin, "Segway's Breakdown," *Wired*, March 2003, http://archive.wired.com/wired/archive/11.03/segway.html; Douglas A. McIntyre, "The 10 Biggest Tech Failures of the Last Decade," *Time*, May 14, 2009, http://content.time.com/time/specials/packages/article/0,28804,1898610_1898625_1898641,00.html.

30 **Some years earlier, two entertainers:** Personal interviews with Rick Ludwin, February 24 and April 4, 2015; Phil Rosenthal, "NBC Executive Stands Apart by Taking Stands," *Chicago Tribune*, August 21, 2005, http://articles.chicagotribune.com/2005-08-21/business/0508210218_1_warren-littlefield-rick-ludwin-head-of-nbc-entertainment; Brian Lowry, "From Allen to Fallon, Exec Has Worked with All 6 'Tonight Show' Hosts," *Variety*, February 17, 2014, http://variety.com/2014/tv/news/from-allen-to-fallon-exec-has-worked-with-all-the-tonight-show-hosts-1201109027; Warren Littlefield, *Top of the Rock: Inside the Rise and Fall of Must See TV* (New York: Doubleday, 2012); Stephen Battaglio, "The Biz: The Research Memo That Almost Killed *Seinfeld*," *TV Guide*, June 27, 2014, www.tvguide.com/news/seinfeld-research-memo-1083639; Jordan Ecarma, "5 Hit TV Shows That Almost Didn't Happen," *Arts.Mic*, April 26, 2013, http://mic.com/articles/38017/

5-hit-tv-shows-that-almost-didn-t-happen; "From the Archives: Seinfeld on 60 Minutes," *CBS News*, March 1, 2015, www.cbsnews.com/news/jerry-seinfeld-on -60-minutes; Louisa Mellor, "Seinfeld's Journey from Flop to Acclaimed Hit," *Den of Geek*, November 10, 2014, www.denofgeek.us/tv/seinfeld/241125/seinfeld-s -journey-from-flop-to-acclaimed-hit; David Kronke, "There's Nothing to It," *Los Angeles Times*, January 29, 1995, http://articles.latimes.com/1995-01-29/ entertainment/ca-25549_1_jerry-seinfeld; James Sterngold, "*Seinfeld* Producers Wonder, Now What?" *New York Times*, January 27, 1998, www.nytimes.com/1998/ 01/27/movies/seinfeld-producers-wonder-now-what.html.

31 **87 percent were completely unique:** Laura J. Kornish and Karl T. Ulrich, "Opportunity Spaces in Innovation: Empirical Analysis of Large Samples of Ideas," *Management Science* 57 (2011): 107–128.

32 **creative forecasting:** Justin M. Berg, "Balancing on the Creative High-Wire: Forecasting the Success of Novel Ideas in Organizations," unpublished doctoral dissertation, University of Pennsylvania, 2015.

33 **High school seniors:** For a review, see David Dunning, Chip Heath, and Jerry M. Suls, "Flawed Self-Assessment: Implications for Health, Education, and the Workplace," *Psychological Science in the Public Interest* 5 (2004): 69–106.

33 **Entrepreneurs: When 3,000:** Arnold C. Cooper, Carolyn Y. Woo, and William C. Dunkelberg, "Entrepreneurs' Perceived Chances for Success," *Journal of Business Venturing* 3 (1988): 97–108; Noam Wasserman, "How an Entrepreneur's Passion Can Destroy a Startup," *Wall Street Journal*, August 25, 2014, www.wsj .com/articles/how-an-entrepreneur-s-passion-can-destroy-a-startup-1408912044.

34 **even geniuses have trouble:** Dean Keith Simonton, "Creativity as Blind Variation and Selective Retention: Is the Creative Process Darwinian?," *Psychological Inquiry* 10 (1999): 309–28.

34 **"Beethoven's own favorites":** Dean Keith Simonton, "Creative Productivity, Age, and Stress: A Biographical Time-Series Analysis of 10 Classical Composers," *Journal of Personality and Social Psychology* 35 (1977): 791–804.

34 **Kozbelt pored over letters:** Aaron Kozbelt, "A Quantitative Analysis of Beethoven as Self-Critic: Implications for Psychological Theories of Musical Creativity," *Psychology of Music* 35 (2007): 144–68.

35 **"proved to constitute 'blind alleys'":** Dean Keith Simonton, "Creativity and Discovery as Blind Variation: Campbell's (1960) BVSR Model After the Half-Century Mark," *Review of General Psychology* 15 (2011): 158–74.

35 **"The odds of producing an influential":** Dean Keith Simonton, "Creative Productivity: A Predictive and Explanatory Model of Career Trajectories and Landmarks," *Psychological Review* 104 (1997): 66–89.

36 **London Philharmonic Orchestra:** London Philharmonic Orchestra and David Parry, *The 50 Greatest Pieces of Classical Music*, X5 Music Group, November 23, 2009.

36 **In a study of over 15,000:** Aaron Kozbelt, "Longitudinal Hit Ratios of Classical Composers: Reconciling 'Darwinian' and Expertise Acquisition Perspectives on Lifespan Creativity," *Psychology of Aesthetics, Creativity, and the Arts* 2 (2008): 221–35.

36 **"the most important possible thing":** Ira Glass, "The Gap," accessed on April 14, 2015, at https://vimeo.com/85040589.

37 **"Those periods in which":** Dean Keith Simonton, "Thomas Edison's Creative Career: The Multilayered Trajectory of Trials, Errors, Failures, and Triumphs," *Psychology of Aesthetics, Creativity, and the Arts* 9 (2015): 2–14.

37 **"especially novel ideas":** Robert I. Sutton, *Weird Ideas That Work: 11½ Practices for Promoting, Managing, and Sustaining Innovation* (New York: Simon & Schuster, 2001).

37 **to achieve originality:** Teresa M. Amabile, "How to Kill Creativity," *Harvard Business Review*, September–October (1998): 77–87; Teresa M. Amabile, Sigal G. Barsade, Jennifer S. Mueller, and Barry M. Staw, "Affect and Creativity at Work," *Administrative Science Quarterly* 50 (2005): 367–403.

37 **Upworthy:** Upworthy, "How to Make That One Thing Go Viral," December 3, 2012, www.slideshare.net/Upworthy/how-to-make-that-one-thing-go-viral-just-kidding, and "2 Monkeys Were Paid Unequally; See What Happens Next," November 11, 2013, www.upworthy.com/2-monkeys-were-paid-unequally-see-what-happens-next.

37 **creative careers were closed to women:** Dean Keith Simonton, "Leaders of American Psychology, 1879–1967: Career Development, Creative Output, and Professional Achievement," *Journal of Personality and Social Psychology* 62 (1992): 5–17.

38 **first ideas are often the most conventional:** Brian J. Lucas and Loran F. Nordgren, "People Underestimate the Value of Persistence for Creative Performance," *Journal of Personality and Social Psychology* 109 (2015): 232–43.

38 ***Daily Show* cocreator Lizz Winstead:** Personal interview with Lizz Winstead, February 8, 2015.

39 **minimum viable product:** Eric Ries, *The Lean Startup: How Today's Entrepreneurs Use Continuous Innovation to Create Radically Successful Businesses* (New York: Crown, 2011).

40 **false negatives are common:** Charalampos Mainemelis, "Stealing Fire: Creative Deviance in the Evolution of New Ideas," *Academy of Management Review* 35 (2010): 558–78; Aren Wilborn, "5 Hilarious Reasons Publishers Rejected Classic Best-Sellers," *Cracked,* February 13, 2013, www.cracked.com/article_20285_5 -hilarious-reasons-publishers-rejected-classic-best-sellers.html; Berg, "Balancing on the Creative High-Wire."

40 **first instinct is often to reject novelty:** Jennifer S. Mueller, Shimul Melwani, and Jack A. Goncalo, "The Bias Against Creativity: Why People Desire But Reject Creative Ideas," *Psychological Science* 23 (2012): 13–17.

41 **the more expertise and experience people gain, the more entrenched they become:** Erik Dane, "Reconsidering the Trade-Off Between Expertise and Flexibility: A Cognitive Entrenchment Perspective," *Academy of Management Review* 35 (2010): 579–603.

45 **"If you're gonna make connections":** Drake Baer, "In 1982, Steve Jobs Presented an Amazingly Accurate Theory About Where Creativity Comes From," *Business Insider,* February 20, 2015, www.businessinsider.com/steve-jobs-theory-of-creativity -2015-2.

46 **engagement in the arts among Nobel Prize winners:** Robert Root-Bernstein, Lindsay Allen, Leighanna Beach, Ragini Bhadula, Justin Fast, Chelsea Hosey, Benjamin Kremkow, Jacqueline Lapp, Kaitlin Lonc, Kendell Pawelec, Abigail Podufaly, Caitlin Russ, Laurie Tennant, Eric Vrtis, and Stacey Weinlander, "Arts Foster Scientific Success: Avocations of Nobel, National Academy, Royal Society, and Sigma Xi Members," *Journal of Psychology of Science and Technology* 1 (2008): 51–63.

47 **A representative study of thousands:** Laura Niemi and Sara Cordes, "The Arts and Economic Vitality: Leisure Time Interest in Art Predicts Entrepreneurship and Innovation at Work," manuscript under review for publication, 2015.

48 **only Galileo "was able":** Dean Keith Simonton, "Foresight, Insight, Oversight, and Hindsight in Scientific Discovery: How Sighted Were Galileo's Telescopic Sightings?," *Psychology of Aesthetics, Creativity, and the Arts* 6 (2012): 243–54.

48 **Research on highly creative adults:** Donald W. MacKinnon, "The Nature and Nurture of Creative Talent," *American Psychologist* 17 (1962): 484–95, and "Personality and the Realization of Creative Potential," *American Psychologist* 20 (1965): 273–81.

48 **time spent abroad:** Frédéric C. Godart, William W. Maddux, Andrew V. Shipilov, and Adam D. Galinsky, "Fashion with a Foreign Flair: Professional Experiences Abroad Facilitate the Creative Innovations of Organizations," *Academy of Management Journal* 58 (2015): 195–220.

48 **"chill or wave of excitement":** Robert R. McCrae, "Aesthetic Chills as a Universal Marker of Openness to Experience," *Motivation and Emotion* 31 (2007): 5–11; Laura A. Maruskin, Todd M. Thrash, and Andrew J. Elliot, "The Chills as a Psychological Construct: Content Universe, Factor Structure, Affective Composition, Elicitors, Trait Antecedents, and Consequences," *Journal of Personality and Social Psychology* 103 (2012): 135–57; Paul J. Silvia and Emily C. Nusbaum, "On Personality and Piloerection: Individual Differences in Aesthetic Chills and Other Unusual Aesthetic Experiences," *Psychology of Aesthetics, Creativity, and the Arts* 5 (2011): 208–14;. Nusbaum and Silvia, "Shivers and Timbres: Personality and the Experience of Chills from Music," *Social Psychological and Personality Science* 2 (2011): 199–204; Oliver Grewe, Reinhard Kopiez, and Eckart Altenmüller, "The Chill Parameter: Goose Bumps and Shivers as Promising Measures in Emotion Research," *Music Perception* 27 (2009): 61–74; Brian S. Connelly, Deniz S. Ones, Stacy E. Davies, and Adib Birkland, "Opening Up Openness: A Theoretical Sort Following Critical Incidents Methodology and a Meta-Analytic Investigation of the Trait Family Measures," *Journal of Personality Assessment* 96 (2014): 17–28.

48 **"I acquired a strong taste":** Charles Darwin, *Charles Darwin: His Life Told in an Autobiographical Chapter, and in a Selected Series of His Published Letters* (London: John Murray, 1908).

50   **Jobs "thought the machine":** Steve Kemper, *Reinventing the Wheel: A Story of Genius, Innovation, and Grand Ambition* (New York: Harper Collins, 2005).

50   **Do diverse experiences:** Angela Ka-yee Leung, William W. Maddux, Adam D. Galinsky, and Chi-yue Chiu, "Multicultural Experience Enhances Creativity: The When and How," *American Psychologist* 63 (2008): 169–81; William W. Maddux and Adam D. Galinsky, "Cultural Borders and Mental Barriers: The Relationship Between Living Abroad and Creativity," *Journal of Personality and Social Psychology* 96 (2009): 1047–61.

51   **our intuitions are only accurate:** Erik Dane, Kevin W. Rockmann, and Michael G. Pratt, "When Should I Trust My Gut? Linking Domain Expertise to Intuitive Decision-Making Effectiveness," *Organizational Behavior and Human Decision Processes* 119 (2012): 187–94.

53   **intuitions are only trustworthy:** Daniel Kahneman and Gary Klein, "Conditions for Intuitive Expertise: A Failure to Disagree," *American Psychologist* 64 (2009): 515–26.

54   **The more successful people have been:** Pino G. Audia, Edwin A. Locke, and Ken G. Smith, "The Paradox of Success: An Archival and a Laboratory Study of Strategic Persistence Following Radical Environmental Change," *Academy of Management Journal* 43 (2000): 837–53.

54   **five dozen angel investors:** Cheryl Mitteness, Richard Sudek, and Melissa S. Cardon, "Angel Investor Characteristics That Determine Whether Perceived Passion Leads to Higher Evaluations of Funding Potential," *Journal of Business Venturing* 27 (2012): 592606.

55   **intuition operates rapidly:** Daniel Kahneman, *Thinking, Fast and Slow* (New York: Macmillan, 2011).

55   **"Passionate people":** Eric Schmidt and Jonathan Rosenberg, *How Google Works* (New York: Grand Central, 2014).

57   **The four founders weren't hindered:** Personal interviews with Lon Binder, December 30, 2014, and Neil Blumenthal and Dave Gilboa, February 2, 2015.

61   **As an inventor:** Adam Higginbotham, "Dean Kamen's Mission to Bring Unlimited Clean Water to the Developing World," *Wired*, August 13, 2013, www.wired.co.uk/

magazine/archive/2013/08/features/engine-of-progress; Christopher Helman, "Segway Inventor Dean Kamen Thinks His New Stirling Engine Will Get You off the Grid for Under $10K," *Forbes*, July 2, 2014, www.forbes.com/sites/ christopherhelman/2014/07/02/dean-kamen-thinks-his-new-stirling-engine-could -power-the-world; Erico Guizzo, "Dean Kamen's 'Luke Arm' Prosthesis Receives FDA Approval," *IEEE Spectrum*, May 13, 2014, http://spectrum.ieee.org/automaton/ biomedical/bionics/dean-kamen-luke-arm-prosthesis-receives-fda-approval.

3: Out on a Limb

62 **Out on a Limb:** Susan J. Ashford, Nancy P. Rothbard, Sandy Kristin Piderit, and Jane E. Dutton, "Out on a Limb: The Role of Context and Impression Management in Selling Gender-Equity Issues," *Administrative Science Quarterly* 43 (1998): 23–57.

62 **"Great spirits have":** *The Ultimate Quotable Einstein*, ed. Alice Calaprice (Princeton, NJ: Princeton University Press, 2011).

63 **an online system for:** Personal interviews with Carmen Medina, August 14, 2014, and March 2, 2015; personal interview with Susan Benjamin, April 3, 2015; Lois Kelly and Carmen Medina, *Rebels at Work: A Handbook for Leading Change from Within* (New York: O'Reilly Media, 2014).

64 **a platform called Intellipedia:** "Don Burke and Sean P. Dennehy," Service to America Medals, 2009, http://servicetoamericamedals.org/honorees/view_profile. php?profile=215; "CIA Adopting Web 2.0 Tools Despite Resistance," *Space War*, June 12, 2009, www.spacewar.com/reports/CIA_adopting_Web_2.0_tools_despite _resistance_999.html; Steve Vogel, "For Intelligence Officers, A Wiki Way to Connect the Dots," *Washington Post*, August 27, 2009, www.washingtonpost.com/ wp-dyn/content/article/2009/08/26/AR2009082603606.html; Robert K. Ackerman, "Intellipedia Seeks Ultimate Information Sharing," *SIGNAL*, October 2007, www.afcea.org/content/?q=intellipedia-seeks-ultimate-information-sharing.

65 **initiative that gets penalized:** Scott E. Seibert, Maria L. Kraimer, and J. Michael Crant, "What Do Proactive People Do? A Longitudinal Model Linking Proactive Personality and Career Success," *Personnel Psychology* 54 (2001): 845–74.

65 **as self-righteous:** Benoît Monin, Pamela J. Sawyer, and Matthew J. Marquez, "The Rejection of Moral Rebels: Resenting Those Who Do the Right Thing," *Journal of Personality and Social Psychology* 95 (2008): 76–93.

65 **power without status:** Alison R. Fragale, Jennifer R. Overbeck, and Margaret A. Neale, "Resources Versus Respect: Social Judgments Based on Targets' Power and Status Positions," *Journal of Experimental Social Psychology* 47 (2011): 767–75.

66 **using their power in ways that degraded others:** Nathanael J. Fast, Nir Halevy, and Adam D. Galinsky, "The Destructive Nature of Power Without Status," *Journal of Experimental Social Psychology* 48 (2012): 391–94.

66 **Francis Ford Coppola:** Jon Lewis, "If History Has Taught Us Anything . . . Francis Ford Coppola, Paramount Studios, and *The Godfather Parts I, II,* and *III*," in *Francis Ford Coppola's The Godfather Trilogy,* ed. Nick Browne (Cambridge: Cambridge University Press, 2000), and *Whom God Wishes to Destroy: Francis Coppola and the New Hollywood* (Durham, NC: Duke University Press, 1997).

67 **called idiosyncrasy credits:** Edwin P. Hollander, "Conformity, Status, and Idiosyncrasy Credit," *Psychological Review* 65 (1958): 117–27; see also Hannah Riley Bowles and Michele Gelfand, "Status and the Evaluation of Workplace Deviance," *Psychological Science* 21 (2010): 49–54.

67 **more status and competence when they donned a T-shirt and a beard:** Silvia Bellezza, Francesca Gino, and Anat Keinan, "The Red Sneakers Effect: Inferring Status and Competence from Signals of Nonconformity," *Journal of Consumer Research* 41 (2014): 35–54.

69 **powerless communication:** Alison R. Fragale, "The Power of Powerless Speech: The Effects of Speech Style and Task Interdependence on Status Conferral," *Organizational Behavior and Human Decision Processes* 101 (2006): 243–61; Adam Grant, *Give and Take: Why Helping Others Drives Our Success* (New York: Viking Press, 2013).

70 **when we're aware:** Marian Friestad and Peter Wright, "The Persuasion Knowledge Model: How People Cope with Persuasion Attempts," *Journal of Consumer Research* 21 (1994): 1–31.

70 **"Every time I would":** Personal interviews with Rufus Griscom, January 29 and February 26, 2015.

71 **gauge the intelligence:** Teresa M. Amabile, "Brilliant But Cruel: Perceptions of Negative Evaluators," *Journal of Experimental Social Psychology* 19 (1983): 146–56.

72 **when experts express doubt:** Uma R. Karmarkar and Zakary L. Tormala, "Believe Me, I Have No Idea What I'm Talking About: The Effects of Source Certainty on Consumer Involvement and Persuasion," *Journal of Consumer Research* 36 (2010): 1033–49.

73 **it makes you more trustworthy:** See R. Glen Hass and Darwyn Linder, "Counterargument Availability and the Effects of Message Structure on Persuasion," *Journal of Personality and Social Psychology* 23 (1972): 219–33.

74 **We use ease of retrieval:** Norbert Schwarz, Herbert Bless, Fritz Strack, Gisela Klumpp, Helga Rittenauer-Schatka, and Annette Simons, "Ease of Retrieval as Information: Another Look at the Availability Heuristic," *Journal of Personality and Social Psychology* 61 (1991): 195–202.

74 **they actually liked him more:** Geoffrey Haddock, "It's Easy to Like or Dislike Tony Blair: Accessibility Experiences and the Favourability of Attitude Judgments," *British Journal of Psychology* 93 (2002): 257–67.

76 **tap out the rhythm of a song:** Elizabeth L. Newton, "Overconfidence in the Communication of Intent: Heard and Unheard Melodies," Ph.D. dissertation, Stanford University (1990); Chip Heath and Dan Heath, *Made to Stick: Why Some Ideas Survive and Others Die* (New York: Random House, 2007).

76 **John Kotter studied change agents:** John P. Kotter, *Leading Change* (Boston: Harvard Business School Press, 1996).

77 **The mere exposure effect:** Robert B. Zajonc, "Attitudinal Effects of Mere Exposure," *Journal of Personality and Social Psychology Monographs* 9 (1968): 1–27.

77 **the more familiar a face:** Robert F. Bornstein, "Exposure and Affect: Overview and Meta-Analysis of Research, 1968–1987," *Psychological Bulletin* 106 (1989): 265–89; Robert B. Zajonc, "Mere Exposure: A Gateway to the Subliminal," *Current Directions in Psychological Science* 10 (2001): 224–28; Eddie Harmon-Jones and John J. B. Allen, "The Role of Affect in the Mere Exposure Effect: Evidence from Psychophysiological and Individual Differences Approaches," *Personality and Social Psychology Bulletin* 27 (2001): 889–98.

77 **when people looked at photographs:** Theodore H. Mita, Marshall Dermer, and Jeffrey Knight, "Reversed Facial Images and the Mere-Exposure Hypothesis," *Journal of Personality and Social Psychology* 35 (1977): 597–601.

78 **"Familiarity doesn't breed":** Personal interview with Howard Tullman, December 16, 2014.

79 **there are four different options:** Ethan R. Burris, James R. Detert, and Dan S. Chiaburu, "Quitting Before Leaving: The Mediating Effects of Psychological Attachment and Detachment on Voice," *Journal of Applied Psychology* 93 (2008): 912–22.

79 **exit, voice, persistence, and neglect:** Caryl E. Rusbult, Dan Farrell, Glen Rogers, and Arch G. Mainous III, "Impact of Exchange Variables on Exit, Voice, Loyalty, and Neglect: An Integrative Model of Responses to Declining Job Satisfaction," *Academy of Management Journal* 31 (1988): 599–627; Michael J. Withey and William H. Cooper, "Predicting Exit, Voice, Loyalty, and Neglect," *Administrative Science Quarterly* 34 (1989): 521–39.

80 **these choices are based on feelings of control and commitment:** Subrahmaniam Tangirala and Rangaraj Ramanujam, "Exploring Nonlinearity in Employee Voice: The Effects of Personal Control and Organizational Identification," *Academy of Management Journal* 51 (2008): 1189–1203.

81 **a supportive boss:** Fred O. Walumbwa and John Schaubroeck, "Leader Personality Traits and Employee Voice Behavior: Mediating Roles of Ethical Leadership and Work Group Psychological Safety," *Journal of Applied Psychology* 94 (2009): 1275–86.

81 **"agreeable people value cooperation":** Jeffrey A. LePine and Linn Van Dyne, "Voice and Cooperative Behavior as Contrasting Forms of Contextual Performance: Evidence of Differential Relationships with Big Five Personality Characteristics and Cognitive Ability," *Journal of Applied Psychology* 86 (2001): 326–36.

81 **typically the last people we seek:** Tiziana Cascario and Miguel Sousa Lobo, "Competent Jerks, Lovable Fools, and the Formation of Social Networks," *Harvard Business Review* June (2005): 92–99.

81 **bad user interface:** Robert Sutton, "Porcupines with Hearts of Gold," *BusinessWeek*, July 14, 2008, www.businessweek.com/business_at_work/bad_bosses/archives/2008/07/porcupines_with.html.

81 **Agreeable people were happiest:** Stéphane Côté and Debbie S. Moskowitz, "On the Dynamic Covariation between Interpersonal Behavior and Affect: Prediction

from Neuroticism, Extraversion, and Agreeableness," *Journal of Personality and Social Psychology* 75 (1998): 1032–46.

82 **when managers have a track record of challenging the status quo:** Zhen Zhang, Mo Wang, and Junqi Shi, "Leader-Follower Congruence in Proactive Personality and Work Outcomes: The Mediating Role of Leader-Member Exchange," *Academy of Management Journal* 55 (2012): 111–30; see also Nathanael J. Fast, Ethan R. Burris, and Caroline A. Bartel, "Managing to Stay in the Dark: Managerial Self-Efficacy, Ego Defensiveness, and the Aversion to Employee Voice," *Academy of Management Journal* 57 (2014): 1013–34; Mark J. Somers and Jose C. Casal, "Organizational Commitment and Whistle-Blowing: A Test of the Reformer and the Organization Man Hypotheses," *Group & Organization Management* 19 (1994): 270–84.

82 **middle-status conformity effect:** George C. Homans, *The Human Group* (New York: Harcourt, Brace, 1950) and *Social Behavior: Its Elementary Forms* (New York: Harcourt, Brace, and World, 1961).

83 **sacrificing anything professionally:** Personal conversations with Larry Page on September 15 and 16, 2014.

83 **security analysts:** Damon J. Phillips and Ezra W. Zuckerman, "Middle-Status Conformity: Theoretical Restatement and Empirical Demonstration in Two Markets," *American Journal of Sociology* 107 (2001): 379–429.

84 **the middle of the status hierarchy actually makes us less original:** Michelle M. Duguid and Jack A. Goncalo, "Squeezed in the Middle: The Middle Status Trade Creativity for Focus," *Journal of Personality and Social Psychology* 109, no. 4 (2015), 589–603.

85 **strong gender-role stereotypes:** Anne M. Koenig, Alice H. Eagly, Abigail A. Mitchell, and Tiina Ristikari, "Are Leader Stereotypes Masculine? A Meta-Analysis of Three Research Paradigms," *Psychological Bulletin* 127 (2011): 616–42.

85 **"labeled bossy":** Sheryl Sandberg, *Lean In: Women, Work, and the Will to Lead* (New York: Knopf, 2013).

85 **voicing new revenue-generating ideas:** Sheryl Sandberg and Adam Grant, "Speaking While Female," *New York Times*, January 12, 2015, www.nytimes.com/

2015/01/11/opinion/sunday/speaking-while-female.html; Adam M. Grant, "Rocking the Boat But Keeping It Steady: The Role of Emotion Regulation in Employee Voice," *Academy of Management Journal* 56 (2013): 1703–23.

85 **male executives who talk more:** Victoria L. Brescoll, "Who Takes the Floor and Why: Gender, Power, and Volubility in Organizations," *Administrative Science Quarterly* 56 (2011): 622–41.

85 **when women offer suggestions:** Ethan R. Burris, "The Risks and Rewards of Speaking Up: Managerial Responses to Employee Voice," *Academy of Management Journal* 55 (2012): 851–75.

85 **in male-dominated organizations, women pay a price:** Taeya M. Howell, David A. Harrison, Ethan R. Burris, and James R. Detert, "Who Gets Credit for Input? Demographic and Structural Status Cues in Voice Recognition," *Journal of Applied Psychology*, forthcoming (2015).

85 **Sexual harassment, she concludes:** Jennifer L. Berdahl, "The Sexual Harassment of Uppity Women," *Journal of Applied Psychology* 92 (2007): 425–37.

86 **they're being communal:** Jens Mazei, Joachim Hüffmeier, Philipp Alexander Freund, Alice F. Stuhlmacher, Lena Bilke, and Guido Hertel, "A Meta-Analysis on Gender Differences in Negotiation Outcomes and Their Moderators," *Psychological Bulletin* 141 (2015): 85–104; Emily T. Amanatullah and Michael W. Morris, "Negotiating Gender Roles: Gender Differences in Assertive Negotiating Are Mediated by Women's Fear of Backlash and Attenuated When Negotiating on Behalf of Others," *Journal of Personality and Social Psychology* 98 (2010): 256–67; Hannah Riley Bowles, Linda Babcock, and Kathleen L. McGinn, "Constraints and Triggers: Situational Mechanics of Gender in Negotiation," *Journal of Personality and Social Psychology* 89 (2005): 951–65.

86 **double minority group members:** Ashleigh Shelby Rosette, "Failure Is Not an Option for Black Women: Effects of Organizational Performance on Leaders with Single Versus Dual-Subordinate Identities," *Journal of Experimental Social Psychology* 48 (2012): 1162–67.

86 **black women defy categories:** Robert W. Livingston, Ashleigh Shelby Rosette, and Ella F. Washington, "Can an Agentic Black Woman Get Ahead? The Impact of Race and Interpersonal Dominance on Perceptions of Female Leaders," *Psychological Science* 23 (2012): 354–58.

87 **"Apple being successful depended on":** Personal interview with Donna Dubinsky, June 20, 2014; Todd D. Jick and Mary Gentile, "Donna Dubinsky and Apple Computer, Inc. (A)," Harvard Business School, Case 9-486-083, December 11, 1995.

89 **Jobs promoted every one of them:** Walter Isaacson, *Steve Jobs* (New York: Simon & Schuster, 2013).

89 **"Voice feeds" :** Albert O. Hirschman, *Exit, Voice, and Loyalty: Responses to Decline in Firms, Organizations, and States* (Cambridge, MA: Harvard University Press, 1970).

91 **the mistakes we regret:** Thomas Gilovich and Victoria Husted Medvec, "The Temporal Pattern to the Experience of Regret," *Journal of Personality and Social Psychology* 67 (1994): 357–65, and "The Experience of Regret: What, When, and Why," *Psychological Review* 102 (1995): 379–95.

4: Fools Rush In

92 **"Never put off till tomorrow":** *Quote Investigator*, January 17, 2013, http://quoteinvestigator.com/2013/01/17/put-off.

92 **"He worked on it all night":** Clarence B. Jones, *Behind the Dream: The Making of the Speech That Transformed a Nation* (New York: Palgrave Macmillan, 2011); Coretta Scott King, *My Life with Martin Luther King, Jr.* (New York: Henry Holt & Co., 1993); Drew Hansen, *The Dream: Martin Luther King, Jr., and the Speech That Inspired a Nation* (New York: Harper Perennial, 2005); Carmine Gallo, "How Martin Luther King Improvised 'I Have a Dream,'" *Forbes*, August 27, 2013, www.forbes.com /sites/carminegallo/2013/08/27/public-speaking-how-mlk-improvised-second-half-of-dream-speech; Frank Hagler, "50 Incredible Facts—and Photos—from the March on Washington," *Policy.Mic*, August 28, 2013, mic.com/articles/60815/ 50-incredible-facts-and-photos-from-the-march-on-washington; David J. Garrow, *Bearing the Cross: Martin Luther King, Jr., and the Southern Christian Leadership Conference* (New York: William Morrow, 1986).

93 **it takes longer to write:** "If I Had More Time, I Would Have Written a Shorter Letter," *Quote Investigator*, April 28, 2012, quoteinvestigator.com/2012/04/28/shorter-letter.

94 **procrastination might be conducive to originality:** Jihae Shin, "Putting Work Off Pays Off: The Hidden Benefits of Procrastination for Creativity," manuscript under review, 2015.

96 **"cannot produce a work of genius according to a schedule":** William A. Pannapacker, "How to Procrastinate Like Leonardo da Vinci," *Chronicle Review*, February 20, 2009.

97 **"accomplish most when they work the least":** Giorgio Vasari, *Lives of the Most Excellent Painters, Sculptors, and Architects, from Cimabue to Our Times* (New York: Modern Library Classics, 1568/2006).

97 **moments where we're unfocused:** Mareike B. Wieth and Rose T. Zacks, "Time of Day Effects on Problem Solving: When the Non-Optimal Is Optimal," *Thinking & Reasoning* 17 (2011): 387–401.

98 **The science stars:** Rena Subotnik, Cynthia Steiner, and Basanti Chakraborty, "Procrastination Revisited: The Constructive Use of Delayed Response," *Creativity Research Journal* 12 (1999): 151–60.

98 **"a form of incubation":** Ut Na Sio and Thomas C. Ormerod, "Does Incubation Enhance Problem Solving? A Meta-Analytic Review," *Psychological Bulletin* 135 (2009): 94–120.

98 **Abraham Lincoln's Gettysburg Address:** Peggy Noonan, "The Writing of a Great Address," *Wall Street Journal*, July 5, 2013, www.wsj.com/articles/ SB10001424127887324399404578583991319014114; Ronald C. White, Jr., *The Eloquent President: A Portrait of Lincoln Through His Words* (New York: Random House, 2011).

99 **the Zeigarnik effect:** Bluma Zeigarnik, *"Das Behalten erledigter und unerledigter Handlungen,"* *Psychologische Forschung* 9 (1927): 1–85; see Kenneth Savitsky, Victoria Husted Medvec, and Thomas Gilovich, "Remembering and Regretting: The Zeigarnik Effect and the Cognitive Availability of Regrettable Actions and Inactions," *Personality and Social Psychology Bulletin* 23 (1997): 248–57.

99 **"I love deadlines," Douglas Adams said:** M. J. Simpson, *Hitchhiker: A Biography of Douglas Adams* (Boston: Justin, Charles & Co., 2005).

100 **the most creative architects:** Donald W. MacKinnon, "The Nature and Nurture of Creative Talent," *American Psychologist* 17 (1962): 484–95, and "Personality and the Realization of Creative Potential," *American Psychologist* 20 (1965): 273–81.

100 **a study of pizza chains:** Adam M. Grant, Francesca Gino, and David A. Hofmann, "Reversing the Extraverted Leadership Advantage: The Role of Employee Proactivity," *Academy of Management Journal* 54 (2011): 528–50.

101 **companies in India:** Sucheta Nadkarni and Pol Herrmann, "CEO Personality, Strategic Flexibility, and Firm Performance: The Case of the Indian Business Process Outsourcing Industry," *Academy of Management Journal* 53 (2010): 1050–73.

101 **evaluated their strategies at the midpoint:** Anita Williams Woolley, "Effects of Intervention Content and Timing on Group Task Performance," *Journal of Applied Behavioral Science* 34 (1998): 30–46.

101 **the midpoint of a task:** Connie J. G. Gersick, "Marking Time: Predictable Transitions in Task Groups," *Academy of Management Journal* 32 (1989): 274–309, and "Revolutionary Change Theories: A Multilevel Exploration of the Punctuated Equilibrium Paradigm," *Academy of Management Review* 16 (1991): 10–36.

101 **halftimes can be so influential:** Nancy Katz, "Sports Teams as a Model for Workplace Teams: Lessons and Liabilities," *Academy of Management Executive* 15 (2001): 56–67.

103 **"The number one thing":** Bill Gross, "The Single Biggest Reason Why Startups Succeed," TED Talks, June 2015, www.ted.com/talks/bill_gross_the_single_biggest _reason_why_startups_succeed/transcript.

103 **a first-mover advantage:** Lisa E. Bolton, "Believing in First Mover Advantage," manuscript under review.

103 **These edges create barriers:** Marvin B. Lieberman and David B. Montgomery, "First-Mover Advantages," *Strategic Management Journal* 9 (1988): 41–58; Montgomery and Lieberman, "First-Mover (Dis)advantages: Retrospective and Link with the Resource-Based View," *Strategic Management Journal* 19 (1998): 1111–25.

104 **the downsides of being the first mover:** Peter N. Golder and Gerard J. Tellis, "Pioneer Advantage: Marketing Logic or Marketing Legend?" *Journal of Marketing Research* 30 (1993): 158–70.

105   **When originals rush:** Jeanette Brown, "What Led to Kozmo's Final Delivery," *Bloomberg Business*, April 15, 2001, www.bloomberg.com/bw/stories/2001-04-15/what-led-to-kozmos-final-delivery; Greg Bensinger, "In Kozmo.com's Failure, Lessons for Same-Day Delivery," *Wall Street Journal*, December 3, 2012, http://blogs.wsj.com/digits/2012/12/03/in-kozmo-coms-failure-lessons-for-same-day-deliver; Diane Seo, "The Big Kozmo KO," *Salon*, July 21, 2000, www.salon.com/2000/07/21/kozmo; Stephanie Miles, "Strategy, Inefficiencies Hurt Kozmo, Say Its Competitors in New York," *Wall Street Journal*, April 17, 2011, www.wsj.com/articles/SB987187139726234932; Jeremy Stahl, "The Kozmo Trap," *Slate*, May 14, 2012, http://hive.slate.com/hive/10-rules-starting-small-business/article/the-kozmo-trap; Jayson Blair, "Behind Kozmo's Demise: Thin Profit Margins," *New York Times*, April 13, 2001, www.nytimes.com/2001/04/13/nyregion/behind-kozmo-s-demise-thin-profit-margins.html.

105   **fail because of premature scaling:** Boonsri Dickinson, "Infographic: Most Startups Fail Because of Premature Scaling," *ZDNet*, September 1, 2011, www.zdnet.com/article/infographic-most-startups-fail-because-of-premature-scaling.

105   **"Wouldn't you rather be second":** Toronto Public Library, "Malcolm Gladwell, Part 3," May 28, 2012, https://www.youtube.com/watch?v=QyL9H4wJ0VE; Laura Petrecca, "Malcolm Gladwell Advocates Being Late," *USA Today*, June 20, 2011, content.usatoday.com/communities/livefrom/post/2011/06/malcolm-gladwell-talks-innovation-and-being-late-at-cannes/1#.VVc6ykZ2M5w.

106   **study of software startups:** Elizabeth G. Pontikes and William P. Barnett, "When to Be a Nonconformist Entrepreneur? Organizational Responses to Vital Events," University of Chicago Working Paper No. 12-59 (2014).

106   **Moving too fast:** Steve Kemper, *Reinventing the Wheel: A Story of Genius, Innovation, and Grand Ambition* (New York: HarperCollins, 2005).

106   **"If it didn't look dorky":** Personal interview with Bill Sahlman, March 11, 2015.

107   **pioneers had lower survival rates:** Stanislav D. Dobrev and Aleksios Gotsopoulos, "Legitimacy Vacuum, Structural Imprinting, and the First Mover Disadvantage," *Academy of Management Journal* 53 (2010): 1153–74.

107   **"We had to wait for Amazon":** Personal interview with Neil Blumenthal, June 25, 2014.

107 **Hungarian physician Ignaz Semmelweis:** Steven D. Levitt and Stephen J. Dubner, *SuperFreakonomics: Global Cooling, Patriotic Prostitutes, and Why Suicide Bombers Should Buy Life Insurance* (New York: William Morrow, 2009).

108 **"A new scientific truth":** Max Planck, *Scientific Autobiography and Other Papers* (New York: Philosophical Library, 1949).

108 **First-mover advantages:** Marvin B. Lieberman, "Did First-Mover Advantages Survive the Dot-Com Crash?," Anderson School of Management working paper (2007).

108 **odds of success aren't higher:** Pieter A. VanderWerf and John F. Mahon, "Meta-Analysis of the Impact of Research Methods on Findings of First Mover Advantage," *Management Science* 43 (1997): 1510–19.

108 **when the market is uncertain:** William Boulding and Markus Christen, "Sustainable Pioneering Advantage? Profit Implications of Market Entry Order," *Marketing Science* 22 (2003): 371–92.

108 **"People under 35":** Jessica Stillman, "Older Entrepreneurs Get a Bum Rap," *Inc.*, December 3, 2012, www.inc.com/jessica-stillman/older-entrepreneurs-vs-young-founders.html.

108 **"A person who has not made":** David Wessel, "The 'Eureka' Moments Happen Later," *Wall Street Journal*, September 5, 2012, www.wsj.com/articles/SB10000872396390443589304577633243828684650.

109 **"To punish me":** Walter Isaacson, *Einstein: His Life and Universe* (New York: Simon & Schuster, 2008).

109 **When companies run suggestion boxes:** Birgit Verworn, "Does Age Have an Impact on Having Ideas? An Analysis of the Quantity and Quality of Ideas Submitted to a Suggestion System," *Creativity and Innovation Management* 18 (2009): 326–34.

109 **average founder is thirty-eight:** Claire Cain Miller, "The Next Mark Zuckerberg Is Not Who You Might Think," *New York Times*, July 2, 2015, www.nytimes.com/2015/07/02/upshot/the-next-mark-zuckerberg-is-not-who-you-might-think.html.

110 **writer E. M. Forster:** Karl E. Weick, *The Social Psychology of Organizing*, 2nd ed. (Reading, MA: Addison-Wesley, 1979).

110   **conceptual innovators are sprinters:** David Galenson, *Old Masters and Young Geniuses: The Two Life Cycles of Artistic Creativity* (Princeton, NJ: Princeton University Press, 2011).

110   **economists who won the Nobel Prize:** Bruce A. Weinberg and David W. Galenson, "Creative Careers: The Life Cycles of Nobel Laureates in Economics," National Bureau of Economic Research Working Paper No. 11799 (November 2005).

110   **most often reproduced poems:** David W. Galenson, "Literary Life Cycles: The Careers of Modern American Poets," National Bureau of Economic Research Working Paper No. 9856 (July 2003); see also Dean Keith Simonton, "Creative Life Cycles in Literature: Poets Versus Novelists or Conceptualists Versus Experimentalists?," *Psychology of Aesthetics, Creativity, and the Arts* 1 (2007): 133–39.

110   **independent study of every physicist:** Benjamin F. Jones, E. J. Reedy, and Bruce A. Weinberg, "Age and Scientific Genius," National Bureau of Economic Research Working Paper No. 19866 (January 2014); see also Benjamin F. Jones and Bruce A. Weinberg, "Age Dynamics in Scientific Creativity," *Proceedings of the National Academy of Sciences* 108 (2011): 18910–914.

111   **when you have a hammer:** Abraham H. Maslow, *The Psychology of Science* (New York: Harper and Row, 1966).

113   **"putting old things in new combinations":** Weick, *The Social Psychology of Organizing.*

113   **"the dedicated tortoises undaunted by the blur of the hares":** Daniel H. Pink, "What Kind of Genius Are You?" *Wired*, July 2006, http://archive.wired.com/wired/archive/14.07/genius.html.

5: Goldilocks and the Trojan Horse

114   **"Now, the Star-Belly Sneetches":** Dr. Seuss, *The Sneetches and Other Stories* (New York: Random House, 1961).

114   **no one did more for women's suffrage:** Andrea Moore Kerr, *Lucy Stone: Speaking Out for Equality* (Rutgers, NJ: Rutgers University Press, 1992); Jean H. Baker, *Sisters: The Lives of America's Suffragists* (New York: Hill and Wang, 2006); Sally G. McMillen, *Lucy Stone: An Unapologetic Life* (Oxford: Oxford University

Press, 2015); Lisa Tetrault, *The Myth of Seneca Falls: Memory and the Women's Suffrage Movement, 1848–1898* (Chapel Hill, NC: University of North Carolina Press, 2014); Elinor Rice Hays, *Morning Star: A Biography of Lucy Stone, 1818–1893* (New York: Harcourt, Brace & World, 1961); Alice Stone Blackwell, *Lucy Stone: Pioneer of Woman's Rights* (Boston: Little, Brown, 1930); Elizabeth Frost-Knappman and Kathryn Cullen-DuPont, *Women's Suffrage in America* (New York: Facts on File, 1992/2005); Suzanne M. Marilley, *Woman Suffrage and the Origins of Liberal Feminism in the United States* (Boston: Harvard University Press, 1997); Catherine Gilbert Murdock, *Domesticating Drink: Women, Men, and Alcohol in America, 1870–1940* (Baltimore: Johns Hopkins University Press, 2003); Carolyn De Swarte Gifford, *Writing Out My Heart: Selections from the Journal of Frances E. Willard, 1855–96* (Urbana: University of Illinois Press, 1995); Joan Smyth Iversen, *The Antipolygamy Controversy in U.S. Women's Movements, 1880–1925: A Debate on the American Home* (New York: Routledge, 1997); Ida Husted Harper, *The Life and Work of Susan B. Anthony, Volume I* (Indianapolis: Bowen-Merrill Company, 1899); Ann D. Gordon, *The Selected Papers of Elizabeth Cady Stanton and Susan B. Anthony* (Rutgers, NJ: Rutgers University Press, 1997).

114 **In 1855, she took a stand:** Claudia Goldin and Maria Shim, "Making a Name: Women's Surnames at Marriage and Beyond," *Journal of Economic Perspectives* 18 (2004): 143–60.

117 **the concept of horizontal hostility:** Judith B. White and Ellen J. Langer, "Horizontal Hostility: Relations Between Similar Minority Groups," *Journal of Social Issues* 55 (1999): 537–59; Judith B. White, Michael T. Schmitt, and Ellen J. Langer, "Horizontal Hostility: Multiple Minority Groups and Differentiation from the Mainstream," *Group Processes & Intergroup Relations* 9 (2006): 339–58; Hank Rothgerber, "Horizontal Hostility Among Non-Meat Eaters," *PLOS ONE* 9 (2014): 1–6.

118 **The more strongly you identify:** Jolanda Jetten, Russell Spears, and Tom Postmes, "Intergroup Distinctiveness and Differentiation: A Meta-Analytic Integration," *Journal of Personality and Social Psychology* 86 (2004): 862–79.

120 **The group that sang together:** Scott S. Wiltermuth and Chip Heath, "Synchrony and Cooperation," *Psychological Science* 20 (2009): 1–5.

120 **In seeking alliances:** Wooseok Jung, Brayden G. King, and Sarah A. Soule, "Issue Bricolage: Explaining the Configuration of the Social Movement Sector, 1960–1995," *American Journal of Sociology* 120 (2014): 187–225.

120 **positive and negative experiences are amplified:** Erica J. Boothby, Margaret S. Clark, and John A. Bargh, "Shared Experiences Are Amplified," *Psychological Science* 25 (2014): 2209–16.

121 **The suffragists who formed alliances:** Holly J. McCammon and Karen E. Campbell, "Allies on the Road to Victory: Coalition Formation Between the Suffragists and the Woman's Christian Temperance Union," *Mobilization: An International Journal* 7 (2002): 231–51.

124 **"'this actually can work'":** Personal interview with Meredith Perry, November 13, 2014; Google Zeitgeist, September 16, 2014; Jack Hitt, "An Inventor Wants One Less Wire to Worry About," *New York Times*, August 17, 2013, www.nytimes.com/ 2013/08/18/technology/an-inventor-wants-one-less-wire-to-worry-about.html ?pagewanted=all; Julie Bort, "A Startup That Raised $10 Million for Charging Gadgets Through Sound Has Sparked a Giant Debate in Silicon Valley," *Business Insider,* November 2, 2014, www.businessinsider.com/startup-ubeams-10-million -debate-2014-11.

124 **we should start with *why*:** Simon Sinek, *Start with Why: How Great Leaders Inspire Everyone to Take Action* (New York: Portfolio, 2011).

124 **become tempered radicals:** Debra E. Meyerson and Maureen A. Scully, "Tempered Radicalism and the Politics of Ambivalence and Change," *Organization Science* 6 (1995): 585–600.

125 **people with extreme political views:** Philip M. Fernbach, Todd Rogers, Craig R. Fox, and Steven A. Sloman, "Political Extremism Is Supported by an Illusion of Understanding," *Psychological Science* 24 (2013): 939–46.

125 **"That's when we threw the strike":** Personal interviews with Josh Steinman, December 10, 2014, and Scott Stearney, December 29, 2014.

125 **foot-in-the-door technique:** For a review, see Robert B. Cialdini, *Influence: Science and Practice*, 4th ed. (Boston: Allyn and Bacon, 2001).

126 **"The 99 Percent":** Srdja Popovic, *Blueprint for Revolution: How to Use Rice Pudding, Lego Men, and Other Nonviolent Techniques to Galvanize Communities, Overthrow Dictators, or Simply Change the World* (New York: Spiegel & Grau, 2015).

128 **insiders and outsiders have distinct ideas about who represents a coalition:**
Blake E. Ashforth and Peter H. Reingen, "Functions of Dysfunction: Managing the
Dynamics of an Organizational Duality in a Natural Food Cooperative,"
Administrative Science Quarterly 59 (2014): 474–516.

128 **"Keep your friends close":** Mario Puzo and Francis Ford Coppola, *The Godfather:
Part II*, directed by Francis Ford Coppola, Paramount Pictures, 1974.

129 **Psychologists call them ambivalent relationships:** Michelle K. Duffy, Daniel C.
Ganster, and Milan Pagon, "Social Undermining in the Workplace," *Academy of
Management Journal* 45 (2002): 331–51; see also Huiwen Lian, D. Lance Ferris,
and Douglas J. Brown, "Does Taking the Good with the Bad Make Things Worse?
How Abusive Supervision and Leader-Member Exchange Interact to Impact Need
Satisfaction and Organizational Deviance," *Organizational Behavior and Human
Decision Processes* 117 (2012): 41–52.

131 **ambivalent relationships are literally unhealthier:** Bert N. Uchino, Julianne
Holt-Lunstad, Timothy W. Smith, and Lindsey Bloor, "Heterogeneity in Social
Networks: A Comparison of Different Models Linking Relationships to
Psychological Outcomes," *Journal of Social and Clinical Psychology*, 23 (2004):
123–39; Bert N. Uchino, Julianne Holt-Lunstad, Darcy Uno, and Jeffrey B.
Flinders, "Heterogeneity in the Social Networks of Young and Older Adults:
Prediction of Mental Health and Cardiovascular Reactivity During Acute Stress,"
Journal of Behavioral Medicine 24 (2001): 361–82.

132 **more sensitive to gains and losses in esteem:** Elliot Aronson and Darwyn
Linder, "Gain and Loss of Esteem as Determinants of Interpersonal
Attractiveness," *Journal of Experimental Social Psychology* 1 (1965): 156–71.

132 **"We find it more rewarding":** Elliot Aronson, *The Social Animal*, 10th ed. (New
York: Worth Publishers, 2007).

132 **people were most persuaded:** Harold Sigall and Elliot Aronson, "Opinion
Change and the Gain-Loss Model of Interpersonal Attraction," *Journal of
Experimental Social Psychology* 3 (1967): 178–88.

132 **"appears to stand up to critical scrutiny":** Ithai Stern and James D. Westphal,
"Stealthy Footsteps to the Boardroom: Executives' Backgrounds, Sophisticated

Interpersonal Influence Behavior, and Board Appointments," *Administrative Science Quarterly* 55 (2010): 278–319.

132 **Essayist Chuck Klosterman:** Chuck Klosterman, "The Importance of Being Hated," *Esquire*, April 1, 2004, www.esquire.com/features/chuck-klostermans -america/ESQ0404-APR_AMERICA.

135 **"Of course it was *Hamlet*":** Personal interviews with Rob Minkoff, October 17 and November 13, 2014.

136 **promising ideas begin from novelty:** Justin M. Berg, "The Primal Mark: How the Beginning Shapes the End in the Development of Creative Ideas," *Organizational Behavior and Human Decision Processes* 125 (2014): 1–17.

138 **a form of "public motherhood":** Paula Baker, "The Domestication of Politics: Women and American Political Society, 1780–1920," *American Historical Review* 89 (1984): 620–47.

141 **The justice argument:** Holly J. McCammon, Lyndi Hewitt, and Sandy Smith, "'No Weapon Save Argument': Strategic Frame Amplification in the U.S. Woman Suffrage Movements," *The Sociological Quarterly* 45 (2004): 529–56; Holly J. McCammon, "'Out of the Parlors and Into the Streets': The Changing Tactical Repertoire of the U.S. Women's Suffrage Movements," *Social Forces* 81 (2003): 787–818; Lyndi Hewitt and Holly J. McCammon, "Explaining Suffrage Mobilization: Balance, Neutralization, and Range in Collective Action Frames, 1892–1919," *Mobilization: An International Journal* 9 (2004): 149–66.

141 **so did the passage of suffrage laws:** Holly J. McCammon, "Stirring Up Suffrage Sentiment: The Formation of the State Woman's Suffrage Organizations, 1866–1914," *Social Forces* 80 (2001): 449–80; Holly J. McCammon, Karen E. Campbell, Ellen M. Granberg, and Christine Mowery, "How Movements Win: Gendered Opportunity Structures and U.S. Women's Suffrage Movements, 1866–1919," *American Sociological Review* 66 (2001): 49–70; Holly J. McCammon and Karen E. Campbell, "Winning the Vote in the West: The Political Successes of the Women's Suffrage Movements, 1866–1919," *Gender & Society* 15 (2001): 55–82.

143 **To build coalitions:** Herbert C. Kelman, "Group Processes in the Resolution of International Conflicts: Experiences from the Israeli-Palestinian Case,"

American Psychologist 52 (1997): 212–20, and "Looking Back at My Work on Conflict Resolution in the Middle East," *Peace and Conflict* 16 (2010): 361–87.

6: Rebel with a Cause

146 **"We are not our brother's keeper":** Harry Allen Overstreet and Bonaro Wilkinson Overstreet, *The Mind Goes Forth: The Drama of Understanding* (New York: Norton, 1956).

146 **Stealing a base:** Ano Katsunori, "Modified Offensive Earned-Run Average with Steal Effect for Baseball," *Applied Mathematics and Computation* 120 (2001): 279–88; Josh Goldman, "Breaking Down Stolen Base Break-Even Points," *Fan Graphs*, November 3, 2011, www.fangraphs.com/blogs/breaking-down-stolen -base-break-even-points/.

146 **Stealing home is even riskier:** Dan Rosenheck, "Robinson Knew Just When to Be Bold on the Base Path," *New York Times*, April 17, 2009, www.nytimes.com /2009/04/19/sports/baseball/19score.html; Dave Anderson, "Why Nobody Steals Home Anymore," *New York Times*, April 16, 1989, www.nytimes.com/1989/04/16 /sports/sports-of-the-times-why-nobody-steals-home-anymore.html; Bryan Grosnick, "Grand Theft Home Plate: Stealing Home in 2012," *Beyond the Box Score*, July 27, 2012, www.beyondtheboxscore.com/2012/7/27/3197011/grand-theft-home -plate-stealing-home-in-2012; Shane Tourtellotte, "And That Ain't All, He Stole Home!" *Hardball Times*, March 2, 2012, www.hardballtimes.com/and-that-aint -all-he-stole-home; Manny Randhawa, "Harrison Dazzles with Steal of Home," April 28, 2013, MiLB.com, www.milb.com/news/print.jsp?ymd=20130428& content_id=46029428&vkey=news_t484&fext=.jsp&sid=t484; Anthony McCarron, "Jacoby Ellsbury's Steal of Home Against Yankees Is a Page from Another Era," *New York Daily News*, April 27, 2009, www.nydailynews.com/sports/baseball/yankees /jacoby-ellsbury-steal-home-yankees-page-era-article-1.359870.

147 **your odds of getting injured:** Robert Preidt, "'Plays at the Plate' Riskiest for Pro Baseball Players," *HealthDay*, January 26, 2014, consumer.healthday.com/fitness -information-14/baseball-or-softball-health-news-240/briefs-emb-1-21-baseball -collision-injuries-ijsm-wake-forest-release-batch-1109-684086.html.

147 **steals leader:** *Baseball Almanac*, "Single Season Leaders for Stolen Bases," www .baseball-almanac.com/hitting/hisb2.shtml, and "Career Leaders for Stolen Bases," www.baseball-almanac.com/hitting/hisb1.shtml.

148 **breaking the color barrier:** Jackie Robinson, *I Never Had It Made* (New York: HarperCollins, 1972/1995); Arnold Rampersad, *Jackie Robinson: A Biography* (New York: Ballantime Books, 1997); Roger Kahn, *Rickey & Robinson: The True, Untold Story of the Integration of Baseball* (New York: Rodale Books, 2014); Harvey Frommer, *Rickey and Robinson: The Men Who Broke Baseball's Color Barrier* (New York: Taylor Trade Publishing, 1982/2003).

148 **ten players have stolen at least 70 bases in two different seasons:** Rickey Henderson: Robert Buderi, "Crime Pays for Rickey Henderson, Who's (Base) Stealing His Way Into the Record Book," *People*, August 23, 1982, www.people .com/people/archive/article/0,20082931,00.html; Lou Brock: "Lou Brock Biography," *ESPN*, espn.go.com/mlb/player/bio/_/id/19568/lou-brock; Vince Coleman: William C. Rhoden, "Coleman Is a Man in a Hurry," *New York Times*, www.nytimes.com/1985/06/12/sports/coleman-is-a-man-in-a-hurry.html; Maury Wills: Bill Conlin, "The Maury Wills We Never Knew," *Chicago Tribune*, February 24, 1991, articles.chicagotribune.com/1991-02-24/sports/9101180148_1 _maurice-morning-wills-maury-wills-bases; Ron LeFlore: Bill Staples and Rich Herschlag, *Before the Glory: 20 Baseball Heroes Talk About Growing Up and Turning Hard Times Into Home Runs* (Deerfield Beach, FL: Health Communications, Inc.: 1997); Omar Moreno: Personal communication with Jim Trdinich, February 1, 2015; Tim Raines: Ron Fimrite, "Don't Knock the Rock," *Sports Illustrated*, June 25, 1984, www.si.com/vault/1984/06/25/619862/dont -knock-the-rock; Willie Wilson: Willie Wilson, *Inside the Park: Running the Base Path of Life* (Olathe, KS: Ascend Books, 2013); Marquis Grissom: Jerome Holtzman, "Marquis Grissom Is Newest Hero of the Fall," *Chicago Tribune*, October 24, 1997, http://articles.chicagotribune.com/1997-10-24/sports/ 9710240033_1_american-league-champion-marquis-grissom-bases; Kenny Lofton: Associated Press, "Former Wildcat Lofton Debuts with Atlanta, Goes 2-for-4," *Arizona Daily Wildcat*, March 28, 1997, http://wc.arizona.edu/papers/90/ 122/20_1_m.html.

150 **brothers who played professional baseball:** Frank J. Sulloway and Richard L. Zweigenhaft, "Birth Order and Risk Taking in Athletics: A Meta-Analysis and Study of Major League Baseball," *Personality and Social Psychology Review* 14 (2010): 402–16.

150 **"father of modern base-stealing":** David Falkner, *Great Time Coming: The Life of Jackie Robinson, from Baseball to Birmingham* (New York: Simon & Schuster, 1995).

151 **"a certain amount of nerve":** Rod Carew, *Carew* (New York: Simon & Schuster, 1979); Martin Miller, "Rod Carew Becomes Champion for the Abused," *Los Angeles Times*, December 12, 1994, http://articles.latimes.com/1994-12-12/local/me-8068_1_rod-carew.

151 **third ranked, Paul Molitor:** McCarron, "Jacoby Ellsbury's Steal of Home"; Ken Rosenthal, "You Can Go Home Again, Says Molitor," *Baltimore Sun*, April 6, 1996, articles.baltimoresun.com/1996-04-06/sports/1996097010_1_molitor-twins-orioles; Jim Souhan, "My Day with Molitor in 1996," *Star Tribune*, November 4, 2014, www.startribune.com/souhan-blog-my-day-with-molitor-in-1996/281481701; Bill Koenig, "Molitor Is Safe at Home," *USA Today*, June 6, 1996, usatoday30.usatoday.com/sports/baseball/sbbw0442.htm.

151 **two dozen major scientific revolutions:** Frank J. Sulloway, *Born to Rebel: Birth Order, Family Dynamics, and Creative Lives* (New York: Vintage, 1997), "Birth Order and Evolutionary Psychology: A Meta-Analytic Overview," *Psychological Inquiry* 6 (1995): 75–80, and "Sources of Scientific Innovation: A Meta-Analytic Approach (Commentary on Simonton, 2009)," *Perspectives on Psychological Science* 4 (2009): 455–59.

152 **Overall, laterborns were twice:** Frank J. Sulloway, *"Born to Rebel* and Its Critics," *Politics and the Life Sciences* 19 (2000): 181–202, and "Birth Order and Political Rebellion: An Assessment, with Biographical Data on Political Activists" (2002), www.sulloway.org/politics.html.

154 **logic of consequence:** James March, *A Primer on Decision-Making: How Decisions Happen* (New York: Free Press, 1994); see also J. Mark Weber, Shirli Kopelman, and David M. Messick, "A Conceptual Review of Decision Making in Social Dilemmas: Applying a Logic of Appropriateness," *Personality and Social Psychology Review* 8 (2004): 281–307.

154 **advantages of being firstborn:** Roger D. Clark and Glenn A. Rice, "Family Constellations and Eminence: The Birth Orders of Nobel Prize Winners," *Journal of Psychology: Interdisciplinary and Applied* 110 (1981): 281–87; Richard L. Zweigenhaft, "Birth Order, Approval-Seeking and Membership in Congress," *Journal of Individual Psychology* 31 (1975): 205–10; Rudy B. Andeweg and Steef B. Van Den Berg, "Linking Birth Order to Political Leadership: The Impact of Parents or Sibling Interaction?," *Political Psychology* 24 (2003): 605–23; Blema S. Steinberg, "The Making of Female Presidents and Prime Ministers: The Impact of Birth

Order, Sex of Siblings, and Father-Daughter Dynamics," *Political Psychology* 22 (2001): 89–110; Del Jones, "First-born Kids Become CEO Material," *USA Today*, September 4, 2007, http://usatoday30.usatoday.com/money/companies/management/2007-09-03-ceo-birth_N.htm; Ben Dattner, "Birth Order and Leadership," www.dattnerconsulting.com/birth.html.

154 **Laterborns have faster salary growth:** Marco Bertoni and Giorgio Brunello, "Laterborns Don't Give Up: The Effects of Birth Order on Earnings in Europe," *IZA Discussion Paper No. 7679*, October 26, 2013, http://papers.ssrn.com/sol3/papers.cfm?abstract_id=2345596.

155 **birth order was a better predictor:** Delroy J. Paulhus, Paul D. Trapnell, and David Chen, "Birth Order Effects on Personality and Achievement Within Families," *Psychological Science* 1999 (10): 482–88; Sulloway, "*Born to Rebel* and Its Critics," and "Why Siblings Are Like Darwin's Finches: Birth Order, Sibling Competition, and Adaptive Divergence Within the Family," in *The Evolution of Personality and Individual Differences,* eds. David M. Buss and Patricia H. Hawley (New York: Oxford University Press, 2010); Laura M. Argys, Daniel I. Rees, Susan L. Averett, and Benjama Witoonchart, "Birth Order and Risky Adolescent Behavior," *Economic Inquiry* 44 (2006): 215–33; Daniela Barni, Michele Roccato, Alessio Vieno, and Sara Alfieri, "Birth Order and Conservatism: A Multilevel Test of Sulloway's 'Born to Rebel' Thesis," *Personality and Individual Differences* 66 (2014): 58–63.

156 **When identical twins grow up:** Steven Pinker, "What Is the Missing Ingredient—Not Genes, Not Upbringing—That Shapes the Mind?," *Edge*, edge.org/response-detail/11078, and *The Blank Slate: The Modern Denial of Human Nature* (New York: Penguin Books, 2003); Eric Turkheimer and Mary Waldron, "Nonshared Environment: A Theoretical, Methodological, and Quantitative Review," *Psychological Bulletin* 126 (2000): 78–108; Robert Plomin and Denise Daniels, "Why Are Children in the Same Family So Different from Each Other?," *International Journal of Epidemiology* 40 (2011): 563–82.

156 **adopted siblings don't resemble:** Thomas J. Bouchard, Jr., and John C. Loehlin, "Genes, Evolution, and Personality," *Behavior Genetics* 31 (2001): 243–73; John C. Loehlin, *Genes and Environment in Personality Development* (Newbury Park, CA: Sage, 1992); John C. Loehlin, Robert R. McCrae, Paul T. Costa, Jr., and Oliver P. John, "Heritabilities of Common and Measure-Specific Components of the Big Five Personality Factors," *Journal of Research in Personality* 32 (1998): 431–53.

157 **"The niche of the responsible":** Sulloway, *Born to Rebel*; Helen Koch, "Some
Personality Correlates of Sex, Sibling Position, and Sex of Sibling Among Five- and
Six-Year-Old Children," *Genetic Psychology Monographs* 52 (1955): 3–50; Frank
Dumont, *A History of Personality Psychology: Theory, Science, and Research from
Hellenism to the Twenty-First Century* (Cambridge: Cambridge University Press, 2010);
"How is Personality Formed? A Talk with Frank J. Sulloway," *Edge*, May 17, 1998,
https://edge.org/conversation/how-is-personality-formed-.

157 **comedians tend to be more original and rebellious:** Gil Greengross and
Geoffrey F. Miller, "The Big Five Personality Traits of Professional Comedians
Compared to Amateur Comedians, Comedy Writers, and College Students,"
Personality and Individual Differences 47 (2009): 79–83; Gil Greengross, Rod A.
Martin, and Geoffrey Miller, "Personality Traits, Intelligence, Humor Styles, and
Humor Production Ability of Professional Stand-Up Comedians Compared to
College Students," *Psychology of Aesthetics, Creativity, and the Arts* 6 (2012): 74–82.

158 **people laugh when:** A. Peter McGraw and Caleb Warren, "Benign Violations:
Making Immoral Behavior Funny," *Psychological Science* 21 (2010): 1141–49.

158 **Jim Carrey's father:** Jim Carrey, "Official Commencement Address Graduating Class
of 2014 from Maharishi University of Management," May 24, 2014. www.mum.edu/
whats-happening/graduation-2014/full-jim-carrey-address-video-and-transcript.

158 **"I never had a job":** *Seinfeld*, "The Calzone," NBC, April 25, 1996.

158 **Comedy Central's 2004 list:** Comedy Central, "100 Greatest Stand-ups of All
Time," www.listology.com/list/comedy-central-100-greatest-standups-all-time.

158 **When I tracked the birth order of these hundred original comedians:** Adam
M. Grant, "Funny Babies: Great Comedians Are Born Last in Big Families,"
working paper (2015).

159 **more older brothers:** Ray Blanchard, "Fraternal Birth Order and the Maternal
Immune Hypothesis of Male Homosexuality," *Hormones and Behavior* 40 (2001):
105–14, and "Quantitative and Theoretical Analyses of the Relation Between
Older Brothers and Homosexuality in Men," *Journal of Theoretical Biology* 21
(2004): 173–87; James M. Cantor, Ray Blanchard, Andrew D. Paterson, and
Anthony F. Bogaert, "How Many Gay Men Owe Their Sexual Orientation to
Fraternal Birth Order?," *Archives of Sexual Behavior* 31 (2002): 63–71; Ray

Blanchard and Richard Lippa, "Birth Order, Sibling Sex Ratio, Handedness, and Sexual Orientation of Male and Female Participants in a BBC Internet Research Project," *Archives of Sexual Behavior* 36 (2007): 163–176; Anthony F. Bogaert, Ray Blanchard, and Lesley E. Crosthwait, "Interaction of Birth Order, Handedness, and Sexual Orientation in the Kinsey Interview Data," *Behavioral Neuroscience* 121 (2007): 845–53; Alicia Garcia-Falgueras and Dick F. Swaab, "Sexual Hormones and the Brain: An Essential Alliance for Sexual Identity and Sexual Orientation," *Endocrine Development* 17 (2010): 22–35.

160 **parents tend to start out:** Robert B. Zajonc, "Family Configuration and Intelligence," *Science* 192 (1976): 227–36, and "Validating the Confluence Model," *Psychological Bulletin* 93 (1983): 457–80; Robert B. Zajonc and Patricia R. Mullally, "Birth Order: Reconciling Conflicting Effects," *American Psychologist* 52 (1997): 685–799; Heidi Keller and Ulrike Zach, "Gender and Birth Order as Determinants of Parental Behaviour," *International Journal of Behavioral Development* 26 (2002): 177–84; J. Jill Suitor and Karl Pillemer, "Mothers' Favoritism in Later Life: The Role of Children's Birth Order," *Research on Aging* 29 (2007): 32–55.

160 **The poster victim:** Andre Agassi, *Open: An Autobiography* (New York: Knopf, 2009). For evidence that the children treated with the greatest hostility by parents are the most likely to rebel, see Katherine Jewsbury Conger and Rand D. Conger, "Differential Parenting and Change in Sibling Differences in Delinquency," *Journal of Family Psychology* 8 (1994): 287–302.

161 **"We were going to make fun":** Personal interview with Lizz Winstead, February 8, 2015, and Lizz Winstead, *Lizz Free or Die: Essays* (New York: Riverhead, 2012).

162 **"I'm from a very large family":** Jim Gaffigan, "The Youngest Child," *Comedy Central Presents*, July 11, 2000, www.cc.com/video-clips/g92efr/comedy-central-presents-the-youngest-child; see also Ben Kharakh, "Jim Gaffigan, Comedian and Actor," *Gothamist*, July 17, 2006, http://gothamist.com/2006/07/17/jim_gaffigan_co.php#.

162 **only children grow up:** Sulloway, "Why Siblings Are Like Darwin's Finches"; Catherine A. Salmon and Martin Daly, "Birth Order and Familial Sentiment: Middleborns Are Different," *Evolution and Human Behavior* 19 (1998): 299–312.

163 **"50 discipline encounters":** Martin L. Hoffman, *Empathy and Moral Development: Implications for Caring and Justice* (New York: Cambridge University Press, 2000).

163 ***"Explained* is the word":** Samuel P. Oliner and Pearl Oliner, *The Altruistic Personality: Rescuers of Jews in Nazi Europe* (New York: Touchstone, 1992); Samuel P. Oliner, "Ordinary Heroes," *Yes! Magazine*, November 5, 2001, www.yesmagazine.org/issues/can-love-save-the-world/ordinary-heroes; see also Eva Fogelman, *Conscience and Courage: Rescuers of Jews During the Holocaust* (New York: Doubleday, 2011).

164 **Parents of highly creative children:** John S. Dacey, "Discriminating Characteristics of the Families of Highly Creative Adolescents," *The Journal of Creative Behavior* 23 (1989): 263–71.

164 **"place emphasis on moral values":** Teresa M. Amabile, *Growing Up Creative: Nurturing a Lifetime of Creativity* (Buffalo, NY: Creative Education Foundation, 1989).

164 **teenagers defy rules when they're enforced in a controlling manner:** Maarten Vansteenkiste, Bart Soenens, Stijn Van Petegem, and Bart Duriez, "Longitudinal Associations Between Adolescent Perceived Degree and Style of Parental Prohibition and Internalization and Defiance," *Developmental Psychology* 50 (2014): 229–36; see also Sharon S. Brehm and Jack W. Brehm, *Psychological Reactance: A Theory of Freedom and Control* (New York: Academic Press, 1981).

164 **a factor that distinguished the creative:** Donald W. MacKinnon, "The Nature and Nurture of Creative Talent," *American Psychologist* 17 (1962): 484–95, and "Personality and the Realization of Creative Potential," *American Psychologist* 20 (1965): 273–81.

165 **"Guilt is the gift":** John Skow, "Erma in Bomburbia: Erma Bombeck," *Time*, July 2, 1984.

166 **merely mentioning *patients*:** Adam M. Grant and David A. Hofmann, "It's Not All About Me: Motivating Hand Hygiene Among Health Care Professionals by Focusing on Patients," *Psychological Science* 22 (2011): 1494–99.

167 **explanations of our impact:** Carolyn Zahn-Wexler, Marian Radke-Yarrow, and Robert A. King, "Child Rearing and Children's Prosocial Initiations Toward Victims of Distress," *Child Development* 50 (1979): 319–30; Seth Izen, "Childhood Discipline and the Development of Moral Courage," unpublished master's thesis, University of Massachusetts Lowell, www.uml.edu/docs/Childhood%20Discipline%

20and%20the%20Development%20of%20Moral%20Courage%20Thesis_tcm18-90752
.pdf; see also Eleanor E. Maccoby, "The Role of Parents in the Socialization of
Children: An Historical Overview," *Developmental Psychology* 28 (1992): 1006–17.

168 ***character* praise:** Joan E. Grusec and Erica Redler, "Attribution, Reinforcement, and
Altruism: A Developmental Analysis," *Developmental Psychology* 16 (1980): 525–34.

168 **Children who received character praise:** Adam Grant, "Raising a Moral Child,"
New York Times, April 11, 2014, www.nytimes.com/2014/04/12/opinion/sunday/
raising-a-moral-child.html.

169 **even among very young children:** Christopher J. Bryan, Allison Master, and
Gregory M. Walton, "'Helping' Versus 'Being a Helper': Invoking the Self to
Increase Helping in Young Children," *Child Development* 85 (2014): 1836–42.

169 **appeals to character are effective:** Christopher J. Bryan, Gabrielle S. Adams, and
Benoît Monin, "When Cheating Would Make You a Cheater: Implicating the Self
Prevents Unethical Behavior," *Journal of Experimental Psychology: General* 142
(2013): 1001–5.

169 **give up in the face of failure:** Carol S. Dweck, *Mindset: The New Psychology of
Success* (New York: Random House, 2006).

170 **Having a role model:** Penelope Lockwood and Ziva Kunda, "Increasing the
Salience of One's Best Selves Can Undermine Inspiration by Outstanding Role
Models," *Journal of Personality and Social Psychology* 76 (1999): 214–28; see also
Albert Bandura, *Self-Efficacy: The Exercise of Control* (New York: Freeman, 1997).

171 **Mentioning a mentor:** Bill E. Peterson and Abigail J. Stewart, "Antecedents and
Contexts of Generativity Motivation at Midlife," *Psychology and Aging* 11 (1996): 21–33.

172 **Malala Yousafzai was moved:** Jodi Kantor, "Malala Yousafzai: By the Book," *New
York Times*, August 19, 2014, www.nytimes.com/2014/08/24/books/review/malala
-yousafzai-by-the-book.html.

172 **King was inspired by Gandhi:** Rufus Burrow Jr., *Extremist for Love: Martin
Luther King Jr., Man of Ideas and Nonviolent Social Action* (Minneapolis, MN:
Fortress Press, 2014).

172   **as was Nelson Mandela:** "Nelson Mandela, the 'Gandhi of South Africa,' Had Strong Indian Ties," *Economic Times*, December 6, 2013, articles.economictimes .indiatimes.com/2013-12-06/news/44864354_1_nelson-mandela-gandhi-memorial -gandhian-philosophy.

172   **Elon Musk . . . *Lord of the Rings*:** Tad Friend, "Plugged In: Can Elon Musk Lead the Way to an Electric-Car Future?" *New Yorker*, August 24, 2009, www.newyorker .com/magazine/2009/08/24/plugged-in.

172   **Peter Thiel . . . *Lord of the Rings*:** Julian Guthrie, "Entrepreneur Peter Thiel Talks 'Zero to One,'" *SFGate*, September 21, 2014, www.sfgate.com/living/article/ Entrepreneur-Peter-Thiel-talks-Zero-to-One-5771228.php.

172   **Sheryl Sandberg . . . *A Wrinkle in Time*:** "Sheryl Sandberg: By the Book," *New York Times*, March 14, 2013, www.nytimes.com/2013/03/17/books/review/sheryl -sandberg-by-the-book.html.

172   **Jeff Bezos . . . *A Wrinkle in Time*:** "Jeffrey P. Bezos Recommended Reading": www.achievement.org/autodoc/bibliography/WrinkleinT_1.

172   **Mark Zuckerberg . . . *Ender's Game*:** Alyson Shontell, "The Books That Inspired Tech's Most Influential People," *Business Insider*, June 26, 2013, www.businessinsider .com/the-books-that-influenced-techs-most-influencial-ceos-2013-6?op=1.

172–73   **Jack Ma . . . *Ali Baba and the Forty Thieves*:** Helen H. Wang, "Alibaba Saga III: Jack Ma Discovered the Internet," *Forbes*, July 17, 2014, www.forbes.com/sites/ helenwang/2014/07/17/alibaba-saga-iii/.

173   **when children's stories emphasize original achievements:** Richard DeCharms and Gerald H. Moeller, "Values Expressed in American Children's Readers, 1800–1950," *Journal of Abnormal and Social Psychology* 64 (1962): 136–42; see also David C. McClelland, *The Achieving Society* (Princeton, NJ: Van Nostrand Co., 1961); Stefan Engeser, Falko Rheinberg, and Matthias Möller, "Achievement Motive Imagery in German Schoolbooks: A Pilot Study Testing McClelland's Hypothesis," *Journal of Research in Personality* 43 (2009): 110–13; Stefan Engeser, Ina Hollricher, and Nicola Baumann, "The Stories Children's Books Tell Us: Motive-Related Imagery in Children's Books and Their Relation to Academic Performance and Crime Rates," *Journal of Research in Personality* 47 (2013): 421–26.

173   **"grow up and contribute":** Dean Keith Simonton, *Greatness: Who Makes History and Why* (New York: Guilford Press, 1994).

173   **making the impossible seem possible:** Mark Strauss, "Ten Inventions Inspired by Science Fiction," *Smithsonian* magazine, March 15, 2012, www.smithsonianmag .com/science-nature/ten-inventions-inspired-by-science-fiction-128080674/?no-ist.

174   **reading *Harry Potter* can improve:** Loris Vezzali, Sofia Stathi, Dino Giovannini, Dora Capozza, and Elena Trifiletti, "The Greatest Magic of Harry Potter: Reducing Prejudice," *Journal of Applied Social Psychology* 45 (2015): 105–21.

7: Rethinking Groupthink

175   **"In fact, the only sin":** Ralph Waldo Emerson, *Society and Solitude: Twelve Chapters* (New York: Houghton, Mifflin, 1893).

175   **Edwin Land, the founder of Polaroid:** Mary Tripsas and Giovanni Gavetti, "Capabilities, Cognition, and Inertia: Evidence from Digital Imaging," *Strategic Management Journal* 21 (2000): 1147–61; Victor K. McElheny, *Insisting on the Impossible: The Life of Edwin Land* (New York: Basic Books, 1999); Milton P. Dentch, *Fall of an Icon: Polaroid After Edwin H. Land: An Insider's View of the Once Great Company* (New York: Riverhaven Books, 2012); Christopher Bonanos, *Instant: The Story of Polaroid* (Princeton, NJ: Princeton Architectural Press, 2012); Peter C. Wensberg, *Land's Polaroid: A Company and the Man Who Invented It* (Boston: Houghton Mifflin, 1987); David Sheff, "Steve Jobs," *Playboy*, February 1985, http://longform.org/stories/playboy-interview-steve-jobs; Brian Dumaine, "How Polaroid Flashed Back," *Fortune*, February 16, 1987, http://archive.fortune .com/magazines/fortune/fortune_archive/1987/02/16/68669/index.htm.

177   **a group becomes that cohesive:** Charles A. O'Reilly and Jennifer A. Chatman, "Culture as Social Control: Corporations, Cults, and Commitment," *Research in Organizational Behavior* 18 (1996): 157–200.

178   **Had Kennedy's advisers:** Irving Janis, *Groupthink: Psychological Studies of Policy Decisions and Fiascoes* (Boston: Houghton Mifflin, 1973); Cass R. Sunstein, *Why Societies Need Dissent* (Boston: Harvard University Press, 2003).

178   **problem with the cohesion theory:** Sally Riggs Fuller and Ramon J. Aldag, "Organizational Tonypandy: Lessons from a Quarter Century of the Groupthink

Phenomenon," *Organizational Behavior and Human Decision Processes* 73 (1998): 163–84; Roderick M. Kramer, "Revisiting the Bay of Pigs and Vietnam Decisions 25 Years Later: How Well Has the Groupthink Hypothesis Stood the Test of Time?," *Organizational Behavior and Human Decision Processes* 73 (1998): 236–71; Glen Whyte, "Recasting Janis's Groupthink Model: The Key Role of Collective Efficacy in Decision Fiascoes," *Organizational Behavior and Human Decision Processes* 73 (1998): 185–209; Clark McCauley, "Group Dynamics in Janis's Theory of Groupthink: Backward and Forward," *Organizational Behavior and Human Decision Processes* 73 (1998): 142–62; Randall S. Peterson, Pamela D. Owens, Philip E. Tetlock, Elliott T. Fan, and Paul Martorana, "Group Dynamics in Top Management Teams: Groupthink, Vigilance, and Alternative Models of Organizational Failure and Success," *Organizational Behavior and Human Decision Processes* 73 (1998): 272–305; Philip E. Tetlock, Randall S. Peterson, Charles McGuire, Shi-jie Chang, and Peter Feld, "Assessing Political Group Dynamics: A Test of the Groupthink Model," *Journal of Personality and Social Psychology* 63 (1992): 403–25; Ramon J. Aldag and Sally Riggs Fuller, "Beyond Fiasco: A Reappraisal of the Groupthink Phenomenon and a New Model of Group Decision Processes," *Psychological Bulletin* 113 (1993): 533–52; Richard E. Neustadt and Ernest R. May, *Thinking in Time: The Uses of History for Decision Makers* (New York: Free Press, 1986); Steve W. J. Kozlowski and Daniel R. Ilgen, "Enhancing the Effectiveness of Work Groups and Teams," *Psychological Science in the Public Interest* 7 (2006): 77–124; Anthony R. Pratkanis and Marlene E. Turner, "Methods for Counteracting Groupthink Risk: A Critical Appraisal," *International Journal of Risk and Contingency Management* 2 (2013): 18–38; Francis J. Flynn and Jennifer A. Chatman, "Strong Cultures and Innovation: Oxymoron or Opportunity?" *The International Handbook of Organizational Culture and Climate* (2001): 263–87.

180 **one blueprint was far superior:** James N. Baron and Michael T. Hannan, "Organizational Blueprints for Success in High-Tech Startups: Lessons from the Stanford Project on Emerging Companies," *California Management Review* 44 (2002): 8–36; Michael T. Hannan, James N. Baron, Greta Hsu, and Ozgecan Kocak, "Organizational Identities and the Hazard of Change," *Industrial and Corporate Change* 15 (2006): 755–84.

183 **what got you here won't get you there:** Marshall Goldsmith, *What Got You Here Won't Get You There: How Successful People Become Even More Successful* (New York: Hachette, 2007).

183 **organizations tend to become more homogeneous:** Edgar H. Schein, *Organizational Culture* (San Francisco: Jossey-Bass, 1992); Benjamin Schneider,

"The People Make the Place," *Personnel Psychology* 40 (1987): 437–53; Benjamin Schneider, D. Brent Smith, and Harold W. Goldstein, "Attraction-Selection-Attrition: Toward a Person-Environment Psychology of Organizations," in *Person-Environment Psychology: Models and Perspectives* (2000): 61–85.

183 **in stable industries, large companies:** Jesper Sørensen, "The Strength of Corporate Culture and the Reliability of Firm Performance," *Administrative Science Quarterly* 47 (2002): 70–91.

184 **CEOs sought advice from friends:** Michael L. McDonald and James D. Westphal, "Getting By with the Advice of Their Friends: CEOs' Advice Networks and Firms' Strategic Responses to Poor Performance," *Administrative Science Quarterly* 48 (2003): 1–32.

184 **generated 16 percent more ideas:** Charlan J. Nemeth, Bernard Personnaz, Marie Personnaz, and Jack A. Goncalo, "The Liberating Role of Conflict in Group Creativity: A Study in Two Countries," *European Journal of Social Psychology* 34 (2004): 365–74.

184 **debate and criticism improve:** Kevin Dunbar, "How Scientists Really Reason: Scientific Reasoning in Real-World Laboratories," in *The Nature of Insight*, eds., Robert J. Sternberg and Janet E. Davidson (Cambridge: MIT Press, 1995) 365–95; Chip Heath, Richard P. Larrick, and Joshua Klayman, "Cognitive Repairs: How Organizational Practices Can Compensate for Individual Shortcomings," *Research in Organizational Behavior* 20 (1998): 1–37; Robert S. Dooley and Gerald E. Fryxell, "Attaining Decision Quality and Commitment from Dissent: The Moderating Effects of Loyalty and Competence in Strategic Decision-Making Teams," *Academy of Management Journal* 42 (1999): 389–402.

185 **"Minority viewpoints":** Charlan J. Nemeth, "Differential Contributions of Majority and Minority Influence," *Psychological Review* 93 (1986): 23–32; Stefan Schulz-Hardt, Felix C. Brodbeck, Andreas Mojzisch, Rudolf Kerschreiter, and Dieter Frey, "Group Decision Making in Hidden Profile Situations: Dissent as a Facilitator for Decision Quality," *Journal of Personality and Social Psychology* 91 (2006): 1080–93.

189 **Bridgewater has prevented groupthink:** Personal interviews with Zack Wieder and Mark Kirby, June 24, 2014; personal interviews with Zack Wieder, January 12, February 9 and 16, and April 16, 2015; personal interviews with Ray Dalio, July 31, 2014, and February 12, 2015; and many hours of additional interviews, observations,

videos, and cases from current and former Bridgewater employees between June 2014 and January 2015; Ray Dalio, "Principles," www.bwater.com/home/culture—principles.aspx; Robert Kegan, Lisa Lahey, Andy Fleming, and Matthew Miller, "Making Business Personal," *Harvard Business Review*, April 2014, 45–52; Kevin Roose, "Pursuing Self-Interest in Harmony with the Laws of the Universe and Contributing to Evolution Is Universally Rewarded," *New York Magazine*, April 10, 2001, http://nymag.com/news/business/wallstreet/ray-dalio-2011-4/; Jeffrey T. Polzer and Heidi K. Gardner, "Bridgewater Associates," Harvard Business School Video Case 413-702, May 2013, www.hbs.edu/faculty/Pages/item.aspx?num=44831.

190 **As Jack Handey advised:** Jack Handey, *Saturday Night Live*, 1991.

190 **"Cultural fit":** Lauren A. Rivera, "Guess Who Doesn't Fit In at Work," *The New York Times*, May 30, 2015,: http://www.nytimes.com/2015/05/31/opinion/sunday/guess-who-doesnt-fit-in-at-work.html.

190 **IDEO:** Personal communication with Duane Bray, January 30, 2014.

191 **bring in someone to oppose:** Charlan Jeanne Nemeth, "Minority Influence Theory," in *Handbook of Theories in Social Psychology* 2 (2012): 362–78; Charlan Nemeth, Keith Brown, and John Rogers, "Devil's Advocate Versus Authentic Dissent: Stimulating Quantity and Quality," *European Journal of Social Psychology* 31 (2001): 707–20; personal communication with Charlan Nemeth, January 15, 2015; Roger B. Porter, *Presidential Decision Making: The Economic Policy Board* (Cambridge: Cambridge University Press, 1980).

192 **designated to dissent:** Stefan Schulz-Hardt, Marc Jochims, and Dieter Frey, "Productive Conflict in Group Decision-Making: Genuine and Contrived Dissent as Strategies to Counteract Biased Information Seeking," *Organizational Behavior and Human Decision Processes* 88 (2002): 563–86.

195 **"strong opinions, weakly held":** Paul Saffo, "Strong Opinions, Weakly Held," July 26, 2008, www.skmurphy.com/blog/2010/08/16/paul-saffo-forecasting-is-strong-opinions-weakly-held/.

197 **when employees bring solutions:** Jian Liang, Crystal I. C. Farh, and Jiing-Lih Farh, "Psychological Antecedents of Promotive and Prohibitive Voice: A Two-Wave Examination," *Academy of Management Journal* 55 (2012): 71–92.

197   **a culture of advocacy:** David A. Hofmann, "Overcoming the Obstacles to Cross-Functional Decision Making: Laying the Groundwork for Collaborative Problem Solving," *Organizational Dynamics* (2015); personal conversations with David Hofmann and Jeff Edwards, March 2008.

198   **"Canaries":** Laszlo Bock, *Work Rules! Insights from Google That Will Transform How You Live and Lead* (New York: Twelve, 2015).

199   **"knowing others' preferences":** Andreas Mojzisch and Stefan Schulz-Hardt, "Knowing Others' Preferences Degrades the Quality of Group Decisions," *Journal of Personality and Social Psychology* 98 (2010): 794–808.

199   **when groups consider options:** Andrea B. Hollingshead, "The Rank-Order Effect in Group Decision Making," *Organizational Behavior and Human Decision Processes* 68 (1996): 181–93.

201   **"Argue like you're right":** Quoted in Robert I. Sutton, "It's Up to You to Start a Good Fight," *Harvard Business Review*, August 3, 2010.

203   **At the software company Index Group:** Personal interview with Tom Gerrity, July 12, 2011.

205   **professional theaters:** Zannie G. Voss, Daniel M. Cable, and Glenn B. Voss, "Organizational Identity and Firm Performance: What Happens When Leaders Disagree About 'Who We Are,'" *Organization Science* 17 (2006): 741–55.

205   **The more core principles:** Andrew Carton, Chad Murphy, and Jonathan Clark, "A (Blurry) Vision of the Future: How Leader Rhetoric About Ultimate Goals Influences Performance," *Academy of Management Journal* 57 (2014): 1544–70.

207   **field of evidence-based management:** Trish Reay, Whitney Berta, and Melanie Kazman Kohn, "What's the Evidence on Evidence-Based Management?," *Academy of Management Perspectives* (November 2009): 5–18.

8: Rocking the Boat and Keeping It Steady

210   **"I learned that courage":** Nelson Mandela, *Long Walk to Freedom: The Autobiography of Nelson Mandela* (New York: Little, Brown, 1995).

211 **Instead of visualizing success:** Personal interview with Lewis Pugh, June 10, 2014, and personal communication, February 15, 2015; Lewis Pugh, *Achieving the Impossible* (London: Simon & Schuster, 2010) and *21 Yaks and a Speedo: How to Achieve Your Impossible* (Johannesburg and Cape Town, South Africa: Jonathan Ball Publishers, 2013); "Swimming Toward Success" speech at the World Economic Forum, Davos, Switzerland, January 23, 2014.

211 **effective strategies for managing emotions:** Adam M. Grant, "Rocking the Boat But Keeping It Steady: The Role of Emotion Regulation in Employee Voice," *Academy of Management Journal* 56 (2013): 1703–23.

212 **U.S. government leaders:** Steven Kelman, Ronald Sanders, Gayatri Pandit, and Sarah Taylor, "'I Won't Back Down?' Complexity and Courage in Federal Decision-Making," Harvard Kennedy School of Government RWP13-044 (2013).

212 **dedicated environmentalists:** Scott Sonenshein, Katherine A. DeCelles, and Jane E. Dutton, "It's Not Easy Being Green: The Role of Self-Evaluations in Explaining Support of Environmental Issues," *Academy of Management Journal* 57 (2014): 7–37.

212 **strategic optimism and defensive pessimism:** Julie K. Norem and Nancy Cantor, "Defensive Pessimism: Harnessing Anxiety as Motivation," *Journal of Personality and Social Psychology* 51 (1986): 1208–17; Stacie M. Spencer and Julie K. Norem, "Reflection and Distraction: Defensive Pessimism, Strategic Optimism, and Performance," *Personality and Social Psychology Bulletin* 22 (1996): 354–65; Julie K. Norem and K. S. Shaun Illingworth, "Strategy-Dependent Effects of Reflecting on Self and Tasks: Some Implications of Optimism and Defensive Pessimism," *Journal of Personality and Social Psychology* 65 (1993): 822–35; Julie K. Norem and Edward C. Chang, "The Positive Psychology of Negative Thinking," *Journal of Clinical Psychology* 58 (2002): 993–1001; Tim Jarvis, "The Power of Negative Thinking," *O, The Oprah Magazine*, March 2009, http://www.oprah.com/spirit/Defensive-Pessimism-How-Negative-Thinking-Can-Pay-Off.

214 **when presidents are too optimistic:** A. Timur Sevincer, Greta Wagner, Johanna Kalvelage, and Gabriele Oettingen, "Positive Thinking About the Future in Newspaper Reports and Presidential Addresses Predicts Economic Downturn," *Psychological Science* 25 (2014): 1010–17.

215 **ordinary people list their fears:** Kaya Burgess, "Speaking in Public Is Worse Than Death for Most," *Times* (London), October 30, 2013, www.thetimes.co.uk/

tto/science/article3908129.ece; Karen Kangas Dwyer and Marlina M. Davidson, "Is Public Speaking Really More Feared Than Death?," *Communication Research Reports* 29 (2012): 99–107; Jerry Seinfeld, www.youtube.com/watch?v= kL7fTLjFzAg.

215 *calm* **versus** *excited*: Alison Wood Brooks, "Get Excited: Reappraising Pre-Performance Anxiety as Excitement," *Journal of Experimental Psychology: General* 143 (2014): 1144–58.

216 **a stop system and a go system:** Charles S. Carver and Teri L. White, "Behavioral Inhibition, Behavioral Activation, and Affective Responses to Impending Reward and Punishment: The BIS/BAS Scales," *Journal of Personality and Social Psychology* 67 (1994): 319–33.

216 **"Your stop system":** Susan Cain, "Why You Fear Public Speaking, and What to Do About It," accessed on September 18, 2014, at www.thepowerofintroverts.com/ 2011/02/08/public-speaking-for-introverts-and-other-microphone-averse-people -tip-2.

217 **the unknown is more terrifying:** Jacob B. Hirsh and Michael Inzlicht, "The Devil You Know: Neuroticism Predicts Neural Response to Uncertainty," *Psychological Science* 19 (2008): 962–67.

217 **"they feel more in control":** Olga Khazan, "The Upside of Pessimism," *Atlantic*, September 12, 2014, www.theatlantic.com/health/archive/2014/09/dont-think -positively/379993.

220 **Popovic's approaches to:** Personal interview with Srdja Popovic, February 8, 2015; Srdja Popovic, *Blueprint for Revolution: How to Use Rice Pudding, Lego Men, and Other Nonviolent Techniques to Galvanize Communities, Overthrow Dictators, or Simply Change the World* (New York: Spiegel & Grau, 2015); *Bringing Down a Dictator*, directed by Steven York, WETA, in association with York Zimerman, 2002; Peter McGraw and Joel Warner, *The Humor Code: A Global Search for What Makes Things Funny* (New York: Simon & Schuster, 2014); Srdja Popovic, "Why Dictators Don't Like Jokes," *Foreign Policy*, April 5, 2013; CANVAS library, accessed on December 26, 2014, at www.canvasopedia.org/index.php/library.

220 **developing a Skype vision:** Personal interviews with Josh Silverman, October 24, November 12, and December 2, 2014.

220 ***Outsourcing Inspiration:*** Adam M. Grant and David A. Hofmann, "Outsourcing Inspiration: The Performance Effects of Ideological Messages from Leaders and Beneficiaries," *Organizational Behavior and Human Decision Processes* 116 (2011): 173–87.

222 **inspired to achieve the highest performance:** Adam M. Grant, "Leading with Meaning: Beneficiary Contact, Prosocial Impact, and the Performance Effects of Transformational Leadership," *Academy of Management Journal* 55 (2012): 458–76.

224 **judge the lengths of different lines:** Solomon E. Asch, "Opinions and Social Pressure," *Scientific American* 193 (1955): 31–35, and "Studies of Independence and Conformity: A Minority of One Against a Unanimous Majority," *Psychological Monographs* 70 (1956): 1–70; see also Rod Bond and Peter B. Smith, "Culture and Conformity: A Meta-Analysis of Studies Using Asch's (1952b, 1956) Line Judgment Task," *Psychological Bulletin* 119 (1996): 111–37.

225 **"The first follower":** Derek Sivers, "How to Start a Movement," TED Talks, April 2010, www.ted.com/talks/derek_sivers_how_to_start_a_movement/transcript ?language=en.

225 **"Never doubt that a small group":** Margaret Mead, *The World Ahead: An Anthropologist Anticipates the Future*, ed. Robert B. Textor (New York: Berghahn Books, 2005).

225 **just having one friend:** Sigal G. Barsade and Hakan Ozcelik, "Not Alone But Lonely: Work Loneliness and Employee Performance," working paper (2011).

229 **They were treated so poorly:** Robert I. Sutton, "Breaking the Cycle of Abuse in Medicine," March 13, 2007, accessed on February 24, 2015, at bobsutton.typepad .com/my_weblog/2007/03/breaking_the_cy.html.

230 **"By the time we were ready":** Personal interview with Brian Goshen, September 22, 2014.

231 **championed environmental issues:** Lynne M. Andersson and Thomas S. Bateman, "Individual Environmental Initiative: Championing Natural Environmental Issues in U.S. Business Organizations," *Academy of Management Journal* 43 (2000): 548–70.

232 **sense of urgency:** John Kotter, *Leading Change* (Boston: Harvard Business School Press, 1996).

233 **dramatically shift risk preferences:** Amos Tversky and Daniel Kahneman, "The Framing of Decisions and the Psychology of Choice," *Science* 211 (1981): 453–58; Max Bazerman, *Judgment in Managerial Decision Making* (New York: John Wiley, 1994).

233 **perceive the new behavior as safe or risky:** Alexander J. Rothman, Roger D. Bartels, Jhon Wlaschin, and Peter Salovey, "The Strategic Use of Gain- and Loss-Framed Messages to Promote Healthy Behavior: How Theory Can Inform Practice," *Journal of Communication* 56 (2006): 202–20.

234 **"kill the company" exercise:** Lisa Bodell, *Kill the Company: End the Status Quo, Start an Innovation Revolution* (New York: Bibliomotion, 2012).

234 **"The greatest communicators":** Nancy Duarte, "The Secret Structure of Great Talks," TEDxEast, November 2011, www.ted.com/talks/nancy_duarte_the_secret _structure_of_great_talks.

234 **The exercise capitalizes:** Anita Williams Woolley, "Playing Offense vs. Defense: The Effects of Team Strategic Orientation on Team Process in Competitive Environments," *Organization Science* 22 (2011): 1384–98.

235 **"This great nation":** Franklin Delano Roosevelt's first inaugural address, March 4, 1933.

235 **"one hundred years later":** Martin Luther King, Jr.'s, "I have a dream" speech, August 28, 1963; Clarence B. Jones, *Behind the Dream: The Making of the Speech That Transformed a Nation* (New York: Palgrave Macmillan, 2011); Drew Hansen, *The Dream: Martin Luther King, Jr., and the Speech That Inspired a Nation* (New York: Harper Perennial, 2005).

235 **"King articulates the crowd's":** Patricia Wasielewski, "The Emotional Basis of Charisma," *Symbolic Interaction* 8 (1985): 207–22.

235 **when we're experiencing doubts:** Minjung Koo and Ayelet Fishbach, "Dynamics of Self-Regulation: How (Un)accomplished Goal Actions Affect Motivation," *Journal of Personality and Social Psychology* 94 (2008): 183–95.

236 **"Instead of courage":** Tom Peters, December 30, 2013, www.facebook.com/ permalink.php?story_fbid=10151762619577396&id=10666812395.

237 **"simultaneously hot- and cool-headed":** Debra E. Meyerson and Maureen A. Scully, "Tempered Radicalism and the Politics of Ambivalence and Change," *Organization Science* 6 (1995): 585–600.

237 **surface acting and deep acting:** Arlie Hochschild, *The Managed Heart: Commercialization of Human Feeling* (California: University of California Press, 1983).

237 **method acting:** Constantin Stanislavski, *An Actor Prepares* (New York: Bloomsbury Academic, 1936/2013); Chris Sullivan, "How Daniel Day-Lewis' Notoriously Rigorous Role Preparation Has Yielded Another Oscar Contender," *The Independent*, February 1, 2008.

238 **surface acting burns us out:** Alicia Grandey, "When 'The Show Must Go On': Surface Acting and Deep Acting as Determinants of Emotional Exhaustion and Peer-Rated Service Delivery," *Academy of Management Journal* 46 (2003): 86–96; Ute R. Hülsheger and Anna F. Schewe, "On the Costs and Benefits of Emotional Labor: A Meta-Analysis of Three Decades of Research," *Journal of Occupational Health Psychology* 16 (2011): 361–89.

238 **To prepare citizens:** Aldon D. Morris, *The Origins of the Civil Rights Movement: Black Communities Organizing for Change* (New York: Free Press, 1984); Rufus Burrow, Jr., *Extremist for Love: Martin Luther King Jr., Man of Ideas and Nonviolent Social Action* (Minneapolis, MN: Fortress Press, 2014); Martin Luther King, Jr., "Remarks in Favor of the Montgomery Bus Boycott," June 27, 1956, accessed on February 24, 2015, at www.usnews.com/news/blogs/press-past/2013/ 02/04/remembering-rosa-parks-on-her-100th-birthday; Martin Luther King, Jr., interview with Kenneth Clark, accessed on February 24, 2015, at www.pbs.org/ wgbh/amex/mlk/sfeature/sf_video_pop_03_tr_qt.html.

239 **hitting a pillow:** *Analyze This*, directed by Harold Ramis, Warner Bros., 1999.

239 **To test whether venting helps:** Brad J. Bushman, "Does Venting Anger Feed or Extinguish the Flame? Catharsis, Rumination, Distraction, Anger, and Aggressive Responding," *Personality and Social Psychology Bulletin* 28 (2002): 724–31; Brad J. Bushman, Roy F. Baumeister, and Angela D. Stack, "Catharsis, Aggression, and

Persuasive Influence: Self-Fulfilling or Self-Defeating Prophecies?," *Journal of Personality and Social Psychology* 76 (1999): 367–76; Brad J. Bushman, Angela M. Bonacci, William C. Pedersen, Eduardo A. Vasquez, and Norman Miller, "Chewing on It Can Chew You Up: Effects of Rumination on Triggered Displaced Aggression," *Journal of Personality and Social Psychology* 88 (2005): 969–83.

240 **Catharsis seems to work best:** Timothy D. Wilson, *Redirect: The Surprising New Science of Psychological Change* (New York: Little, Brown, 2011); Jonathan I. Bisson, Peter L. Jenkins, Julie Alexander, and Carol Bannister, "Randomised Controlled Trial of Psychological Debriefing for Victims of Acute Burn Trauma," *British Journal of Psychiatry* 171 (1997): 78–81; Benedict Carey, "Sept. 11 Revealed Psychology's Limits, Review Finds," *New York Times*, July 28, 2011; James W. Pennebaker, *Opening Up: The Healing Power of Expressing Emotions* (New York: Guilford Press, 1997).

241 **channel anger productively:** Andrew Brodsky, Joshua D. Margolis, and Joel Brockner, "Speaking Truth to Power: A Full Cycle Approach," working paper (2015).

242 **Focusing on the victim:** Guy D. Vitaglione and Mark A. Barnett, "Assessing a New Dimension of Empathy: Empathic Anger as a Predictor of Helping and Punishing Desires," *Motivation and Emotion* 27 (2003): 301–25; C. Daniel Batson, Christopher L. Kennedy, Lesley-Anne Nord, E. L. Stocks, D'Yani A. Fleming, Christian M. Marzette, David A. Lishner, Robin E. Hayes, Leah M. Kolchinsky, and Tricia Zerger, "Anger at Unfairness: Is It Moral Outrage?," *European Journal of Social Psychology* 37 (2007): 1272–85; Jennifer J. Kish-Gephart, James R. Detert, Linda Klebe Trevino, and Amy C. Edmondson, "Silenced by Fear: The Nature, Sources, and Consequences of Fear at Work," *Research in Organizational Behavior* 29 (2009): 163–93.

242 **"I arise in the morning":** Israel Shenker, "E. B. White: Notes and Comment by Author," *New York Times*, July 11, 1969: www.nytimes.com/books/97/08/03/lifetimes/white-notes.html.

243 **happiness of pursuit:** Brian R. Little, *Me, Myself, and Us: The Science of Personality and the Art of Well-Being* (New York: PublicAffairs, 2014); Brian R. Little, "Personal Projects and Social Ecology: Lives, Liberties and the Happiness of Pursuit," Colloquium presentation, department of psychology, University of Michigan (1992); Brian R. Little, "Personality Science and the Northern Tilt: As

Positive as Possible Under the Circumstances," in *Designing Positive Psychology: Taking Stock and Moving Forward,* eds. K. M. Sheldon, T. B. Kashdan, and M. F. Steger (New York: Oxford University Press, 228–47).

Action for Impact

247 **rapid-innovation cell:** Personal interviews with Benjamin Kohlmann, November 19 and December 10, 2014.

249 **Innovation tournaments are highly efficient:** Karl Ulrich and Christian Terwiesch, *Innovation Tournaments: Creating and Selecting Exceptional Opportunities* (Boston: Harvard Business School Press, 2009); "Why Some Innovation Tournaments Succeed and Others Fail," *Knowledge@Wharton*, February 20, 2014, knowledge.wharton.upenn .edu/article/innovation-tournaments-succeed-others-fail.

249 ***Picture yourself as the enemy*:** Lisa Bodell, *Kill the Company: End the Status Quo, Start an Innovation Revolution* (New York: Bibliomotion, 2012).

250 **At DreamWorks Animation:** Anita Bruzzese, "DreamWorks Is Believer in Every Employee's Creativity," *USA Today*, July 23, 2012, usatoday30.usatoday.com/money/ jobcenter/workplace/bruzzese/story/2012-07-22/dreamworks-values-innovation-in -all-workers/56376470/1.

250 **add skill variety:** Robert I. Sutton and Andrew Hargadon, "Brainstorming Groups in Context: Effectiveness in a Product Design Firm," *Administrative Science Quarterly* 41 (1996): 685–718.

250 ***Ban the words* like, love, *and* hate:** Personal interviews with Nancy Lublin, December 12, 2014, and February 23, 2015.

253 **Jigsaw Classroom:** Elliot Aronson and Shelley Patnoe, *Cooperation in the Classroom: The Jigsaw Method* (New York: Addison Wesley, 1997).

Index

academic achievement, 155

achievement motivation, 10–11, 13

acting, 237–38

Actions for impact, 245–54

Adams, Ansel, 175

Adams, Douglas, 99*n*

Adams, John, 11

Adams, Scott, 18, 29

Adler, Alfred, 156–57

Adventures of Huckleberry Finn
    (Twain), 112

advocacy, culture of, 197–98, 204

African Americans, 118

    men, voting rights for,
        118–19, 126–27

    women, 86

Agassi, Andre, 160*n*–61*n*

age, 108–13, 152

agreeableness, 81–82

alcohol abuse, 119, 139, 140*n*, 141, 248

Aldag, Ray, 179

Ali Baba and the Forty Thieves, 173

allies, 249

    See also Coalitions

Amabile, Teresa, 51, 71–72, 164

Amazon, 29, 107, 188

ambivalence, 212

American Revolution, 11

Analyze This, 239

Anderson, Carl, 167

Andersson, Lynne, 231

Angelou, Maya, 36

anger, 235–37, 239–42, 248

    civil rights activists and, 212, 238–39, 241

    venting of, 239–41

Anthony, Susan B., 115–16, 118–19, 121,
    126–31, 142–44

anxiety. *See* fear and anxiety

apathy, 234, 236

Apple, 2, 12–13, 17, 26, 190*n*

    Dubinsky at, 87–89, 91

    iPhone, 7, 90, 91

appropriateness, logic of, 154, 166–67, 170

Armstrong, Neil, 14

Aronson, Elliot, 131–32

arts, 46–48, 246

Asch, Solomon, 224–25

Ashforth, Blake, 128, 143

Assad, Bashar al-, 227, 229

autocratic blueprint, 181*n*

Babble, 68–70, 72–74

Bach, Johann Sebastian, 36

Baker, Jean, 8, 116, 140

Barnett, William, 106

Baron, James, 179–81, 183

Barr, Roseanne, 171

Barron's, 189

Barsade, Sigal, 225

baseball, 146–51, 157, 200

Bateman, Thomas, 231

Bay of Pigs, 176–78, 191, 199*n*

Bearing the Cross (Garrow), 102

Beethoven, Ludwig van, 34–36

behavior, praise of, 168–70
Belafonte, Harry, 93
Belgrade, 218, 226, 231
believability, 200–201, 207, 208
Bellezza, Silvia, 67
Benjamin, Susan, 84, 107
Berdahl, Jennifer, 85*n*
Berg, Justin, 24, 32–33, 37*n*, 40–44,
    59, 135–37, 140
Bertoni, Marco, 154
Beyoncé, 114
Bezos, Jeff, 29, 39, 50–51, 60, 172
Binder, Lon, 59
birth order, 148–59, 162, 174
Blair, Tony, 74*n*
Blakely, Sara, 20, 114
Blue Nile, 107
Blueprint for Revolution (Popovic), 226
blueprints, 180, 181*n*, 187*n*
    autocratic, 181*n*
    bureaucratic, 181*n*, 182
    changing, 187*n*
    commitment, 180–83, 181*n*, 187*n*, 188
    professional, 180–82, 181*n*
    star, 180–82, 181*n*
Blumenthal, Neil, 15–16, 20–21,
    58–59, 107
Bock, Laszlo, 198–99
Bodell, Lisa, 250
Bolton, Lisa, 104
Bombeck, Erma, 165
book reviewers, 71–72
books, characters in, 172–74
Booth, Mac, 186
Boothby, Erica, 120*n*
bosses and managers, 80–82
Bowles, Chester, 177
brainstorming, 184*n*
Brando, Marlon, 93

Bridgewater Associates, 187–91, 194–96,
    199–209, 251
Brin, Sergey, 17–18, 83
British Petroleum, 197
Brock, Lou, 147, 149
Brockner, Joel, 241
Brodsky, Andrew, 241
Brooks, Alison Wood, 215, 216
Brooks, Mel, 159
browser preference, 3–6
Brunello, Giorgio, 154
Bryan, Christopher, 169–70
bureaucratic blueprint, 181*n*, 182
Burke, Don, 68, 79*n*
Burton, Diane, 181*n*
Bush, George W., 6
Bushman, Brad, 239–40

Cable, Dan, 205
Cain, Susan, 216
calm, 215, 230*n*
canaries, 198–99
Cantillon, Richard, 14
career success, 154–55
Carew, Rod, 151
Carlin, George, 158
Carrey, Jim, 158
Carrie (King), 18
Carton, Drew, 205
Castro, Fidel, 177
catharsis, 240*n*
Catholic Church, 191, 207
Catt, Carrie Chapman, 115, 144–45
CEOs, 101, 184
character, praise of, 168–70, 252–53
cheating, 169–70
Cheney, Dick, 30
child prodigies, 8–10
Chile, 226

chocolate, 120*n*

Chrome, 4–6

CIA, 26, 62–64, 67–68, 78–79, 82, 84, 86, 89, 91, 107, 247

Cialdini, Robert, 125

circus performances, 33, 40, 42, 44

Citizen Kane, 109

civil rights movement, 11–12, 99, 113
  anger and, 212, 238–39, 241

Civil War, 24, 98

C.K., Louis, 159

Claris, 89

Clinton, Bill, 30, 123

Clipper of the Clouds, The (Verne), 173

coalitions, 27, 114–45
  sharing tactics and, 120–21
  tempered radicalism and, 124–26, 128, 140, 145, 248
  See also movements

cohesion, 177–79

Colbert, Stephen, 159

Cold War, 176

Coleman, Vince, 149

Columbia, 27, 197, 203

comedians, 157–59

commitment, 235–36

commitment blueprint, 180–83, 181*n*, 187*n*, 188

computers, 230*n*

conceptual innovators, 109–12

confidence, 212, 213
  overconfidence, 33–34, 54, 186, 195

confirmation bias, 34, 192

conformity, 3, 225

consensus, 176, 195, 196
  See also groupthink

consequences, 154, 165–66, 170, 253

Constitution, 99, 102

Coombs, Clyde, 18–19

Copernicus, Nicolaus, 12, 151–52

Coppola, Francis Ford, 66

Côté, Stéphane, 81

crafts, learning new, 246

creative destruction, 13

creativity, 3, 10, 11, 14, 31, 95
  life cycles of, 108–13
  procrastination and, 94–98, 100

Crick, Francis, 110

criticism, 184*n*, 190, 196*n*, 252
  See also dissenting opinions; feedback

Crucible, The, 238

Crystal, Billy, 239

Cuba:
  Bay of Pigs invasion of, 176–78, 191, 199*n*
  missile crisis in, 178, 193*n*, 199*n*

Cuban, Mark, 123

cults, 177, 179, 190

cultures, company, 176–78, 251–52
  of advocacy, 197–98, 204
  fit and, 190, 251
  strong, 183, 187, 190
  "think different," 189
  See also Blueprints

cultures, foreign, 48–49, 50*n*, 246

Cummings, E. E., 109, 111

curiosity, 7

Daily Show, The, 38, 161

Dalio, Ray, 189–91, 194–96, 199–200, 202–9, 252

Damascus, 227–29

Dane, Erik, 41, 51

Darwin, Charles, 48*n*, 151, 152

David, Larry, 45, 57

Da Vinci, Leonardo, 96–97, 112

Davis, Raymond, 113

Day-Lewis, Daniel, 238

decision making, 199*n*–200*n*, 208
  democratic, 199
Declaration of Independence, 11,
    98, 99, 102, 242
deep acting, 237–38
Deepwater Horizon, 197
defaults, 6–8, 10, 24, 25, 176, 245
defense, playing offense versus, 234*n*
defensive pessimism, 212–14, 217
déjà vu, 7
democratic decision making, 199
Democrats, 6
De Niro, Robert, 239
Dennehy, Sean, 68, 79*n*
Dentch, Milton, 187
Depression, Great, 235
Deresiewicz, William, 10
devil's advocate, 191–95, 204, 207, 252
dialysis machine, 29, 32, 56
Dilbert (Adams), 18
dilemma actions, 228–29
Dimon, Jamie, 75–76
disagreeableness, 81–82, 247
discipline, parental, 163–65, 169*n*
Disney, 27, 106*n*, 134
  Babble and, 69, 73
  The Lion King and, 134–35, 137–38, 247
dissenting opinions, 176, 185–87, 189–90,
    193–95, 199*n*, 201–2, 225, 247, 252
  devil's advocate and, 191–95, 204, 207, 252
diverse experiences, 50*n*, 246
diversity, 190
Doerr, John, 29, 30, 39, 50–52, 60
Donley, Maureen, 135, 137
DoSomething.org, 250
doubt, 212–14, 235
Downs, Karl, 171–72
Dream, The (Hansen), 101–3
DreamWorks Animation, 250

Dr. Seuss, 114
drug infusion pump, 29–30, 32, 56
Duarte, Nancy, 234
Dubinsky, Donna, 87–91
DuBois, W. E. B., 24
Duffy, Michelle, 130–31
Duguid, Michelle, 84*n*
Dumont, Frank, 157*n*
DuVernay, Ava, 18
Dweck, Carol, 169*n*
Dylan, Bob, 93

Earhart, Amelia, 114
eBay, 19–20, 188
Edison, Thomas, 20, 29, 37, 176
Edwards, Jeff, 197
effort, praise of, 169*n*
Egypt, 220, 223, 226, 228
Einstein, Albert, 36, 62, 108–9, 111, 151, 208
Eisenhower, Dwight, 176
Eisner, Michael, 135
Eliot, T. S., 9, 19
Emancipation Proclamation, 24, 235
Emerson, Ralph Waldo, 175
emotions, 27, 210–43, 248–49
  anger. *See* anger
  faking of, 238
  fear. *See* fear and anxiety
  negative, transforming into positive,
    215–17, 221, 222, 229–30
  and surface versus deep
    acting, 237–38
empathy, 165, 248, 253
Ender's Game (Card), 172
enemies, 128–29, 131–33
engineers, 33
entrepreneurs, 14, 17–18
  arts and, 47
  evaluation and, 33–34

and leading with weaknesses, 68–69, 72*n*

risk and, 20, 22–23

entry interviews, 204, 251

esteem, 132

evaluation and forecasting, 29–61, 78

evidence, quality of, 207

evolution, 151, 152

excitement, transforming fear and anxiety into, 215–17, 221, 222, 230*n*

exit, 79, 80, 89–91, 249

exit interviews, 204, 251

experimental innovators, 109–13

exposure, 78

mere exposure effect, 77–78, 137

eyewear, 1–2, 7–8

Warby Parker, 1–3, 7–8, 14–17, 20–22, 57–60, 107

Facebook, xi, 33, 39

Fallingwater, 113

false negatives, 31, 34, 37*n*, 40, 42–44, 57, 60

false positives, 31, 34, 39, 55, 60

familiarity, 77–79, 137, 247

family, 153

birth order in, 148–59, 162, 174

niche picking in, 156–59, 174, 253

personality differences in, 156

See also parents, parenting

fashion industry, 48–49, 50*n*, 246

Fast Company, 2, 17

fear and anxiety, 213–18, 229, 230, 230*n*, 236, 237, 248

transforming into motivation and excitement, 213, 215–17, 221, 222, 230*n*

feedback, 38–39, 42–43, 60, 194, 198, 202, 203, 246

negative, 190

See also dissenting opinions

Feng, Jie, 17

fictional characters, 172–74

Firefox, 4–6

first movers, 93, 103–8

Fishbach, Ayelet, 235

flexibility, 101

focus groups, 41

Food and Drug Administration, 13

foot-in-the-door technique, 125

Ford, Henry, 20, 39*n*

forecasting and evaluation, 29–61, 78

Forster, E. M., 110

Founders Fund, 123

Fragale, Alison, 65

Franklin, Benjamin, 93, 208

Franklin, Rosalind, 110

Frazier, Kenneth, 233–34

frenemies, 129, 131

Freud, Sigmund, 117, 156, 239

friends, 128–29

Friestad, Marian, 70

Frost, Robert, 109, 111–12

Fuller, Sally Riggs, 179

Gaffigan, Jim, 159, 162

gains, emphasizing losses versus, 232–34

Galenson, David, 109–11

Galileo Galilei, 48, 152

Gandhi, Mahatma, 14, 172, 227

Garrison, William Lloyd, 126*n*

Garrow, David, 102

Gates, Bill, 14, 20

gender:

forecasting and, 37*n*

roles and, 138, 141

speaking up and, 84–88

Gerrity, Tom, 203

Gersick, Connie, 101*n*

Gettysburg Address, 98

Gilboa, Dave, 7–8, 15, 16, 20–22, 58–59

Gino, Francesca, 100

Gladwell, Malcolm, 23, 105–6

Glass, Ira, 36–37

glasses, 1–2, 7–8

  Warby Parker, 1–3, 7–8, 14–17, 20–22,

    57–60, 107

Godart, Frédéric, 48

Godfather, The: Part II, 128

Golder, Peter, 103–4

Goldman Sachs, 204

Goldsmith, Marshall, 182–83

Goncalo, Jack, 84*n*

Google, 2, 17–18, 24–25, 29, 55, 81, 83, 188, 198

  canaries at, 198–99

Google+, 33

Gore, Al, 6

Goshen, Brian, 230*n*

go system, 216–18, 221, 223, 226, 227, 229,

  230*n*, 231, 233, 236, 240

GQ, 2

Great Depression, 235

Greece, 118

Greenert, Jonathan, 125

Griscom, Rufus, 68–70, 72–74, 77, 247

Grissom, Marquis, 149

Gross, Bill, 103

group projects, 253–54

groupthink, 176–79, 185–86, 189, 191, 197,

  202, 204, 209, 254

Grusec, Joan, 168

Guernica (Picasso), 35

guilt, 165, 253

Haddock, Geoffrey, 74*n*

halftimes, 101*n*

Hamlet (Shakespeare), 135, 137–38, 247

handbags, 51

Handey, Jack, 190

Handler, Chelsea, 159

handspring, 90

Hannan, Michael, 181*n*

Hansen, Drew, 101–3

Harry Potter series (Rowling), 40–41, 173–74

Hawkins, Jeff, 90

Heath, Chip, 76, 120

Heath, Dan, 76

Henderson, Rickey, 147, 149

Herrmann, Pol, 100–101

Hewlett-Packard, 13, 17

high school seniors, 33

Hirschman, Albert, 79, 89

Hitchcock, Alfred, 109

Hobson, Mellody, 14

Hochschild, Arlie, 237

Hoffman, Martin, 163, 165*n*

Hofmann, David, 100, 166, 196–98, 221

Hollander, Edwin, 67

Hollingshead, Andrea, 199*n*–200*n*

Holocaust, 163, 165, 168, 170, 253

Homans, George, 83

homosexuality, 159*n*

honest broker, 193*n*

Hope, Bob, 45

horizontal hostility, 117–18

hospitals, 185*n*, 205–6

  hand washing in, 166

Housman, Michael, 4–5

Howe, Julia Ward, 133

humor, 227–30

Huxley, Aldous, 19

idea generation, 31, 34, 39, 44, 84*n*, 245–46

  quantity and, 35–38

  starting point in, 136–37

Idealab, 103

idea meritocracy, 207

idea selection, 31, 44, 56

IDEO, 190*n*

idiosyncrasy credits, 67, 88

I Know Why the Caged Bird Sings (Angelou), 36

improvisation, 100

inaugural addresses, 214*n*

Index Group, 203

information processing, 73–74, 78

in-line skates, 136, 137

innovation tournament, 249

Instacart, 105

intelligence community, 62–64, 68, 70,
    78–79, 107

Intellipedia, 64, 68, 79*n*

Internet, 63, 64, 67

Internet browsers, 3–6

Internet Explorer, 4–6

intuitions, 51, 53–55

Israel-Palestine conflict, 142, 143*n*

Jackson, Mahalia, 100, 102

Janis, Irving, 176–78, 191

Jensen, Greg, 201–3, 205, 207–8

Jefferson, Thomas, 13

Jews, 118
    during Holocaust, 163, 165, 168, 170, 253

Jigsaw Classroom, 253–54

job rotation, 246

Jobs, Steve, 12–14, 17, 26, 45, 64,
    87–90, 189, 208
    Dubinsky and, 87–88, 90
    Land and, 175, 176
    Segway and, 29, 39, 50–55, 106*n*

Johnson, Lyndon, 177

Jones, Clarence, 98–100

Jost, John, 6

Jung, Wooseok, 120–21, 122*n*

Kahneman, Daniel, 53, 55, 233

Kamen, Dean, 32, 38, 39, 50, 52–56, 58,
    60–61, 106

Katzenberg, Jeffrey, 134, 135

Kelman, Herbert, 142, 143

Kemper, Steve, 50, 106*n*

Kennedy, John F., 177, 178, 199*n*

Kennedy, Robert F., 191, 193*n*

Kerouac, Jack, 2, 59

Kerr, Andrea Moore, 131, 133, 145

Khosla, Vinod, 108

"Kill the company" exercise, 234, 250

King, Brayden, 120–21, 122*n*

King, Coretta Scott, 12, 92

King, Martin Luther, Jr., 11–14, 113, 172,
    212, 241–42
    "I Have a Dream" speech of, 12, 92–93,
        98–103, 113, 235
    workshops of, 238–39, 241

King, Stephen, 18

King Lear (Shakespeare), 135

Klein, Gary, 53

Klosterman, Chuck, 132*n*

Knight, Phil, 17

Koch, Helen, 157*n*

Koch, Robert, 107

Kodak, 181

Kohlmann, Ben, 247

Komisar, Randy, 52–54, 56, 60–61, 106*n*

Koo, Minjung, 235

Kotter, John, 76, 232

Kozbelt, Aaron, 34

Kozmo, 105

Kramer, Roderick, 178

Kunda, Ziva, 170

Kurkoski, Jennifer, 24

Kutcher, Ashron, 220–21

Land, Edwin, 19, 175–76, 181–82,
    183–87, 203, 204

Last Supper, The (da Vinci), 97, 112

Lawson, James, 238

leaders, 222

Lean In (Sandberg), 85

LeanIn.Org, xi

Lean Startup, The (Ries), 39*n*

Lee, Aileen, 52, 54, 56

LeFlore, Ron, 149

Legend, John, 18

Lego building experiment, 101*n*

Leno, Jay, 45

Leonardo da Vinci, 96–97, 112

LePine, Jeff, 81

life cycles of creativity, 108–13

Lincoln, Abraham, 23–24, 98

   Emancipation Proclamation of, 24, 235

line length experiment, 224–25

Linge, Mary Kay, 160

Lion King, The, 134–35, 137–38, 247

listing positive features, 73–74

Little, Brian, 243

Littlefield, Warren, 40, 41, 44

Lockwood, Penelope, 170

Lofton, Kenny, 149

logic of appropriateness, 154, 166–67, 170

logic of consequence, 154, 165–66, 170, 253

Lord of the Rings, The (Tolkien), 172

losses, emphasizing gains versus, 232–34

Lowell, Robert, 112

Lubart, Todd, 11

Lublin, Nancy, 250

Lucy Stone League, 114

Ludwin, Rick, 44–46, 49–50, 57

Luther, Martin, 93

Luxottica, 1, 8

Ma, Jack, 172–73

MacKinnon, Donald, 100, 164

Made to Stick (Heath and Heath), 76

Magnavox Odyssey, 104

Maldives, 238

managers and bosses, 80–82

Mandela, Nelson, 172, 210

March, James, 154

March on Washington, 12, 92–93, 98–103

Margolis, Joshua, 241

Maslow, Abraham, 111

May, Brian, 18

Mayer, Marissa, 123

McAdams, Dan, 219

McCammon, Holly, 138, 141

McCrae, Robert, 48*n*

McCune, William, 184

McDonald, Michael, 184

Mead, Margaret, 225

medicine, 207

Medina, Carmen, 62–68, 70–71, 78–82,
   84–87, 89–91, 107, 247

Meena, 172

memory for tasks, 99

mentors, 171, 172

Merck, 233–34

mere exposure effect, 77–78, 137

method acting, 237–38

Meyerson, Debra, 124, 236–37

Michelangelo, 12, 13

microbiology laboratories, 184*n*–85*n*

Microsoft, 20, 222

middle-status conformity effect, 82–84

Mill, Harriet Taylor, 115

Mill, John Stuart, 115

Millay, Edna St. Vincent, 114

Miller, Arthur, 238

Milosevic, Slobodan, 218–20, 223, 226, 227,
   236, 241, 242

Mindset (Dweck), 169*n*

Minkoff, Rob, 134, 135, 137, 141

minorities, 86

Mitteness, Cheryl, 54

Mojzisch, Andreas, 199*n*

Molitor, Paul, 151
Mona Lisa (da Vinci), 96, 112
Moreno, Omar, 149
Morita, Akio, 183–84
Morse, Meroë, 182
motivation, 218, 248
    converting anxiety into, 213, 215, 217
movements, 126
    former adversaries and, 132
    resistance, 219–20, 223, 225–27
    status and, 121*n*–22*n*
    See also Coalitions
movie rentals, 105
Moyers, Bill, 177
Mozart, Wolfgang Amadeus, 36
Mubarak, Hosni, 228
Musk, Elon, 172
My Left Foot, 238

Nadkarni, Sucheta, 100–101
NASA, 27, 197, 203
Navy, U.S., 125, 247
NBC, 34, 40, 45, 50
negative thinking, 212, 214, 214*n*
neglect, 79–80, 89, 249
Nemeth, Charlan, 185, 191–94
Netflix, 105
network effects, 108
Neustadt, Richard, 178
new skills, learning, 246
Newton, Isaac, 151
New Yorker, 23
New York Times, 71
niches, 156–59, 174, 253
Nicolay, John, 98
Nike, 2
Nintendo, 104–5
Nobel Peace Prize, 143*n*
Nobel Prize, 46–47, 110, 113, 123, 154, 232, 233

Norem, Julie, 212–13, 217
North Pole, 27, 210–11, 214, 217

O'Brien, Conan, 45
"O Canada," 120
Occupy Wall Street, 125–26
odyssey, 104
offense, playing defense versus, 234*n*
Office, The, 45
O'Keeffe, Georgia, 114
Oliner, Pearl, 163–65, 168
Oliner, Samuel, 163–65, 168
Omidyar, Pierre, 19–20
openness, 47*n*–48*n*
opinions:
    believability and, 200–201, 207, 208
    dissenting. *See* Dissenting opinions
opposite day, 250
optimism, 214
    in presidents, 214*n*
    strategic, 212–13
originality, 3, 13–14, 16, 23–28
    achievement motivation and, 10–11
Osborn, Alex, 184*n*
Oslo Accords, 143*n*
Otpor!, 219, 223, 226–28, 232,
    235–36, 241, 242
overconfidence, 33–34, 54, 186, 195
Overstreet, Bonaro, 146
Overstreet, Harry, 146
Ozcelik, Hakan, 225

Page, Larry, 17–18, 83
Palestine-Israel conflict, 142, 143*n*
Palm Computing, 90, 186
parents, parenting, 159–70, 252–54
    discipline and, 163–65, 169*n*
    as role models, 170–71
    values and, 167–71

Park, Joseph, 105
Parker, Sarah Jessica, 114
Parks, Rosa, 12, 93, 153, 238
passion, 32, 55–57, 180
Pasteur, Louis, 107
Patel, Priya, 221*n*
Paul, Alice, 145
pen design, 136–37
Pennebaker, James, 240*n*
Perry, Meredith, 122–24, 140–41, 248
persistence, 79, 80, 89, 249
pessimism, defensive, 212–14, 217
Peters, Tom, 236
Peterson, Bill, 171
Phillips, Damon, 83
photography:
    digital, 183, 184, 186, 187
    Polaroid and, 175–76, 179, 181–87,
        199, 203, 209
Picasso, Pablo, 35, 36
Pink, Daniel, 113
Pinker, Steven, 156
Pinochet, Augusto, 226
pioneers, 103–8
Planck, Max, 107–8
PlayStation, 186
Poitier, Sidney, 93
Poland, 227
Polaroid, 175–76, 179, 181–87,
    199, 203, 209
police officers, 130
politicians, 151, 154
Pontikes, Elizabeth, 106
Popovic, Srdja, 126, 218–20, 223, 226–31,
    235–36, 238, 241, 242
Porter, Roger, 193*n*
positive features, listing, 73–74
power, 65, 66, 68, 86, 88

praise, 168–70, 252–53
presidents, 23–24
    inaugural addresses of, 214*n*
Presley, Elvis, 230*n*
problems and solutions, 197, 251
procrastination, x, 26, 93–102, 108, 246
    improvisation and, 100
    planning and, 102
professional blueprint, 180–82, 181*n*
professors, 33, 67
prototypes, 41, 42
public speaking, 215
Pugh, Lewis, 210–12, 214, 217–18, 237–38

quantity, 35–38
    quality and, 37
Queen, 18
Quiet (Cain), 216
Quillen, Robert, 148

radicalism, tempered, 124–26,
    128, 140, 145, 248
Raffiee, Joseph, 17
Raines, Tim, 149
Rakove, Jack, 11
Rebele, Reb, 60
rebels, 152, 153, 155, 157, 161*n*, 162
Reebok, 186
Reingen, Peter, 128, 143
Reinventing the Wheel (Kemper), 106
Reiser, Paul, 42
relationships, 128–31
    ambivalent, 129–31
Republicans, 6
reputation, 186
respect, 66, 67, 88
revolutions and resistance movements,
    219–20, 223, 225–27

Rickey, Branch, 19, 172

Ride, Sally, 14

Ries, Eric, 39*n*

risk, 14, 16–23, 26, 40, 43, 83, 106, 209, 234
  birth order and, 150, 153–56
  comedians and, 158
  parenting and, 160, 162
  portfolios of, 18–20, 25, 66–67, 246–47
  reputational, 186

Rivera, Lauren, 190*n*

Rivers, Joan, 158

Robinson, Jackie, 19, 93, 146–48, 150,
  153–54, 157, 159–60, 162, 167, 171–72

Robinson, Mack, 157

Robinson, Mallie, 160, 167, 171

Robinson, Willa Mae, 160

Rock, Chris, 158

Rockefeller, Nelson, 99

Rogers, Howard, 182

role models, 170–74, 252

roller blading, 136, 137

Roman Catholic Church, 191, 207

Roosevelt, Eleanor, 253–54

Roosevelt, Franklin D., 234–35

Rosenberg, Jonathan, 55

Rosette, Ashleigh, 86, 87

Rottenberg, Linda, 20

Rowling, J. K., 40–41, 174

Rustin, Bayard, 238

Safari, 4–6

Saffo, Paul, 195

Sahlman, Bill, 52, 56, 106*n*

Salovey, Peter, 233

Sandberg, Sheryl, ix–xii, 85, 114, 172

Santayana, George, 144

Sarick, Leslie, 69, 77

Sarick Effect, 69–75, 77

Saturday Night Live, 46, 190

Schmidt, Eric, 55

Schneider, Benjamin, 182

Schulz-Hardt, Stefan, 199*n*

Schumpeter, Joseph, 13

Schwartz, Shalom, 205

Schwarz, Norbert, 74

science, 207

Science Talent Search, 97–98

scientists, 151–52, 154

Scully, Maureen, 124, 236–37

Segway, 29–32, 38, 39, 50–56, 60, 106*n*

Seinfeld, 31, 39–42, 42*n*, 44–46, 49–50, 57

Seinfeld, Jerry, 45, 57, 158, 215

self-confidence, 212, 213
  overconfidence, 33–34, 54, 186, 195

self-doubt, 212–14, 235

Selma, 18

Semmelweis, Ignaz, 107

September 11 terrorist attacks, 64, 107, 240*n*

Serbia, 218–20, 223, 226, 227,
  231–32, 235–36, 242

Serial, 37

settlers, 103–7

sexual harassment, 85*n*

Shakespeare, William, 35–36, 135

shapers, 208–9

sharing, 120–21

Shaw, George Bernard, 1

Shin, Jihae, 94–95

siblings:
  birth order of, 148–59, 162, 174
  niche picking and, 156–59, 174, 253
  parenting and, 159–70

Silicon Valley, 125, 180–82, 187*n*

Silverman, Josh, 220–21, 222

Simonton, Dean, 34–37, 48, 155, 173

sincerity, 193

Sinek, Simon, 124
singing, 120, 216
Sistine Chapel, 11, 12
Sivers, Derek, 225
Sixtus V, Pope, 191
Skype, 220–22
smartphones, 7, 90
    iPhone, 7, 90, 91
Smiley, Glenn, 238–39
Smith, Rick, 20
Snoop Dogg, 123
social approval, 23
solutions, focus on, 197, 251
Sonenshein, Scott, 212
songs:
    singing, 120, 216
    tapping rhythm to, 75–76
Sony, 183, 186
Sørensen, Jesper, 183
Soske, Trina, 201–3, 205, 207
Soule, Sarah, 120–21, 122*n*
Spanx, 20, 114
speaking up, 62–91, 196*n*, 201–2, 205
    women and, 84–88
    See also dissenting opinions
Sperry, Roger, 109, 111
Stanislavski, Constantin, 237
Stanton, Elizabeth Cady, 115–16, 118–19,
    121, 126–31, 142, 144
star blueprint, 180–82, 181*n*
Star Trek, 173
status, 65–68, 82–83, 86, 88, 202
    movements and, 121*n*–22*n*
Stearney, Scott, 125
Steinman, Josh, 125
Sternberg, Robert, 11
Stewart, Abigail, 171
Stewart, Jon, 158

"Still I Rise" (Angelou), 36
stock market, 83, 181, 182
Stone, Lucy, 114–16, 118–19, 121, 127–31,
    133–34, 141–45
stop system, 216–17, 229, 240
strategic flexibility, 101
strategic optimism, 212–13
Streisand, Barbra, 161*n*
Subotnik, Rena, 97–98
Sulloway, Frank, 150–52, 156*n*, 157, 162
support, 225–27
surface acting, 237, 238
surgeons, 229
Sutton, Robert, 37, 229
Syria, 227–29

Tadic, Boris, 231, 242
Tartikoff, Brandon, 34, 41
teachers, 9–10
Tellis, Gerard, 103–4
tempered radicalism, 124–26, 128,
    140, 145, 248
Thiel, Peter, 106, 123, 172
Thinking, Fast and Slow (Kahneman), 55
This American Life, 36–37
Thoreau, Henry David, 93
three-ring binder, 135–36
Time, 30
time of day, 97*n*
timing, 26, 92–113
    age and, 108–13
    first movers and, 93, 103–8
    procrastination and. *See* procrastination
Titanic, 211
Tormala, Zak, 72*n*
Train, George Francis, 118, 126–27
transparency, 141, 196, 203, 205
Trojan horses, 125, 141, 248

Tullman, Howard, 78

Tversky, Amos, 233

TV Guide, 31

Twain, Mark, 92, 112

Twenty Thousand Leagues Under the Sea (Verne), 173

Twitter, 33, 39

typewriters, 230*n*

Ubeam, 123

Uchino, Bert, 131

undercommunication of ideas, 76–77

university fund-raisers, 221–22

Upworthy, 37–38

urgency, sense of, 231–32, 234, 249–50

values, 118, 120, 124, 140, 167, 190, 253

parents and, 167–71

relative importance of, 205–6

Van Dyne, Linn, 81

vegans and vegetarians, 117–18

Verne, Jules, 173

victims of injustice, focus on, 241–42, 248–49

video game consoles, 104–5

Vietnam War, 176

voice, 79–81, 89–91, 249

See also speaking up

Volkman, Alisa, 68

Voss, Glenn, 205

Voss, Zannie, 205

voting rights:

for African-American men, 118–19, 126–27

for women. *See* women's suffrage

vuja de, 7, 25

Warby Parker, 1–3, 7–8, 14–17, 20–22, 57–60, 107

Warhol, Andy, 176

Washington, George, 11

Wasielewski, Patricia, 235

Waste Land, The (Eliot), 19

Watson, James, 109, 110

weaknesses, leading with, 68–75, 247

web browsers, 3–6

Weick, Karl, 113, 201

Welle, Brian, 24

Welles, Orson, 109

Wells, H. G., 173

Westphal, James, 184

White, E. B., 242

White, Judith, 117

Whyte, Glen, 178, 179

Wieder, Zack, 190–91, 203

Wieth, Mareike, 97*n*

Wikipedia, 64, 68

Willard, Frances, 133–34, 138–41, 248

Wills, Maury, 149

Wilson, Timothy, 240*n*

Wilson, Willie, 149

Wilson, Woodrow, 145

Wiltermuth, Scott, 120

Winner, Ellen, 10

Winstead, Gene, 161

Winstead, Lizz, 38–39, 161–62, 171

wireless power, 122–24, 140–41, 248

Woman's Christian Temperance Union (WCTU), 119–22, 134, 138, 139, 139*n*–40*n*, 145

Woman's Journal, 115

women, 84–85

black, 86

forecasting and, 37*n*

rights for, 115

women (*cont.*)
  sexual harassment and, 85*n*
  speaking up and, 84–88
women's suffrage, 8, 27, 114–16, 118–19, 121,
    126–28, 133–34, 138–45
  home protection and,
    139–41, 248
  two main arguments in, 138–39
  WCTU and, 119–22, 134, 138,
    139, 139*n*–40*n*
Woodhull, Victoria, 127–28
Woolley, Anita, 101*n*, 234*n*
Work Rules! (Bock), 198
Wozniak, Steve, 12–13, 17
Wright, Frank Lloyd, 113
Wright, Peter, 70

Wrinkle in Time, A (L'Engle), 172
Wrzesniewski, Amy, 24

Yahoo, 188
Yankowski, Carl, 186–87
Yousafzai, Malala, 172

Zacks, Rose, 97*n*
Zajonc, Robert, 77, 159
Zappos, 1, 107
Zeigarnik, Bluma, 99
Zeigarnik effect, 99
Zero to One (Thiel), 106
Zuckerberg, Mark, x, 172
Zuckerman, Ezra, 83
Zweigenhaft, Richard, 150